Constitutional Law

Second Edition

2006 Supplement

2006 Supplement

Constitutional Law

Second Edition

Erwin Chemerinsky
Alston & Bird Professor of Law
Duke Law School

76 Ninth Avenue, New York, NY 10011
http://lawschool.aspenpublishers.com

© 2006 Aspen Publishers, Inc.
a Wolters Kluwer business
http://lawschool.aspenpublishers.com

Aspen Publishers
Attn: Permissions Department
76 Ninth Avenue, 7th Floor
New York, NY 10011-5201

Printed in the United States of America.

1 2 3 4 5 6 7 8 9 0

ISBN 0-7355-5768-3

Library of Congress Cataloging-in Publication Data

Chemerinsky, Erwin.
   Constitutional law/Erwin Chemerinsky. — 2nd ed.
      p. cm.
   Includes index.
   ISBN 0-7355-4946-X (casebook)
   ISBN 0-7355-5768-3 (supplement)
   1. Constitutional law—United States—Cases. I. Title.

KF4549.C44 2005
342.73—dc22

                                                    2005007712

About Aspen Publishers

Aspen Publishers, headquartered in New York City, is a leading information provider for attorneys, business professionals, and law students. Written by pre-eminent authorities, our products consist of analytical and practical information covering both U.S. and international topics. We publish in the full range of formats, including updated manuals, books, periodicals, CDs, and online products.

Our proprietary content is complemented by 2,500 legal databases, containing over 11 million documents, available through our Loislaw division. Aspen Publishers also offers a wide range of topical legal and business databases linked to Loislaw's primary material. Our mission is to provide accurate, timely, and authoritative content in easily accessible formats, supported by unmatched customer care.

To order any Aspen Publishers title, go to *http://lawschool.aspenpublishers.com* or call 1-800-638-8437.

To reinstate your manual update service, call 1-800-638-8437.

For more information on Loislaw products, go to *www.loislaw.com* or call 1-800-364-2512.

For Customer Care issues, e-mail *CustomerCare@aspenpublishers.com*; call 1-800-234-1660; or fax 1-800-901-9075.

Aspen Publishers
a Wolters Kluwer business

Contents

Preface

The second edition of the casebook was published in May 2005 and covers cases and developments through the end of October Term 2005, which concluded in June 2006. Thus, this supplement covers the last two years of the Supreme Court, October Terms 2004 and 2005.

This has been a time of momentous developments on the Supreme Court, occasioned by the death of Chief Justice William Rehnquist and the retirement of Justice Sandra Day O'Connor. There are two new members of the Court, Chief Justice John Roberts and Justice Samuel Alito.

The two years also have seen many major developments, which are reflected in the cases included in this supplement. Some of the most important include the following:

- *Gonzales v. Raich*, on the scope of Congress's commerce power and whether Congress may prohibit the cultivation and possession of small amounts of marijuana for medicinal purposes. (Chapter 2)
- *Hamdan v. Rumsfeld*, on the legality of the military tribunals created to try those held as enemy combatants in Guantanamo Bay, Cuba. (Chapter 3)
- *Kelo v. City of New London*, on what constitutes a taking for "public use" and whether a taking for economic development purposes is "public use." (Chapter 6)
- *Johnson v. California*, on whether the routine racial segregation of prisoners warrants strict scrutiny. (Chapter 7)
- *Randall v. Sorrell*, on the constitutionality of a state law restricting campaign contributions and expenditures, and *Rumsfeld v. FAIR*, on whether Congress may compel law schools to allow military recruiters to use campus facilities. (Chapter 9)
- *McCreary County v. ACLU of Kentucky* and *Van Orden v. Perry*, on whether Ten Commandment displays violate the Establishment Clause. (Chapter 10)

In addition to being important clarifications of the doctrines in these areas, these cases raise important underlying questions about how these constitutional provisions—and all of the Constitution—should be interpreted.

With two new Justices, there is the prospect of the Court reconsidering many areas of constitutional law in the years ahead. It is an exciting time to be studying constitutional law. I look forward to continuing to do annual supplements and a new edition every several years. I welcome comments and suggestions from those using this book.

Erwin Chemerinsky

July 2006

Chapter 1

The Federal Judicial Power

B. Limits on the Federal Judicial Power

3. Justiciability Limits

b. Standing

ii. Prudential Standing Limits

The Prohibition of Generalized Grievances (*casebook, p. 58*)

In *DaimlerChrysler Corp. v. Cuno*, 126 S.Ct. 1854 (2006), the Supreme Court reaffirmed and applied the prohibition against taxpayer standing. The case involved the issue of whether a state and local government giving tax benefits to a company to move into the area violated the dormant commerce clause.[1] The United States Court of Appeals for the Sixth Circuit found that there was a violation of the dormant commerce clause; the Supreme Court, however, ordered the case dismissed for lack of standing. The Court said that the plaintiffs were suing solely as taxpayers objecting that the tax benefits were unconstitutional. The Court concluded that such taxpayer standing is not permitted.

DAIMLERCHRYSLER CORP. v. CUNO
126 S.Ct. 1854 (2006)

Chief Justice ROBERTS delivered the opinion of the Court.

Jeeps were first mass-produced in 1941 for the U.S. Army by the Willys-Overland Motor Company in Toledo, Ohio. Nearly 60 years later, the city of Toledo and State of Ohio sought to encourage the current manufacturer of Jeeps—DaimlerChrysler—to expand its Jeep operation in Toledo, by offering local and state tax benefits for new investment. Taxpayers in Toledo sued, alleging that their local and state tax burdens were increased by the tax breaks

---

1. The dormant commerce clause is the principle that state and local governments act unconstitutionally if they place an undue burden on interstate commerce. The dormant commerce clause is discussed in Chapter 4.

for DaimlerChrysler, tax breaks that they asserted violated the Commerce Clause. The Court of Appeals agreed that a state tax credit offered under Ohio law violated the Commerce Clause, and state and local officials and DaimlerChrysler sought review in this Court. We are obligated before reaching this Commerce Clause question to determine whether the taxpayers who objected to the credit have standing to press their complaint in federal court. We conclude that they do not, and we therefore can proceed no further.

Plaintiffs principally claim standing by virtue of their status as Ohio taxpayers, alleging that the franchise tax credit "depletes the funds of the State of Ohio to which the Plaintiffs contribute through their tax payments" and thus "diminish[es] the total funds available for lawful uses and impos[es] disproportionate burdens on" them. On several occasions, this Court has denied federal taxpayers standing under Article III to object to a particular expenditure of federal funds simply because they are taxpayers.

The animating principle behind these cases was announced in their progenitor, *Frothingham v. Mellon* (1923). In rejecting a claim that improper federal appropriations would "increase the burden of future taxation and thereby take [the plaintiff's] property without due process of law," the Court observed that a federal taxpayer's "interest in the moneys of the Treasury is shared with millions of others; is comparatively minute and indeterminable; and the effect upon future taxation, of any payment out of the funds, so remote, fluctuating and uncertain, that no basis is afforded for an appeal to the preventive powers of a court of equity."

This logic is equally applicable to taxpayer challenges to expenditures that deplete the treasury, and to taxpayer challenges to so-called "tax expenditures," which reduce amounts available to the treasury by granting tax credits or exemptions. In either case, the alleged injury is based on the asserted effect of the allegedly illegal activity on public revenues, to which the taxpayer contributes. Standing has been rejected in such cases because the alleged injury is not "concrete and particularized," but instead a grievance the taxpayer "suffers in some indefinite way in common with people generally." In addition, the injury is not "actual or imminent," but instead "conjectural or hypothetical." As an initial matter, it is unclear that tax breaks of the sort at issue here do in fact deplete the treasury: The very point of the tax benefits is to spur economic activity, which in turn increases government revenues. In this very action, the Michigan plaintiffs claimed that they were injured because they lost out on the added revenues that would have accompanied DaimlerChrysler's decision to expand facilities in Michigan.

Plaintiffs' alleged injury is also "conjectural or hypothetical" in that it depends on how legislators respond to a reduction in revenue, if that is the consequence of the credit. Establishing injury requires speculating that elected officials will increase a taxpayer-plaintiff's tax bill to make up a deficit; establishing redressability requires speculating that abolishing the challenged credit will redound to the benefit of the taxpayer because legislators will pass along the supposed increased revenue in the form of tax reductions. Neither sort of speculation suffices to support standing.

A taxpayer-plaintiff has no right to insist that the government dispose of any increased revenue it might experience as a result of his suit by decreasing his tax liability or bolstering programs that benefit him. To the contrary, the decision of how to allocate any such savings is the very epitome of a policy judgment committed to the "broad and legitimate discretion" of lawmakers, which "the courts cannot presume either to control or to predict." Under such circumstances, we have no assurance that the asserted injury is "imminent"— that it is "certainly impending."

The foregoing rationale for rejecting federal taxpayer standing applies with undiminished force to state taxpayers. We indicated as much in *Doremus v. Board of Ed. of Hawthorne* (1952). In that case, we noted our earlier holdings that "the interests of a taxpayer in the moneys of the federal treasury are too indeterminable, remote, uncertain and indirect" to support standing to challenge "their manner of expenditure." We then "reiterate[d]" what we had said in rejecting a federal taxpayer challenge to a federal statute "as equally true when a state Act is assailed: 'The [taxpayer] must be able to show . . . that he has sustained . . . some direct injury . . . and not merely that he suffers in some indefinite way in common with people generally.'" The allegations of injury that plaintiffs make in their complaint furnish no better basis for finding standing than those made in the cases where federal taxpayer standing was denied. Plaintiffs claim that DaimlerChrysler's tax credit depletes the Ohio fisc and "impos[es] disproportionate burdens on [them]." This is no different from similar claims by federal taxpayers we have already rejected under Article III as insufficient to establish standing. For the foregoing reasons, we hold that state taxpayers have no standing under Article III to challenge state tax or spending decisions simply by virtue of their status as taxpayers.

Plaintiffs argue that an exception to the general prohibition on taxpayer standing should exist for Commerce Clause challenges to state tax or spending decisions, analogizing their Commerce Clause claim to the Establishment Clause challenge we permitted in *Flast v. Cohen* (1968). *Flast* held that because "the Establishment Clause . . . specifically limit[s] the taxing and spending power conferred by Art. I, § 8, "a taxpayer will have standing consistent with Article III to invoke federal judicial power when he alleges that congressional action under the taxing and spending clause is in derogation of" the Establishment Clause. But as plaintiffs candidly concede, "only the Establishment Clause" has supported federal taxpayer suits since *Flast*. Quite apart from whether the franchise tax credit is analogous to an exercise of congressional power under Art. I, § 8, plaintiffs' reliance on *Flast* is misguided: Whatever rights plaintiffs have under the Commerce Clause, they are fundamentally unlike the right not to "contribute three pence . . . for the support of any one [religious] establishment." (2 Writings of James Madison 186 (G. Hunt ed.1901)). Indeed, plaintiffs compare the Establishment Clause to the Commerce Clause at such a high level of generality that almost any constitutional constraint on government power would "specifically limit" a State's taxing and spending power for *Flast* purposes. And even if the two clauses are similar in that they often implicate governments' fiscal decisions, a finding that the Commerce Clause satisfies the *Flast* test would leave no principled way of distinguishing those other constitutional provisions that we have recognized constrain governments' taxing and spending decisions. Yet such a broad application of *Flast's* exception to the general prohibition on taxpayer standing would be quite at odds with its narrow application in our precedent and *Flast's* own promise that it would not transform federal courts into forums for taxpayers' "generalized grievances." Plaintiffs thus do not have state taxpayer standing on the ground that their Commerce Clause challenge is just like the Establishment Clause challenge in *Flast*.

Plaintiffs also claim that their status as municipal taxpayers gives them standing to challenge the state franchise tax credit at issue here. The *Frothingham* Court noted with approval the standing of municipal residents to enjoin the "illegal use of the moneys of a municipal corporation," relying on "the peculiar relation of the corporate taxpayer to the corporation" to distinguish such a case from the general bar on taxpayer suits. Plaintiffs here challenged the municipal property tax exemption as municipal taxpayers. That challenge was rejected by the Court of Appeals on the merits, and no issue regarding plaintiffs' standing to bring it has been raised. In plaintiffs' challenge to the state franchise tax credit, however, they identify no municipal action contributing to any claimed injury.

[P]laintiffs claim that because state law requires revenues from the franchise tax to be distributed to local governments. But plaintiffs' challenge is still to the state law and state decision, not those of their municipality. We have already explained why a state taxpayer lacks standing to challenge a state fiscal decision on the grounds that it might affect his tax liability. All plaintiffs have done in recasting their claims as ones brought by municipal taxpayers whose municipalities receive funding from the State—the level of which might be affected by the same state fiscal decision—is introduce yet another level of conjecture to their already hypothetical claim of injury.

All the theories plaintiffs have offered to support their standing to challenge the franchise tax credit are unavailing. Because plaintiffs have no standing to challenge that credit, the lower courts erred by considering their claims against it on the merits.

e. The Political Question Doctrine

i. The Political Question Doctrine Defined

WHAT IS A POLITICAL QUESTION: THE ISSUES OF PARTISAN GERRYMANDERING AND PARTISAN GERRYMANDERING

In *Vieth v. Jubelirer* (2004) (casebook p. 81), the Supreme Court, by a 5-4 margin and without a majority opinion, held that challenges to partisan gerrymandering are non-justiciable political questions. Justice Scalia, writing for himself and three other Justices, concluded that such challenges are always non-justiciable political questions because there inherently are not judicially discoverable or manageable standards. Justice Kennedy, concurring in the judgment, said that no such standards could be identified at this time, but that in the future standards might be found and then such challenges would be justiciable.

In *League of United Latin American Citizens v. Perry* (2006), the Court again dismissed a challenge to partisan gerrymandering. After Republicans gained control of the Texas legislature in 2002, they redrew districts for Congress so as to maximize likely seats for Republicans. This replaced a plan that was drawn by a federal district court in 2001. The redistricting was very successful. The Texas congressional delegation went from 17 Democrats and 15 Republicans in the 2002 election to 11 Democrats and 21 Republicans in the 2004 election.

Many lawsuits were brought and raised three major issues:

1) Is partisan gerrymandering a non-justiciable political question and if it is justiciable, does it violate equal protection?
2) Is the mid-decade redistricting unconstitutional?
3) Did Texas violate the Voting Rights Act by diluting the voting strength of minority voters?

LEAGUE OF UNITED LATIN AMERICAN CITIZENS v. PERRY
126 S.Ct. 2594 (2006)

Justice KENNEDY announced the judgment of the Court.

In Davis v. Bandemer (1986), the Court held that an equal protection challenge to a political gerrymander presents a justiciable case or controversy, but there was disagreement over what substantive standard to apply. That disagreement persists. A plurality of the Court in *Vieth v. Jubelirer* [2004] would have held such challenges to be nonjusticiable political questions, but a majority declined to do so. We do not revisit the justiciability holding but do proceed to examine whether appellants' claims offer the Court a manageable, reliable measure of fairness for determining whether a partisan gerrymander violates the Constitution.

Appellants claim that Plan 1374C, enacted by the Texas Legislature in 2003, is an unconstitutional political gerrymander. A decision, they claim, to effect mid-decennial redistricting, when solely motivated by partisan objectives, violates equal protection and the First Amendment because it serves no legitimate public purpose and burdens one group because of its political opinions and affiliation. The mid-decennial nature of the redistricting, appellants say, reveals the legislature's sole motivation. Unlike *Vieth*, where the legislature acted in the context of a required decennial redistricting, the Texas Legislature voluntarily replaced a plan that itself was designed to comply with new census data.

Because Texas had "no constitutional obligation to act at all" in 2003, it is hardly surprising, according to appellants, that the District Court found "[t]here is little question but that the single-minded purpose of the Texas Legislature in enacting Plan 1374C was to gain partisan advantage" for the Republican majority over the Democratic minority.

A rule, or perhaps a presumption, of invalidity when a mid-decade redistricting plan is adopted solely for partisan motivations is a salutary one, in appellants' view, for then courts need not inquire about, nor parties prove, the discriminatory effects of partisan gerrymandering—a matter that has proved elusive since *Bandemer*. Adding to the test's simplicity is that it does not quibble with the drawing of individual district lines but challenges the decision to redistrict at all.

For a number of reasons, appellants' case for adopting their test is not convincing. To begin with, the state appellees dispute the assertion that partisan gain was the "sole" motivation for the decision to replace Plan 1151C. There is some merit to that criticism, for the pejorative label overlooks indications that partisan motives did not dictate the plan in its entirety. The legislature does seem to have decided to redistrict with the sole purpose of achieving a Republican congressional majority, but partisan aims did not guide every line it drew. As the District Court found, the contours of some contested district lines were drawn based on more mundane and local interests. The state appellees also contend, and appellants do not contest, that a number of line-drawing requests by Democratic state legislators were honored.

Evaluating the legality of acts arising out of mixed motives can be complex, and affixing a single label to those acts can be hazardous, even when the actor is an individual performing a discrete act. When the actor is a legislature and the act is a composite of manifold choices, the task can be even more daunting. Even setting this skepticism aside, a successful claim attempting to identify unconstitutional acts of partisan gerrymandering must do what appellants' sole-motivation theory explicitly disavows: show a burden, as measured by a reliable standard, on the complainants' representational rights. For this reason, a majority of the Court rejected a test proposed in *Vieth* that is markedly similar to the one appellants present today.

The sole-intent standard offered here is no more compelling when it is linked to the circumstance that Plan 1374C is mid-decennial legislation. The text and structure of the Constitution and our case law indicate there is nothing inherently suspect about a legislature's decision to replace mid-decade a court-ordered plan with one of its own. And even if there were, the fact of mid-decade redistricting alone is no sure indication of unlawful political gerrymanders. Under appellants' theory, a highly effective partisan gerrymander that coincided with decennial redistricting would receive less scrutiny than a bumbling, yet solely partisan, mid-decade redistricting. More concretely, the test would leave untouched the 1991 Texas redistricting, which entrenched a party on the verge of minority status, while striking down the 2003 redistricting plan, which resulted in the majority Republican Party capturing a larger share of the seats. A test that treats these two similarly effective power plays in such different ways does not have the reliability appellants ascribe to it.

Furthermore, compared to the map challenged in *Vieth*, which led to a Republican majority in the congressional delegation despite a Democratic majority in the statewide vote, Plan 1374C can be seen as making the party balance more congruent to statewide party power. To be sure, there is no constitutional requirement of proportional representation, and equating a party's statewide share of the vote with its portion of the congressional delegation is a rough measure at best. Nevertheless, a congressional plan that more closely reflects the distribution of state party power seems a less likely vehicle for partisan discrimination than one that entrenches an electoral minority. By this measure, Plan 1374C can be seen as fairer than the plan that survived in *Vieth* and the two previous Texas plans—all three of which would pass the modified sole-intent test that Plan 1374C would fail.

In the absence of any other workable test for judging partisan gerrymanders, one effect of appellants' focus on mid-decade redistricting could be to encourage partisan excess at the outset of the decade, when a legislature redistricts pursuant to its decennial constitutional duty and is then immune from the charge of sole-motivation. If mid-decade redistricting were barred or at least subject to close judicial oversight, opposition legislators would also have every incentive to prevent passage of a legislative plan and try their luck with a court that might give them a better deal than negotiation with their political rivals.

In sum, we disagree with appellants' view that a legislature's decision to override a valid, court-drawn plan mid-decade is sufficiently suspect to give shape to a reliable standard for identifying unconstitutional political gerrymanders. We conclude that appellants have established no legally impermissible use of political classifications. For this reason, they state no claim on which relief may be granted for their statewide challenge.

[Justice Kennedy's opinion went on to conclude that the drawing of one district did violate the Voting Rights Act by diluting the voting strength of Latino voters].

Justice STEVENS, with whom Justice BREYER joins concurring in part and dissenting in part.

This is a suit in which it is perfectly clear that judicially manageable standards enable us to decide the merits of a statewide challenge to a political gerrymander. Applying such standards, I shall explain why the wholly unnecessary replacement of the neutral plan fashioned by the three-judge court (Plan 1151C or Balderas Plan) with Plan 1374C, which creates districts with less compact shapes, violates the Voting Rights Act, and fragments communities of interest—all for purely partisan purposes—violated the State's constitutional duty to govern impartially. Prior misconduct by the Texas Legislature neither excuses nor justifies that violation.

The maintenance of existing district boundaries is advantageous to both voters and candidates. Changes, of course, must be made after every census to equalize the population of each district or to accommodate changes in the size of a State's congressional delegation. Similarly, changes must be made in response to a finding that a districting plan violates §2 or §5 of the Voting Rights Act. But the interests in orderly campaigning and voting, as well as in maintaining communication between representatives and their constituents, underscore the importance of requiring that any decision to redraw district boundaries—like any other state action that affects the electoral process—must, at the very least, serve some legitimate governmental purpose. A purely partisan desire "to minimize or cancel out the voting strength of racial or political elements of the voting population," is not such a purpose. Because a desire to minimize the strength of Texas Democrats was the sole motivation for the adoption of Plan 1374C, the plan cannot withstand constitutional scrutiny.

The districting map that Plan 1374C replaced, Plan 1151C, was not only manifestly fair and neutral, it may legitimately be described as a milestone in Texas' political history because it put an end to a long history of Democratic misuse of power in that State. For decades after the Civil War, the political party associated with the former Commander in Chief of the Union Army attracted the support of former slaves and a handful of "carpetbaggers," but had no significant political influence in Texas. The Democrats maintained their political power by excluding black voters from participating in primary elections, by the artful management of multimember electoral schemes, and, most recently, by outrageously partisan gerrymandering. Unfortunately, some of these tactics are not unique to Texas Democrats; the apportionment scheme they devised in the 1990's is only one example of the excessively gerrymandered districting plans that parties with control of their States' governing bodies have implemented in recent years.

Despite the Texas Democratic Party's sordid history of manipulating the electoral process to perpetuate its stranglehold on political power, the Texas Republican Party managed to become the State's majority party by 2002. If, after finally achieving political strength in Texas, the Republicans had adopted a new plan in order to remove the excessively partisan Democratic gerrymander of the 1990's, the decision to do so would unquestionably have been supported by a neutral justification. But that is not what happened. Instead, Texas Republicans abandoned a neutral apportionment map for the sole purpose of manipulating district boundaries to maximize their electoral advantage and thus create their own impermissible stranglehold on political power.

The unique question of law that is raised in this appeal is one that the Court has not previously addressed. That narrow question is whether it was unconstitutional for Texas to replace a lawful districting plan "in the middle of a decade, for the sole purpose of maximizing partisan advantage." This question is both different from, and simpler than, the principal question presented in *Vieth v. Jubelirer*, in which the "'lack of judicially discoverable and manageable standards'" prevented the plurality from deciding the merits of a statewide challenge to a political gerrymander.

The legislature's decision to redistrict at issue in this litigation was entirely inconsistent with these principles. By taking an action for the sole purpose of advantaging Republicans and disadvantaging Democrats, the State of Texas violated its constitutional obligation to govern impartially.

[Justice Stevens then went on to conclude that there was a violation of the Voting Rights Act.]

Justice SOUTER, with whom Justice GINSBURG joins, concurring in part and dissenting in part.

I join the principal opinion, rejecting the one-person, one-vote challenge to Plan 1374C based simply on its mid-decade timing, and I also join [the part of the opinion], in which the Court preserves the principle that partisan gerrymandering can be recognized as a violation of equal protection. I see nothing to be gained by working through these cases on the standard I would have applied in *Vieth*, because here as in *Vieth* we have no majority for any single criterion of impermissible gerrymander (and none for a conclusion that Plan 1374C is unconstitutional across the board). I therefore treat the broad issue of gerrymander much as the subject of an improvident grant of certiorari.

[Justice Souter then went on to conclude that there was a violation of the Voting Rights Act.]

Chief Justice ROBERTS, with whom Justice ALITO joins, concurring in part, concurring in the judgment in part, and dissenting in part.

I agree with the determination that appellants have not provided "a reliable standard for identifying unconstitutional political gerrymanders." The question whether any such standard exists—that is, whether a challenge to a political gerrymander presents a justiciable case or controversy—has not been argued in these cases. I therefore take no position on that question, which has divided the Court, see *Vieth v. Jubelirer* (2004), and I join the Court's disposition without specifying whether appellants have failed to state a claim on which relief can be granted, or have failed to present a justiciable controversy.

[Chief Justice Roberts then dissented as to whether there was a violation of the Voting Rights Act.]

Justice SCALIA, with whom Justice THOMAS joins, and with whom THE CHIEF JUSTICE and Justice ALITO join [in part], concurring in the judgment in part and dissenting in part.

As I have previously expressed, claims of unconstitutional partisan gerrymandering do not present a justiciable case or controversy. See *Vieth v. Jubelirer* (2004) (plurality opinion). Justice Kennedy's discussion of appellants' political-gerrymandering claims ably demonstrates that, yet again, no party or judge has put forth a judicially discernable standard by which to evaluate them. Unfortunately, the opinion then concludes that the appellants have failed to state a claim as to political gerrymandering, without ever articulating what the elements of such a claim consist of. That is not an available disposition of this appeal. We must either conclude that the claim is nonjusticiable and dismiss it, or else set forth a standard and measure appellant's claim against it. Instead, we again dispose of this claim in a way that provides no guidance to lower-court judges and perpetuates a cause of action with no discernible content. We should simply dismiss appellants' claims as nonjusticiable.

[Justice Scalia then went on to dissent as to whether there was a violation of the Voting Rights Act.]

Chapter 2

The Federal Legislative Power

B. The Commerce Power

4. 1990s-???: Narrowing of the Commerce Power and Revival of the Tenth Amendment as a Constraint on Congress

a. What Is Congress's Authority to Regulate "Commerce Among the States"? (casebook, p. 153)

In *Gonzales v. Raich*, excerpted below, the Supreme Court considered the constitutionality of whether Congress, pursuant to its commerce power, can criminally prohibit and punish cultivation and possession of small amounts of marijuana for medical purposes. In upholding the law at issue here, Justice Stevens's majority opinion argues that the ruling is consistent with earlier decisions such as *Wickard v. Filburn*, *United States v. Lopez*, and *United States v. Morrison*. In appraising *Gonzales v. Raich*, it is important to consider whether this decision is consistent with these precedents, or whether there is tension between it and especially *Lopez* and *Morrison*, which narrowed the scope of Congress's commerce power.

GONZALES v. RAICH
125 S. Ct. 2195 (2005)

Justice STEVENS delivered the opinion of the Court.

California is one of at least nine States that authorize the use of marijuana for medicinal purposes. The question presented in this case is whether the power vested in Congress by Article I, § 8, of the Constitution "[t]o make all Laws which shall be necessary and proper for carrying into Execution" its authority to "regulate Commerce with foreign Nations, and among the several States" includes the power to prohibit the local cultivation and use of marijuana in compliance with California law.

I

California has been a pioneer in the regulation of marijuana. In 1913, California was one of the first States to prohibit the sale and possession of marijuana, and at the end of the century, California became the first State to authorize limited use of the drug for medicinal purposes. In 1996, California voters passed Proposition 215, now codified as the Compassionate Use Act of 1996. The proposition was designed to ensure that "seriously ill" residents of the State have access to marijuana for medical purposes, and to encourage Federal and State Governments to take steps towards ensuring the safe and affordable distribution of the drug to patients in need. The Act creates an exemption from criminal prosecution for physicians, as well as for patients and primary caregivers who possess or cultivate marijuana for medicinal purposes with the recommendation or approval of a physician.

Respondents Angel Raich and Diane Monson are California residents who suffer from a variety of serious medical conditions and have sought to avail themselves of medical marijuana pursuant to the terms of the Compassionate Use Act. They are being treated by licensed, board-certified family practitioners, who have concluded, after prescribing a host of conventional medicines to treat respondents' conditions and to alleviate their associated symptoms, that marijuana is the only drug available that provides effective treatment. Both women have been using marijuana as a medication for several years pursuant to their doctors' recommendation, and both rely heavily on cannabis to function on a daily basis. Indeed, Raich's physician believes that forgoing cannabis treatments would certainly cause Raich excruciating pain and could very well prove fatal.

On August 15, 2002, county deputy sheriffs and agents from the federal Drug Enforcement Administration (DEA) came to Monson's home. After a thorough investigation, the county officials concluded that her use of marijuana was entirely lawful as a matter of California law. Nevertheless, after a 3-hour standoff, the federal agents seized and destroyed all six of her cannabis plants. Respondents thereafter brought this action against the Attorney General of the United States and the head of the DEA seeking injunctive and declaratory relief prohibiting the enforcement of the federal Controlled Substances Act (CSA) to the extent it prevents them from possessing, obtaining, or manufacturing cannabis for their personal medical use.

The case is made difficult by respondents' strong arguments that they will suffer irreparable harm because, despite a congressional finding to the contrary, marijuana does have valid therapeutic purposes. The question before us, however, is not whether it is wise to enforce the statute in these circumstances; rather, it is whether Congress' power to regulate interstate markets for medicinal substances encompasses the portions of those markets that are supplied with drugs produced and consumed locally. Well-settled law controls our answer. The CSA is a valid exercise of federal power, even as applied to the troubling facts of this case. We accordingly vacate the judgment of the Court of Appeals.

II

Shortly after taking office in 1969, President Nixon declared a national "war on drugs." As the first campaign of that war, Congress set out to enact legislation that would consolidate various drug laws on the books into a comprehensive statute, provide meaningful regulation over legitimate sources of drugs to prevent diversion into illegal channels, and strengthen law enforcement tools against the traffic in illicit drugs. That effort culminated in the passage of the Comprehensive Drug Abuse Prevention and Control Act of 1970.

[Subsequently, Congress enacted the CSA and] Congress devised a closed regulatory system making it unlawful to manufacture, distribute, dispense, or possess any controlled substance except in a manner authorized by the CSA. The CSA categorizes all controlled substances into five schedules. The drugs are grouped together based on their accepted medical uses, the potential for abuse, and their psychological and physical effects on the body. Each schedule is associated with a distinct set of controls regarding the manufacture, distribution, and use of the substances listed therein. The CSA and its implementing regulations set forth strict requirements regarding registration, labeling and packaging, production quotas, drug security, and recordkeeping.

In enacting the CSA, Congress classified marijuana as a Schedule I drug. Schedule I drugs are categorized as such because of their high potential for abuse, lack of any accepted medical use, and absence of any accepted safety for use in medically supervised treatment. These three factors, in varying gradations, are also used to categorize drugs in the other four schedules. For example, Schedule II substances also have a high potential for abuse which may lead to severe psychological or physical dependence, but unlike Schedule I drugs, they have a currently accepted medical use.

III

Respondents in this case do not dispute that passage of the CSA, as part of the Comprehensive Drug Abuse Prevention and Control Act, was well within Congress' commerce power. Nor do they contend that any provision or section of the CSA amounts to an unconstitutional exercise of congressional authority. Rather, respondents' challenge is actually quite limited; they argue that the CSA's categorical prohibition of the manufacture and possession of marijuana as applied to the intrastate manufacture and possession of marijuana for medical purposes pursuant to California law exceeds Congress' authority under the Commerce Clause.

In assessing the validity of congressional regulation, none of our Commerce Clause cases can be viewed in isolation. As charted in considerable detail in *United States v. Lopez*, our understanding of the reach of the Commerce Clause, as well as Congress' assertion of authority thereunder, has evolved over time. Cases decided during that "new era," which now spans more than a century, have identified three general categories of regulation in which Congress is authorized to engage under its commerce power. First, Congress can regulate the channels of interstate commerce. Second, Congress has authority to regulate and protect the instrumentalities of interstate commerce, and persons or things in interstate commerce. Third, Congress has the power to regulate activities that substantially affect interstate commerce. Only the third category is implicated in the case at hand.

Our case law firmly establishes Congress' power to regulate purely local activities that are part of an economic "class of activities" that have a substantial effect on interstate commerce. See, e.g., *Wickard v. Filburn* (1942). As we stated in *Wickard*, "even if appellee's activity be local and though it may not be regarded as commerce, it may still, whatever its nature, be reached by Congress if it exerts a substantial economic effect on interstate commerce." We have never required Congress to legislate with scientific exactitude. When Congress decides that the "'total incidence'" of a practice poses a threat to a national market, it may regulate the entire class. In this vein, we have reiterated that when "'a general regulatory statute bears a substantial relation to commerce, the de minimis character of individual instances arising under that statute is of no consequence.'"

Our decision in *Wickard* is of particular relevance. In *Wickard*, we upheld the application of regulations promulgated under the Agricultural Adjustment Act of 1938, which were designed to control the volume of wheat moving in interstate and foreign commerce in order to avoid surpluses and consequent abnormally low prices. *Wickard* thus establishes that Congress can regulate purely intrastate activity that is not itself "commercial," in that it is not produced for sale, if it concludes that failure to regulate that class of activity would undercut the regulation of the interstate market in that commodity.

The similarities between this case and *Wickard* are striking. Like the farmer in *Wickard*, respondents are cultivating, for home consumption, a fungible commodity for which there is an established, albeit illegal, interstate market. Just as the Agricultural Adjustment Act was designed "to control the volume [of wheat] moving in interstate and foreign commerce in order to avoid surpluses . . ." and consequently control the market price, a primary purpose of the CSA is to control the supply and demand of controlled substances in both lawful and unlawful drug markets. In *Wickard*, we had no difficulty concluding that Congress had a rational basis for believing that, when viewed in the aggregate, leaving homeconsumed wheat outside the regulatory scheme would have a substantial influence on price and market conditions. Here too, Congress had a rational basis for concluding that leaving home-consumed marijuana outside federal control would similarly affect price and market conditions.

More concretely, one concern prompting inclusion of wheat grown for home consumption in the 1938 Act was that rising market prices could draw such wheat into the interstate market, resulting in lower market prices. The parallel concern making it appropriate to include marijuana grown for home consumption in the CSA is the likelihood that the high demand in the interstate market will draw such marijuana into that market. While the diversion of homegrown wheat tended to frustrate the federal interest in stabilizing prices by regulating the volume of commercial transactions in the interstate market, the diversion of homegrown marijuana tends to frustrate the federal interest in eliminating commercial transactions in the interstate market in their entirety. In both cases, the regulation is squarely within Congress' commerce power because production of the commodity meant for home consumption, be it wheat or marijuana, has a substantial effect on supply and demand in the national market for that commodity.[1]

Nonetheless, respondents suggest that *Wickard* differs from this case in three respects: (1) the Agricultural Adjustment Act, unlike the CSA, exempted small farming operations; (2) *Wickard* involved a "quintessential economic activity"— a commercial farm—whereas respondents do not sell marijuana; and (3) the *Wickard* record made it clear that the aggregate production of wheat for use on farms had a significant impact on market prices. Those differences, though factually accurate, do not diminish the precedential force of this Court's reasoning. The fact that Wickard's own impact on the market was "trivial by itself" was not a sufficient reason for removing him from the scope of federal regulation. That the Secretary of Agriculture elected to exempt even smaller farms from regulation does not speak to his power to regulate all those whose aggregated production was significant, nor did that fact play any role in the Court's analysis. Moreover, even though Wickard was indeed a commercial farmer, the activity he was engaged in—the cultivation of wheat for home consumption—was not treated by the Court as part of his commercial farming operation. And while it is true that the record in the *Wickard* case itself established the causal connection between the production for local use and the national market, we have before us findings by Congress to the same effect.

In assessing the scope of Congress' authority under the Commerce Clause, we stress that the task before us is a modest one. We need not determine whether respondents' activities, taken in the aggregate, substantially affect interstate commerce in fact, but only whether a "rational basis" exists for so concluding. Given the enforcement difficulties that attend distinguishing between marijuana cultivated locally and marijuana grown elsewhere, 21 U.S.C. § 801(5), and concerns about diversion into illicit channels, we have no difficulty concluding that Congress had a rational basis for believing that failure to regulate the intrastate manufacture and possession of marijuana would leave a gaping hole in the CSA. Thus, as in *Wickard*, when it enacted comprehensive legislation to regulate the interstate market in a fungible commodity, Congress was acting well within its authority to "make all Laws which shall be necessary and proper" to "regulate Commerce . . . among the several States." U.S. Const.,

---

1. To be sure, the wheat market is a lawful market that Congress sought to protect and stabilize, whereas the marijuana market is an unlawful market that Congress sought to eradicate. This difference, however, is of no constitutional import. It has long been settled that Congress' power to regulate commerce includes the power to prohibit commerce in a particular commodity. [Footnote by the Court.]

Art. I, § 8. That the regulation ensnares some purely intrastate activity is of no moment. As we have done many times before, we refuse to excise individual components of that larger scheme.

IV

To support their contrary submission, respondents rely heavily on two of our more recent Commerce Clause cases. In their myopic focus, they overlook the larger context of modern-era Commerce Clause jurisprudence preserved by those cases. Moreover, even in the narrow prism of respondents' creation, they read those cases far too broadly. Those two cases, of course, are United States v. Lopez (1995) and *United States v. Morrison* (2000). As an initial matter, the statutory challenges at issue in those cases were markedly different from the challenge respondents pursue in the case at hand. Here, respondents ask us to excise individual applications of a concededly valid statutory scheme. In contrast, in both *Lopez* and *Morrison*, the parties asserted that a particular statute or provision fell outside Congress' commerce power in its entirety. This distinction is pivotal for we have often reiterated that "[w]here the class of activities is regulated and that class is within the reach of federal power, the courts have no power 'to excise, as trivial, individual instances' of the class."

Unlike those at issue in *Lopez* and *Morrison*, the activities regulated by the CSA are quintessentially economic. "Economics" refers to "the production, distribution, and consumption of commodities." Webster's Third New International Dictionary (1966). The CSA is a statute that regulates the production, distribution, and consumption of commodities for which there is an established, and lucrative, interstate market. Prohibiting the intrastate possession or manufacture of an article of commerce is a rational (and commonly utilized) means of regulating commerce in that product. Such prohibitions include specific decisions requiring that a drug be withdrawn from the market as a result of the failure to comply with regulatory requirements as well as decisions excluding Schedule I drugs entirely from the market. Because the CSA is a statute that directly regulates economic, commercial activity, our opinion in *Morrison* casts no doubt on its constitutionality.

V

Respondents also raise a substantive due process claim and seek to avail themselves of the medical necessity defense. These theories of relief were set forth in their complaint but were not reached by the Court of Appeals. We therefore do not address the question whether judicial relief is available to respondents on these alternative bases. We do note, however, the presence of another avenue of relief. As the Solicitor General confirmed during oral argument, the statute authorizes procedures for the reclassification of Schedule I drugs. But perhaps even more important than these legal avenues is the democratic process, in which the voices of voters allied with these respondents may one day be heard in the halls of Congress.

Justice SCALIA, concurring in the judgment.

I agree with the Court's holding that the Controlled Substances Act (CSA) may validly be applied to respondents' cultivation, distribution, and possession of marijuana for personal, medicinal use. I write separately because my understanding of the doctrinal foundation on which that holding rests is, if not inconsistent with that of the Court, at least more nuanced.

Since *Perez v. United States* (1971), our cases have mechanically recited that the Commerce Clause permits congressional regulation of three categories: (1) the channels of interstate commerce; (2) the instrumentalities of interstate commerce, and persons or things in interstate commerce; and (3) activities that "substantially affect" interstate commerce. The first two categories are self-evident, since they are the ingredients of interstate commerce itself. The third category, however, is different in kind, and its recitation without explanation is misleading and incomplete.

It is misleading because, unlike the channels, instrumentalities, and agents of interstate commerce, activities that substantially affect interstate commerce are not themselves part of interstate commerce, and thus the power to regulate them cannot come from the Commerce Clause alone. Rather, Congress's regulatory authority over intrastate activities that are not themselves part of interstate commerce (including activities that have a substantial effect on interstate commerce) derives from the Necessary and Proper Clause. And the category of "activities that substantially affect interstate commerce" is incomplete because the authority to enact laws necessary and proper for the regulation of interstate commerce is not limited to laws governing intrastate activities that substantially affect interstate commerce. Where necessary to make a regulation of interstate commerce effective, Congress may regulate even those intrastate activities that do not themselves substantially affect interstate commerce.

Today's principal dissent objects that, by permitting Congress to regulate activities necessary to effective interstate regulation, the Court reduces *Lopez* and *Morrison* to "little more than a drafting guide." I think that criticism unjustified. Unlike the power to regulate activities that have a substantial effect on interstate commerce, the power to enact laws enabling effective regulation of interstate commerce can only be exercised in conjunction with congressional regulation of an interstate market, and it extends only to tho measures necessary to make the interstate regulation effective. As *Lopez* itself states, and the Court affirms today, Congress may regulate noneconomic intrastate activities only where the failure to do so "could . . . undercut" its regulation of interstate commerce. This is not a power that threatens to obliterate the line between "what is truly national and what is truly local."

Lopez and *Morrison* affirm that Congress may not regulate certain "purely local" activity within the States based solely on the attenuated effect that such activity may have in the interstate market. But those decisions do not declare noneconomic intrastate activities to be categorically beyond the reach of the Federal Government. Neither case involved the power of Congress to exert control over intrastate activities in connection with a more comprehensive scheme of regulation.

To dismiss this distinction as "superficial and formalistic," (O'Connor, J., dissenting), is to misunderstand the nature of the Necessary and Proper Clause, which empowers Congress to enact laws in effectuation of its enumerated powers that are not within its authority to enact in isolation. See McCulloch v. Maryland (1819). And there are other restraints upon the Necessary and Proper Clause authority. As Chief Justice Marshall wrote in McCulloch v. Maryland, even when the end is constitutional and legitimate, the means must be "appropriate" and "plainly adapted" to that end. Moreover, they may not be otherwise "prohibited" and must be "consistent with the letter and spirit of the constitution." These phrases are not merely hortatory.

III

The application of these principles to the case before us is straightforward. In the CSA, Congress has undertaken to extinguish the interstate market in Schedule I controlled substances, including marijuana. The Commerce Clause unquestionably permits this. The power to regulate interstate commerce "extends not only to those regulations which aid, foster and protect the commerce, but embraces those which prohibit it." To effectuate its objective, Congress has prohibited almost all intrastate activities related to Schedule I substances—both economic activities (manufacture, distribution, possession with the intent to distribute) and noneconomic activities (simple possession). That simple possession is a noneconomic activity is immaterial to whether it can be prohibited as a necessary part of a larger regulation. Rather, Congress's authority to enact all of these prohibitions of intrastate controlled-substance activities depends only upon whether they are appropriate means of achieving the legitimate end of eradicating Schedule I substances from interstate commerce.

By this measure, I think the regulation must be sustained. Not only is it impossible to distinguish "controlled substances manufactured and distributed intrastate" from "controlled substances manufactured and distributed interstate," but it hardly makes sense to speak in such terms. Drugs like marijuana are fungible commodities. As the Court explains, marijuana that is grown at home and possessed for personal use is never more than an instant from the interstate market— and this is so whether or not the possession is for medicinal use or lawful use under the laws of a particular State. Congress need not accept on faith that state law will be effective in maintaining a strict division between a lawful market for "medical" marijuana and the more general marijuana market.

I thus agree with the Court that, however the class of regulated activities is subdivided, Congress could reasonably conclude that its objective of prohibiting marijuana from the interstate market "could be undercut" if those activities were excepted from its general scheme of regulation. That is sufficient to authorize the application of the CSA to respondents.

Justice O'CONNOR, with whom THE CHIEF JUSTICE and Justice THOMAS join as to all but Part III, dissenting.

We enforce the "outer limits" of Congress' Commerce Clause authority not for their own sake, but to protect historic spheres of state sovereignty from excessive federal encroachment and thereby to maintain the distribution of power fundamental to our federalist system of government. *United States v. Lopez* (1995). One of federalism's chief virtues, of course, is that it promotes innovation by allowing for the possibility that "a single courageous State may, if its citizens choose, serve as a laboratory; and try novel social and economic experiments without risk to the rest of the country." *New State Ice Co. v. Liebmann* (1932) (Brandeis, J., dissenting).

This case exemplifies the role of States as laboratories. The States' core police powers have always included authority to define criminal law and to protect the health, safety, and welfare of their citizens. Exercising those powers, California (by ballot initiative and then by legislative codification) has come to its own conclusion about the difficult and sensitive question of whether marijuana should be available to relieve severe pain and suffering. Today the Court sanctions an application of the federal Controlled Substances Act that extinguishes that experiment, without any proof that the personal cultivation, possession, and use of marijuana for medicinal purposes, if economic activity in the first place, has a substantial effect on interstate commerce and is therefore an appropriate subject of federal regulation. In so doing, the Court announces a rule that gives Congress a perverse incentive to legislate broadly pursuant to the Commerce Clause—nestling questionable assertions of its authority into comprehensive regulatory schemes—rather than with precision. That rule and the result it produces in this case are irreconcilable with our decisions in *Lopez* and *Morrison*. Accordingly I dissent.

What is the relevant conduct subject to Commerce Clause analysis in this case? The Court takes its cues from Congress, applying the above considerations to the activity regulated by the Controlled Substances Act (CSA) in general. The Court's decision rests on two facts about the CSA: (1) Congress chose to enact a single statute providing a comprehensive prohibition on the production, distribution, and possession of all controlled substances, and (2) Congress did not distinguish between various forms of intrastate noncommercial cultivation, possession, and use of marijuana. Today's decision suggests that the federal regulation of local activity is immune to Commerce Clause challenge because Congress chose to act with an ambitious, all-encompassing statute, rather than piecemeal. In my view, allowing Congress to set the terms of the constitutional debate in this way, i.e., by packaging regulation of local activity in broader schemes, is tantamount to removing meaningful limits on the Commerce Clause.

The Court's principal means of distinguishing *Lopez* from this case is to observe that the Gun-Free School Zones Act of 1990 was a "brief, single-subject statute," whereas the CSA is "a lengthy and detailed statute creating a comprehensive framework for regulating the production, distribution, and possession of five classes of 'controlled substances.'" Thus, according to the Court, it was possible in *Lopez* to evaluate in isolation the constitutionality of criminalizing local activity (there gun possession in school zones), whereas the local activity that the CSA targets (in this case cultivation and possession of marijuana for personal medicinal use) cannot be separated from the general drug control scheme of which it is a part.

Today's decision allows Congress to regulate intrastate activity without check, so long as there is some implication by legislative design that regulating intrastate activity is essential (and the Court appears to equate "essential" with "necessary") to the interstate regulatory scheme. Seizing upon our language in *Lopez* that the statute prohibiting gun possession in school zones was "not an essential part of a larger regulation of economic activity, in which the regulatory scheme could be undercut unless the intrastate activity were regulated," the Court appears to reason that the placement of local activity in a comprehensive scheme confirms that it is essential to that scheme. If the Court is right, then *Lopez* stands for nothing more than a drafting guide: Congress should have described the relevant crime as "transfer or possession of a firearm anywhere in the nation"—thus including commercial and noncommercial activity, and clearly encompassing some activity with assuredly substantial effect on interstate commerce. Had it done so, the majority hints, we would have sustained its authority to regulate possession of firearms in school zones. Furthermore, today's decision suggests we would readily sustain a congressional decision to attach the regulation of intrastate activity to a pre-existing comprehensive (or even not-so-comprehensive) scheme. If so, the Court invites increased federal regulation of local activity even if, as it suggests, Congress would not enact a new interstate scheme exclusively for the sake of reaching intrastate activity. I cannot agree that our decision in *Lopez* contemplated such evasive or overbroad legislative strategies with approval. Until today, such arguments have been made only in dissent.

Lopez and *Morrison* did not indicate that the constitutionality of federal regulation depends on superficial and formalistic distinctions. Likewise I did not understand our discussion of the role of courts in enforcing outer limits of the Commerce Clause for the sake of maintaining the federalist balance our Constitution requires as a signal to Congress to enact legislation that is more extensive and more intrusive into the domain of state power. If the Court always defers to Congress as it does today, little may be left to the notion of enumerated powers.

The hard work for courts, then, is to identify objective markers for confining the analysis in Commerce Clause cases. Here, respondents challenge the constitutionality of the CSA as applied to them and those similarly situated. I agree with the Court that we must look beyond respondents' own activities. Otherwise, individual litigants could always exempt themselves from Commerce Clause regulation merely by pointing to the obvious—that their personal activities do not have a substantial effect on interstate commerce. The task is to identify a mode of analysis that allows Congress to regulate more than nothing (by declining to reduce each case to its litigants) and less than everything (by declining to let Congress set the terms of analysis). The analysis may not be the same in every case, for it depends on the regulatory scheme at issue and the federalism concerns implicated.

A number of objective markers are available to confine the scope of constitutional review here. Both federal and state legislation—including the CSA itself, the California Compassionate Use Act, and other state medical marijuana legislation—recognize that medical and nonmedical (i.e., recreational) uses of drugs are realistically distinct and can be segregated, and regulate them differently. Respondents challenge only the application of the CSA to medicinal use of marijuana. Moreover, because fundamental structural concerns about dual sovereignty animate our Commerce Clause cases, it is relevant that this case involves the interplay of federal and state regulation in areas of criminal law and social policy, where "States lay claim by right of history and expertise." Under our precedents, the conduct is economic and, in the aggregate, substantially affects interstate commerce. Even if intrastate cultivation and possession of marijuana for one's own medicinal use can properly be characterized as economic, and I question whether it can, it has not been shown that such activity substantially affects interstate commerce. Similarly, it is neither self-evident nor demonstrated that regulating such activity is necessary to the interstate drug control scheme.

The Court's definition of economic activity is breathtaking. It defines as economic any activity involving the production, distribution, and consumption of commodities. And it appears to reason that when an interstate market for a commodity exists, regulating the intrastate manufacture or possession of that commodity is constitutional either because that intrastate activity is itself economic, or because regulating it is a rational part of regulating its market. Putting to one side the problem endemic to the Court's opinion—the shift in focus from the activity at issue in this case to the entirety of what the CSA regulates—the Court's definition of economic activity for purposes of Commerce Clause jurisprudence threatens to sweep all of productive human activity into federal regulatory reach.

Even assuming that economic activity is at issue in this case, the Government has made no showing in fact that the possession and use of homegrown marijuana for medical purposes, in California or elsewhere, has a substantial effect on interstate commerce. Similarly, the Government has not shown that regulating such activity is necessary to an interstate regulatory scheme. Whatever the specific theory of "substantial effects" at issue (i.e., whether the activity substantially affects interstate commerce, whether its regulation is necessary to an interstate regulatory scheme, or both), a concern for dual sovereignty requires that Congress' excursion into the traditional domain of States be justified.

That is why characterizing this as a case about the Necessary and Proper Clause does not change the analysis significantly. Congress must exercise its authority under the Necessary and Proper Clause in a manner consistent with basic constitutional principles. Likewise, that authority must be used in a manner consistent with the notion of enumerated powers—a structural principle that is as much part of the Constitution as the Tenth Amendment's explicit textual command. Accordingly, something more than mere assertion is required when Congress purports to have power over local activity whose connection to an intrastate market is not self-evident. Otherwise, the Necessary and Proper Clause will always be a back door for unconstitutional federal regulation. Indeed, if it were enough in "substantial effects" cases for the Court to supply conceivable justifications for intrastate regulation related to an interstate market, then we could have surmised in *Lopez* that guns in school zones are "never more than an instant from the interstate market" in guns already subject to extensive federal regulation, recast *Lopez* as a Necessary and Proper Clause case, and thereby upheld the Gun-Free School Zones Act of 1990.

There is simply no evidence that homegrown medicinal marijuana users constitute, in the aggregate, a sizable enough class to have a discernable, let alone substantial, impact on the national illicit drug market—or otherwise to threaten the CSA regime.

The Government has not overcome empirical doubt that the number of Californians engaged in personal cultivation, possession, and use of medical marijuana, or the amount of marijuana they produce, is enough to threaten the federal regime. Nor has it shown that Compassionate Use Act marijuana users have been or are realistically likely to be responsible for the drug's seeping into the market in a significant way. The Government does cite one estimate that there were over 100,000 Compassionate Use Act users in California in 2004, but does not explain, in terms of proportions, what their presence means for the national illicit drug market.

Relying on Congress' abstract assertions, the Court has endorsed making it a federal crime to grow small amounts of marijuana in one's own home for one's own medicinal use. This overreaching stifles an express choice by some States, concerned for the lives and liberties of their people, to regulate medical marijuana differently. If I were a California citizen, I would not have voted for the medical marijuana ballot initiative; if I were a California legislator I would not have supported the Compassionate Use Act. But whatever the wisdom of California's experiment with medical marijuana, the federalism principles that have driven our Commerce Clause cases require that room for experiment be protected in this case. For these reasons I dissent.

Justice THOMAS, dissenting.

Respondents Diane Monson and Angel Raich use marijuana that has never been bought or sold, that has never crossed state lines, and that has had no demonstrable effect on the national market for marijuana. If Congress can regulate this under the Commerce Clause, then it can regulate virtually anything—and the Federal Government is no longer one of limited and enumerated powers.

I

Respondents' local cultivation and consumption of marijuana is not "Commerce . . . among the several States." By holding that Congress may regulate activity that is neither interstate nor commerce under the Interstate Commerce Clause, the Court abandons any attempt to enforce the Constitution's limits on federal power. The majority supports this conclusion by invoking, without explanation, the Necessary and Proper Clause. Regulating respondents' conduct, however, is not "necessary and proper for carrying into Execution" Congress' restrictions on the interstate drug trade. Thus, neither the Commerce Clause nor the Necessary and Proper Clause grants Congress the power to regulate respondents' conduct.

As I explained at length in *United States v. Lopez* (1995), the Commerce Clause empowers Congress to regulate the buying and selling of goods and services trafficked across state lines. The Clause's text, structure, and history all indicate that, at the time of the founding, the term "'commerce' consisted of selling, buying, and bartering, as well as transporting for these purposes." Commerce, or trade, stood in contrast to productive activities like manufacturing and agriculture.

Even the majority does not argue that respondents' conduct is itself "Commerce among the several States." Monson and Raich neither buy nor sell the marijuana that they consume. They cultivate their cannabis entirely in the State of California—it never crosses state lines, much less as part of a commercial transaction. Certainly no evidence from the founding suggests that "commerce" included the mere possession of a good or some purely personal activity that did not involve trade or exchange for value. In the early days of the Republic, it would have been unthinkable that Congress could prohibit the local cultivation, possession, and consumption of marijuana.

On this traditional understanding of "commerce," the Controlled Substances Act (CSA) regulates a great deal of marijuana trafficking that is interstate and commercial in character. The CSA does not, however, criminalize only the interstate buying and selling of marijuana. Instead, it bans the entire market— intrastate or interstate, noncommercial or commercial—for marijuana. Respondents are correct that the CSA exceeds Congress' commerce power as applied to their conduct, which is purely intrastate and noncommercial.

More difficult, however, is whether the CSA is a valid exercise of Congress' power to enact laws that are "necessary and proper for carrying into Execution" its power to regulate interstate commerce. The Necessary and Proper Clause is not a warrant to Congress to enact any law that bears some conceivable connection to the exercise of an enumerated power. Nor is it, however, a command to Congress to enact only laws that are absolutely indispensable to the exercise of an enumerated power.

On its face, a ban on the intrastate cultivation, possession and distribution of marijuana may be plainly adapted to stopping the interstate flow of marijuana. Unregulated local growers and users could swell both the supply and the demand sides of the interstate marijuana market, making the market more difficult to regulate. But respondents do not challenge the CSA on its face. Instead, they challenge it as applied to their conduct. The question is thus whether the intrastate ban is "necessary and proper" as applied to medical marijuana users like respondents.

Respondents are not regulable simply because they belong to a large class (local growers and users of marijuana) that Congress might need to reach, if they also belong to a distinct and separable subclass (local growers and users of state-authorized, medical marijuana) that does not undermine the CSA's interstate ban. California's Compassionate Use Act sets respondents' conduct apart from other intrastate producers and users of marijuana.

In sum, neither in enacting the CSA nor in defending its application to respondents has the Government offered any obvious reason why banning medical marijuana use is necessary to stem the tide of interstate drug trafficking. Congress' goal of curtailing the interstate drug trade would not plainly be thwarted if it could not apply the CSA to patients like Monson and Raich. That is, unless Congress' aim is really to exercise police power of the sort reserved to the States in order to eliminate even the intrastate possession and use of marijuana.

The majority prevents States like California from devising drug policies that they have concluded provide much-needed respite to the seriously ill. It does so without any serious inquiry into the necessity for federal regulation or the propriety of "displac[ing] state regulation in areas of traditional state concern." The majority's rush to embrace federal power "is especially unfortunate given the importance of showing respect for the sovereign States that comprise our Federal Union." Our federalist system, properly understood, allows California and a growing number of other States to decide for themselves how to safeguard the health and welfare of their citizens. I would affirm the judgment of the Court of Appeals.

Two high profile cases raised potentially important issues concerning the scope of Congress's commerce clause authority, but each was decided on statutory interpretation grounds without reaching the constitutional issues. In *Gonzales v. Oregon*, 126 S. Ct. 904 (2006), the Court considered the legality of an interpretive rule issued by Attorney General John Ashcroft that physicians who assist with suicide of terminally ill patients pursuant to the Oregon Death With Dignity Act would be violating the federal Controlled Substances Act and could thereby lose the ability to issue prescriptions. The Court, in a 6-3 decision with Justice Kennedy writing for the majority, held that the interpretive rule did not fit within the scope of the Attorney General's authority under the Controlled Substances Act and thus was invalid.

There was no discussion of the Constitution or federalism, except for the following paragraph: "Just as the conventions of expression indicate that Congress is unlikely to alter a statute's obvious scope and division of authority through muffled hints, the background principles of our federal system also belie the notion that Congress would use such an obscure grant of authority to regulate areas traditionally supervised by the States' police power. It is unnecessary even to consider the application of clear statement requirements, or presumptions against pre-emption, to reach this commonsense conclusion. For all these reasons, we conclude the CSA's prescription requirement does not authorize the Attorney General to bar dispensing controlled substances for assisted suicide in the face of a state medical regime permitting such conduct."

The other case that potentially raised commerce clause issues was *Rapanos v. United States*, 126 S.Ct. 2208 (2006), in which the Court considered whether the federal Clean Water Act (CWA) could be applied to intrastate wetlands. Justice Scalia, writing for a plurality of four, gave a narrow construction to the statute and said that the term "navigable waters," under CWA, includes only relatively permanent, standing or flowing bodies of water, not intermittent or ephemeral flows of water, and only those wetlands with a continuous surface connection to bodies that are waters of the United States in their own right are adjacent to such waters and covered by the CWA. Again, the plurality opinion was based on statutory interpretation and not on the commerce clause.

However, at the conclusion of the plurality opinion, Justice Scalia invoked the Constitution: "Even if the phrase 'the waters of the United States' were ambiguous as applied to intermittent flows, our own canons of construction would establish that the Corps' interpretation of the statute is impermissible. As we noted in [*Solid Waste Agency of Northern Cook County v. United States Army Corps of Engineers (SWANCC)*], the Government's expansive interpretation would "result in a significant impingement of the States' traditional and primary power over land and water use." Regulation of land use, as through the issuance of the development permits sought by petitioners in both of these cases, is a quintessential state and local power. The extensive federal jurisdiction urged by the Government would authorize the Corps to function as a de facto regulator of immense stretches of intrastate land—an authority the agency has shown its willingness to exercise with the scope of discretion that would befit a local zoning board. We ordinarily expect a "clear and manifest" statement from Congress to authorize an unprecedented intrusion into traditional state authority. The phrase "the waters of the United States" hardly qualifies.

Likewise, just as we noted in *SWANCC*, the Corps' interpretation stretches the outer limits of Congress's commerce power and raises difficult questions about the ultimate scope of that power. Even if the term "the waters of the United States" were ambiguous as applied to channels that sometimes host ephemeral flows of water (which it is not), we would expect a clearer statement from Congress to authorize an agency theory of jurisdiction that presses the envelope of constitutional validity.

Justice Kennedy concurred in the judgment, and said that the Water Pollution Control Act applies to intrastate waters that have a "significant nexus" to interstate waters. He disagreed with the plurality's approach and said its that reading of the Act "is inconsistent with its text, structure, and purpose." Justice Kennedy said that the significant nexus test he urged also would meet the requirements under the commerce clause.

Justices Stevens, Souter, Ginsburg, and Breyer would have upheld that federal regulation of the intrastate wetlands. As a result, since Justice Kennedy's vote was the narrowest ground upon which a majority agreed, his "significant nexus" test is now to be followed for the application of the CWA.

E. Congress's Power to Authorize Suits Against State Governments

1. Background on the Eleventh Amendment and Sovereign Immunity (casebook, p. 222)

In *Central Virginia Community College v. Katz*, 126 S.Ct. 990 (2006), the Court ruled that sovereign immunity does not apply in bankruptcy courts. Justice Stevens, writing for the Court in a 5-4 decision, stated: "Bankruptcy jurisdiction, as understood today and at the time of the framing, is principally in rem jurisdiction. In bankruptcy, 'the court's jurisdiction is premised on the debtor and his estate, and not on the creditors.' As such, its exercise does not, in the usual case, interfere with state sovereignty even when States' interests are affected.

The text of Article I, § 8, cl. 4, of the Constitution, however, provides that Congress shall have the power to establish 'uniform Laws on the subject of Bankruptcies throughout the United States.' Although the interest in avoiding unjust imprisonment for debt and making federal discharges in bankruptcy enforceable in every State was a primary motivation for the adoption of that provision, its coverage encompasses the entire 'subject of Bankruptcies.' The power granted to Congress by that Clause is a unitary concept rather than an amalgam of discrete segments.

The ineluctable conclusion, then, is that States agreed in the plan of the Convention not to assert any sovereign immunity defense they might have had in proceedings brought pursuant to 'Laws on the subject of Bankruptcies.'

It is interesting to note that this was a 5-4 decision, with Justice O'Connor in the majority. Perhaps the result would have been different with Justice Alito on the Court, and perhaps it will be revisited by the Court in the future.

2. Congress's Power to Authorize Suits Against State Governments

c. Congress's Greater Authority to Legislate Concerning Types of Discrimination and Rights that Receive Heightened Scrutiny (casebook, p. 246)

As the casebook indicates, based on the most recent Supreme Court decisions concerning sovereign immunity, *Nevada Department of Human Resources v. Hibbs* and *Tennessee v. Lane*, Congress has greater authority to legislate under section five of the Fourteenth Amendment when it is dealing with a type of discrimination or a right that receives heightened scrutiny. In *United States v. Georgia*, below, the Court considered, as it did in *Lane*, whether a state government could be sued for violating Title II of the Americans with Disabilities Act. Title II prohibits state and local governments from discriminating against people with disabilities in government programs, services, and activities. In *Lane*, the Court held that state governments can be sued for violating Title II when the fundamental right of access to the courts is implicated.

In *United States v. Georgia*, the Court held that a prisoner who alleged unconstitutional state behavior could sue the state because Congress under section five of the Fourteenth Amendment can provide a remedy for unconstitutional state conduct. Thus, it appears after *United States v. Georgia*, in considering whether a state government can be sued for violating a federal law that authorizes such suits, the initial question is whether the plaintiff alleges a constitutional violation. If so, a state can be sued. If not, the question becomes whether the statute is dealing with a type of discrimination that receives heightened scrutiny or a fundamental right, in which case the lawsuit against the state likely can go forward. But if the plaintiff is not alleging a constitutional violation and the case does not involve a type of discrimination or a right receiving heightened scrutiny, the state can be sued only if Congress finds pervasive unconstitutional state conduct.

UNITED STATES v. GEORGIA
126 S.Ct. 877 (2006)

Justice SCALIA delivered the opinion of the Court.

We consider whether a disabled inmate in a state prison may sue the State for money damages under Title II of the Americans with Disabilities Act of 1990.

Tony Goodman is a paraplegic inmate in the Georgia prison system who, at all relevant times, was housed at the Georgia State Prison in Reidsville. Goodman's pro se complaint and subsequent filings in the District Court included many allegations, both grave and trivial, regarding the conditions of his confinement in the Reidsville prison. Among his more serious allegations, he claimed that he was confined for 23-to-24 hours per day in a 12-by-3-foot cell in which he could not turn his wheelchair around. He alleged that the lack of accessible facilities rendered him unable to use the toilet and shower without assistance, which was often denied. On multiple occasions, he asserted, he had injured himself in attempting to transfer from his wheelchair to the shower or toilet on his own, and, on several other occasions, he had been forced to sit in his own feces and urine while prison officials refused to assist him in cleaning up the waste. He also claimed that he had been denied physical therapy and medical treatment, and denied access to virtually all prison programs and services on account of his disability.

While the Members of this Court have disagreed regarding the scope of Congress's "prophylactic" enforcement powers under § 5 of the Fourteenth Amendment, no one doubts that § 5 grants Congress the power to "enforce . . . the provisions" of the Amendment by creating private remedies against the States for actual violations of those provisions. "Section 5 authorizes Congress to create a cause of action through which the citizen may vindicate his Fourteenth Amendment rights." This enforcement power includes the power to abrogate state sovereign immunity by authorizing private suits for damages against the States. Thus, insofar as Title II creates a private cause of action for damages against the States for conduct that actually violates the Fourteenth Amendment, Title II validly abrogates state sovereign immunity. The Eleventh Circuit erred in dismissing those of Goodman's Title II claims that were based on such unconstitutional conduct.

From the many allegations in Goodman's pro se complaint and his subsequent filings in the District Court, it is not clear precisely what conduct he intended to allege in support of his Title II claims. Because the Eleventh Circuit did not address the issue, it is likewise unclear to what extent the conduct underlying Goodman's constitutional claims also violated Title II. It is therefore unclear whether Goodman's amended complaint will assert Title II claims premised on conduct that does not independently violate the Fourteenth Amendment. Once Goodman's complaint is amended, the lower courts will be best situated to determine in the first instance, on a claim-by-claim basis, (1) which aspects of the State's alleged conduct violated Title II; (2) to what extent such misconduct also violated the Fourteenth Amendment; and (3) insofar as such misconduct violated Title II but did not violate the Fourteenth Amendment, whether Congress's purported abrogation of sovereign immunity as to that class of conduct is nevertheless valid.

Chapter 3

The Federal Executive Power

E. Presidential Power and the War on Terrorism

2. Military Tribunals (casebook, p. 342)

Perhaps the most important decision in October Term 2005 was the Supreme Court's decision in *Hamdan v. Rumsfeld*, below. The case concerned the legality of the military tribunals created by Presidential Executive Order (casebook, p. 343). The United States military captured Yemeni citizen Salim Ahmed Hamdan during its invasion of Afghanistan. There seems no dispute that he was the driver for Bin Laden, although Hamdan does deny any involvement in terrorist activity. The United States detained Hamdan at its naval base in Guantanamo Bay, Cuba. Hamdan was one of the first individuals to be designated for trial in a military tribunal created by Presidential Executive Order.

Hamdan brought a habeas corpus petition arguing that the military tribunal violated his rights under due process and international law. The United States District Court for the District of Columbia granted his habeas petition. The United States Court of Appeals for the District of Columbia Circuit reversed, with then-Judge John Roberts participating.

Subsequent to the grant of certiorari, Congress enacted the Detainee Treatment Act, which said that those in Guantanamo did not have access to habeas corpus and could gain review only in the D.C. Circuit of decisions of the military tribunals.

The Court, in what was essentially a 5-3 ruling, reversed the D.C. Circuit decision and held that the military tribunals created by executive order violated the Geneva Accords and the Uniform Code of Military Justice. (Chief Justice Roberts did not participate because he had been on the panel that decided the case in the D.C. Circuit.) Several aspects of the decision, although important, do not relate to constitutional issues and are not included in the excerpt below. First, the Court held that despite Congress's passage of the Detainee Treatment Act of 2005, the Court had jurisdiction. The Court found that Congress had not clearly indicated that it wanted the restriction on jurisdiction to apply retroactively to cases pending at the time it was adopted. The Court, as a matter of statutory construction, said that Congress did not provide that the provisions restricting jurisdiction would apply retroactively to cases such as this that were already pending in the courts.

Second, the Court rejected the government's argument that abstention was appropriate because the matter was pending in a military tribunal. The Court read *Ex parte Quirin* (casebook, p. 347), which upheld the use of a military tribunal during World War II, as precedent for judicial review.

The core constitutional issue involved whether there was adequate congressional authorization for the Executive Order providing for military tribunals. The Court also considered whether the military tribunals as constituted by the Executive Order met the requirements of international law or the Uniform Code of Military Justice. These aspects of the decision are below.

HAMDAN v. RUMSFELD
126 S.Ct. 2749 (2006)

Justice STEVENS announced the judgment of the Court.

Petitioner Salim Ahmed Hamdan, a Yemeni national, is in custody at an American prison in Guantanamo Bay, Cuba. In November 2001, during hostilities between the United States and the Taliban (which then governed Afghanistan), Hamdan was captured by militia forces and turned over to the U.S. military. In June 2002, he was transported to Guantanamo Bay. Over a year later, the President deemed him eligible for trial by military commission for then-unspecified crimes. After another year had passed, Hamdan was charged with one count of conspiracy "to commit . . . offenses triable by military commission."

Hamdan filed petitions for writs of habeas corpus and mandamus to challenge the Executive Branch's intended means of prosecuting this charge. He concedes that a court-martial constituted in accordance with the Uniform Code of Military Justice (UCMJ) would have authority to try him. His objection is that the military commission the President has convened lacks such authority, for two principal reasons: First, neither congressional Act nor the common law of war supports trial by this commission for the crime of conspiracy—an offense that, Hamdan says, is not a violation of the law of war. Second, Hamdan contends, the procedures that the President has adopted to try him violate the most basic tenets of military and international law, including the principle that a defendant must be permitted to see and hear the evidence against him.

For the reasons that follow, we conclude that the military commission convened to try Hamdan lacks power to proceed because its structure and procedures violate both the UCMJ and the Geneva Conventions. Four of us also conclude, see Part V, infra, that the offense with which Hamdan has been charged is not an "offens[e] that by . . . the law of war may be tried by military commissions."

I

On September 11, 2001, agents of the al Qaeda terrorist organization hijacked commercial airplanes and attacked the World Trade Center in New York City and the national headquarters of the Department of Defense in Arlington, Virginia. Americans will never forget the devastation wrought by these acts. Nearly 3,000 civilians were killed.

Congress responded by adopting a Joint Resolution authorizing the President to "use all necessary and appropriate force against those nations, organizations, or persons he determines planned, authorized, committed, or aided the terrorist attacks . . . in order to prevent any future acts of international terrorism against the United States by such nations, organizations or persons." Authorization for Use of Military Force (AUMF). Acting pursuant to the AUMF, and having determined that the Taliban regime had supported al Qaeda, the President ordered the Armed Forces of the United States to invade Afghanistan. In the ensuing hostilities, hundreds of individuals, Hamdan among them, were captured and eventually detained at Guantanamo Bay.

On November 13, 2001, while the United States was still engaged in active combat with the Taliban, the President issued a comprehensive military order intended to govern the "Detention, Treatment, and Trial of Certain Non-Citizens in the War Against Terrorism." [The Executive Order is found in the casebook at p. 343.]

[II]

The military commission, a tribunal neither mentioned in the Constitution nor created by statute, was born of military necessity. Exigency alone, of course, will not justify the establishment and use of penal tribunals not contemplated by Article I, § 8 and Article III, § 1 of the Constitution unless some other part of that document authorizes a response to the felt need.

Whether the President may constitutionally convene military commissions "without the sanction of Congress" in cases of "controlling necessity" is a question this Court has not answered definitively, and need not answer today. For we held in *Quirin* that Congress had, through Article of War 15, sanctioned the use of military commissions in such circumstances. Article 21 of the UCMJ, the language of which is substantially identical to the old Article 15 and was preserved by Congress after World War II, reads as follows:

> "Jurisdiction of courts-martial not exclusive.
>
> The provisions of this code conferring jurisdiction upon courts-martial shall not be construed as depriving military commissions, provost courts, or other military tribunals of concurrent jurisdiction in respect of offenders or offenses that by statute or by the law of war may be tried by such military commissions, provost courts, or other military tribunals."

We have no occasion to revisit *Quirin's* controversial characterization of Article of War 15 as congressional authorization for military commissions. Contrary to the Government's assertion, however, even *Quirin* did not view the authorization as a sweeping mandate for the President to "invoke military commissions when he deems them necessary." Rather, the *Quirin* Court recognized that Congress had simply preserved what power, under the Constitution and the common law of war, the President had had before 1916 to convene military commissions—with the express condition that the President and those under his command comply with the law of war.[1] That much is evidenced by the Court's inquiry, following its conclusion that Congress had authorized military commissions, into whether the law of war had indeed been complied with in that case.

The Government would have us dispense with the inquiry that the *Quirin* Court undertook and find in either the AUMF or the [Detainee Treatment Act (DTA)] specific, overriding authorization for the very commission that has been convened to try Hamdan. Neither of these congressional Acts, however, expands the President's authority to convene military commissions. First, while we assume that the AUMF activated the President's war powers, see *Hamdi v. Rumsfeld* (2004) (plurality opinion), and that those powers include the authority to convene military commissions in appropriate circumstances, there is nothing in the text or legislative history of the AUMF even hinting that Congress intended to expand or alter the authorization set forth in Article 21 of the UCMJ.

Likewise, the DTA cannot be read to authorize this commission. Although the DTA, unlike either Article 21 or the AUMF, was enacted after the President had convened Hamdan's commission, it contains no language authorizing that tribunal or any other at Guantanamo Bay. The DTA obviously "recognize[s]" the existence of the Guantanamo Bay commissions in the weakest sense, because it references some of the military orders governing them and creates limited judicial review of their "final decision[s]." But the statute also pointedly reserves judgment on whether "the Constitution and laws of the United States are applicable" in reviewing such decisions and whether, if they are, the "standards and procedures" used to try Hamdan and other detainees actually violate the "Constitution and laws."

Together, the UCMJ, the AUMF, and the DTA at most acknowledge a general Presidential authority to convene military commissions in circumstances where justified under the "Constitution and laws," including the law of war. Absent a more specific congressional authorization, the task of this Court is, as it was in *Quirin*, to decide whether Hamdan's military commission is so justified. It is to that inquiry we now turn.

[III]

The common law governing military commissions may be gleaned from past practice and what sparse legal precedent exists. Commissions historically have been used in three situations. First, they have substituted for civilian courts at times and in places where martial law has been declared. Their use in these

---

1. Whether or not the President has independent power, absent congressional authorization, to convene military commissions, he may not disregard limitations that Congress had, in proper exercise of its own war powers, placed on his powers. See *Youngstown Sheet & Tube Co. v. Sawyer* (1952) (Jackson, J., concurring). The Government does not argue otherwise. [Footnote by Justice Stevens]

circumstances has raised constitutional questions. Second, commissions have been established to try civilians "as part of a temporary military government over occupied enemy territory or territory regained from an enemy where civilian government cannot and does not function." Illustrative of this second kind of commission is the one that was established, with jurisdiction to apply the German Criminal Code, in occupied Germany following the end of World War II.

The third type of commission, convened as an "incident to the conduct of war" when there is a need "to seize and subject to disciplinary measures those enemies who in their attempt to thwart or impede our military effort have violated the law of war," has been described as "utterly different" from the other two. Not only is its jurisdiction limited to offenses cognizable during time of war, but its role is primarily a factfinding one—to determine, typically on the battlefield itself, whether the defendant has violated the law of war. The last time the U.S. Armed Forces used the law-of-war military commission was during World War II. In *Quirin*, this Court sanctioned President Roosevelt's use of such a tribunal to try Nazi saboteurs captured on American soil during the War. And in Yamashita, we held that a military commission had jurisdiction to try a Japanese commander for failing to prevent troops under his command from committing atrocities in the Philippines.

Quirin is the model the Government invokes most frequently to defend the commission convened to try Hamdan. That is both appropriate and unsurprising. Since Guantanamo Bay is neither enemy-occupied territory nor under martial law, the law-of-war commission is the only model available. At the same time, no more robust model of executive power exists; *Quirin* represents the high-water mark of military power to try enemy combatants for war crimes.

The charge against Hamdan alleges a conspiracy extending over a number of years, from 1996 to November 2001. All but two months of that more than 5-year-long period preceded the attacks of September 11, 2001, and the enactment of the AUMF—the Act of Congress on which the Government relies for exercise of its war powers and thus for its authority to convene military commissions. Neither the purported agreement with Osama bin Laden and others to commit war crimes, nor a single overt act, is alleged to have occurred in a theater of war or on any specified date after September 11, 2001. None of the overt acts that Hamdan is alleged to have committed violates the law of war.

These facts alone cast doubt on the legality of the charge and, hence, the commission; the offense alleged must have been committed both in a theater of war and during, not before, the relevant conflict. But the deficiencies in the time and place allegations also underscore—indeed are symptomatic of—the most serious defect of this charge: The offense it alleges is not triable by law-of-war military commission. There is no suggestion that Congress has, in exercise of its constitutional authority to "define and punish . . . Offences against the Law of Nations," U.S. Const., Art. I, § 8, cl. 10, positively identified "conspiracy" as a war crime. As we explained in *Quirin*, that is not necessarily fatal to the Government's claim of authority to try the alleged offense by military commission; Congress, through Article 21 of the UCMJ, has "incorporated by reference" the common law of war, which may render triable by military commission certain offenses not defined by statute. When, however, neither the elements of the offense nor the range of permissible punishments is defined by statute or treaty, the precedent must be plain and unambiguous. To demand any less would be to risk concentrating in military hands a degree of adjudicative and punitive power in excess of that contemplated either by statute or by the Constitution. This high standard was met in *Quirin*; the violation there alleged was, by "universal agreement and practice" both in this country and internationally, recognized as an offense against the law of war.

At a minimum, the Government must make a substantial showing that the crime for which it seeks to try a defendant by military commission is acknowledged to be an offense against the law of war. That burden is far from satisfied here. The crime of "conspiracy" has rarely if ever been tried as such in this country by any law-of-war military commission not exercising some other form of jurisdiction, and does not appear in either the Geneva Conventions or the Hague Conventions-the major treaties on the law of war.

[V]

Whether or not the Government has charged Hamdan with an offense against the law of war cognizable by military commission, the commission lacks power to proceed. The UCMJ conditions the President's use of military commissions on compliance not only with the American common law of war, but also with the rest of the UCMJ itself, insofar as applicable, and with the "rules and precepts of the law of nations," including the four Geneva Conventions signed in 1949. The procedures that the Government has decreed will govern Hamdan's trial by commission violate these laws.

These rights [provided by the Presidential Executive Order] are subject, however, to one glaring condition: The accused and his civilian counsel may be excluded from, and precluded from ever learning what evidence was presented during, any part of the proceeding that either the Appointing Authority or the presiding officer decides to "close." Grounds for such closure "include the protection of information classified or classifiable . . . ; information protected by law or rule from unauthorized disclosure; the physical safety of participants in Commission proceedings, including prospective witnesses; intelligence and law enforcement sources, methods, or activities; and other national security interests." Appointed military defense counsel must be privy to these closed sessions, but may, at the presiding officer's discretion, be forbidden to reveal to his or her client what took place therein.

Another striking feature of the rules governing Hamdan's commission is that they permit the admission of any evidence that, in the opinion of the presiding officer, "would have probative value to a reasonable person." Under this test, not only is testimonial hearsay and evidence obtained through coercion fully admissible, but neither live testimony nor witnesses' written statements need be sworn. Moreover, the accused and his civilian counsel may be denied access to evidence in the form of "protected information" (which includes classified information as well as "information protected by law or rule from unauthorized disclosure" and "information concerning other national security interests," so long as the presiding officer concludes that the evidence is "probative" and that its admission without the accused's knowledge would not "result in the denial of a full and fair trial." Finally, a presiding officer's determination that evidence "would not have probative value to a reasonable person" may be overridden by a majority of the other commission members.

Once all the evidence is in, the commission members (not including the presiding officer) must vote on the accused's guilt. A two-thirds vote will suffice for both a verdict of guilty and for imposition of any sentence not including death (the imposition of which requires a unanimous vote). Any appeal is taken to a three-member review panel composed of military officers and designated by the Secretary of Defense, only one member of which need have experience as a judge. The review panel is directed to "disregard any variance from procedures specified in this Order or elsewhere that would not materially have affected the outcome of the trial before the Commission." Once the panel makes its recommendation to the Secretary of Defense, the Secretary can either remand for further proceedings or forward the record to the President with his recommendation as to final disposition. The President then, unless he has delegated the task to the Secretary, makes the "final decision." He may change the commission's findings or sentence only in a manner favorable to the accused.

Hamdan raises both general and particular objections to the procedures set forth in Commission Order No. 1. His general objection is that the procedures' admitted deviation from those governing courts-martial itself renders the commission illegal. Chief among his particular objections are that he may, under the Commission Order, be convicted based on evidence he has not seen or heard, and that any evidence admitted against him need not comply with the admissibility or relevance rules typically applicable in criminal trials and court-martial proceedings.

In part because the difference between military commissions and courts-martial originally was a difference of jurisdiction alone, and in part to protect against abuse and ensure evenhandedness under the pressures of war, the procedures governing trials by military commission historically have been the same as those governing courts-martial. The uniformity principle is not an inflexible one; it does not preclude all departures from the procedures dictated for use by courts-martial. But any departure must be tailored to the exigency that necessitates it. That understanding is reflected in Article 36 of the UCMJ, which provides:

"(a) The procedure, including modes of proof, in cases before courts-martial, courts of inquiry, military commissions, and other military tribunals may be prescribed by the President by regulations which shall, so far as he considers practicable, apply the principles of law and the rules of evidence generally recognized in the trial of criminal cases in the United States district courts, but which may not be contrary to or inconsistent with this chapter.

(b) All rules and regulations made under this article shall be uniform insofar as practicable and shall be reported to Congress."

Article 36 places two restrictions on the President's power to promulgate rules of procedure for courts-martial and military commissions alike. First, no procedural rule he adopts may be "contrary to or inconsistent with" the UCMJ—however practical it may seem. Second, the rules adopted must be "uniform insofar as practicable." That is, the rules applied to military commissions must be the same as those applied to courts-martial unless such uniformity proves impracticable.

Hamdan argues that Commission Order No. 1 violates both of these restrictions; he maintains that the procedures described in the Commission Order are inconsistent with the UCMJ and that the Government has offered no explanation for their deviation from the procedures governing courts-martial, which are set forth in the Manual for Courts-Martial. Among the inconsistencies Hamdan identifies is that between § 6 of the Commission Order, which permits exclusion of the accused from proceedings and denial of his access to evidence in certain circumstances, and the UCMJ's requirement that "[a]ll . . . proceedings" other than votes and deliberations by courts-martial "shall be made a part of the record and shall be in the presence of the accused." Hamdan also observes that the Commission Order dispenses with virtually all evidentiary rules applicable in courts-martial.

Without reaching the question whether any provision of Commission Order No. 1 is strictly "contrary to or inconsistent with" other provisions of the UCMJ, we conclude that the "practicability" determination the President has made is insufficient to justify variances from the procedures governing courts-martial. Subsection (b) of Article 36 was added after World War II, and requires a different showing of impracticability from the one required by subsection (a). Subsection (a) requires that the rules the President promulgates for courts-martial, provost courts, and military commissions alike conform to those that govern procedures in Article III courts,"so far as he considers practicable." Subsection (b), by contrast, demands that the rules applied in courts-martial, provost courts, and military commissions—whether or not they conform with the Federal Rules of Evidence—be "uniform insofar as practicable." Under the latter provision, then, the rules set forth in the Manual for Courts-Martial must apply to military commissions unless impracticable.

The President here has determined, pursuant to subsection (a), that it is impracticable to apply the rules and principles of law that govern "the trial of criminal cases in the United States district courts," to Hamdan's commission. We assume that complete deference is owed that determination. The President has not, however, made a similar official determination that it is impracticable to apply the rules for courts-martial. And even if subsection (b)'s requirements may be satisfied without such an official determination, the requirements of that subsection are not satisfied here.

Nothing in the record before us demonstrates that it would be impracticable to apply court-martial rules in this case. There is no suggestion, for example, of any logistical difficulty in securing properly sworn and authenticated evidence or in applying the usual principles of relevance and admissibility. Assuming arguendo that the reasons articulated in the President's Article 36(a) determination ought to be considered in evaluating the impracticability of applying court-martial rules, the only reason offered in support of that determination is the danger posed by international terrorism. Without for one moment underestimating that danger, it is not evident to us why it should require, in the case of Hamdan's trial, any variance from the rules that govern courts-martial.

The absence of any showing of impracticability is particularly disturbing when considered in light of the clear and admitted failure to apply one of the most fundamental protections afforded not just by the Manual for Courts-Martial but also by the UCMJ itself: the right to be present. Whether or not that departure technically is "contrary to or inconsistent with" the terms of the UCMJ, the jettisoning of so basic a right cannot lightly be excused as "practicable." Under the circumstances, then, the rules applicable in courts-martial must apply. Since it is undisputed that Commission Order No. 1 deviates in many significant respects from those rules, it necessarily violates Article 36(b).

The procedures adopted to try Hamdan also violate the Geneva Conventions. The conflict with al Qaeda is not, according to the Government, a conflict to which the full protections afforded detainees under the 1949 Geneva Conventions apply because Article 2 of those Conventions (which appears in all four Conventions) renders the full protections applicable only to "all cases of declared war or of any other armed conflict which may arise between two or more of the High Contracting Parties." Since Hamdan was captured and detained incident to the conflict with al Qaeda and not the conflict with the Taliban, and since al Qaeda, unlike Afghanistan, is not a "High Contracting Party"— i.e., a signatory of the Conventions, the protections of those Conventions are not, it is argued, applicable to Hamdan.

We need not decide the merits of this argument because there is at least one provision of the Geneva Conventions that applies here even if the relevant conflict is not one between signatories. Article 3, often referred to as Common Article 3 because, like Article 2, it appears in all four Geneva Conventions, provides that in a "conflict not of an international character occurring in the territory of one of the High Contracting Parties, each Party to the conflict shall be bound to apply, as a minimum," certain provisions protecting "[p]ersons taking no active part in the hostilities, including members of armed forces who have laid down their arms and those placed hors de combat by . . . detention." One such provision prohibits "the passing of sentences and the carrying out of executions without previous judgment pronounced by a regularly constituted court affording all the judicial guarantees which are recognized as indispensable by civilized peoples."

Common Article 3, then, is applicable here and, as indicated above, requires that Hamdan be tried by a "regularly constituted court affording all the judicial guarantees which are recognized as indispensable by civilized peoples." While the term "regularly constituted court" is not specifically defined in either Common Article 3 or its accompanying commentary, other sources disclose its core meaning. The commentary accompanying a provision of the Fourth Geneva Convention, for example, defines "'regularly constituted' tribunals" to include "ordinary military courts" and "definitely exclud[e] all special tribunals." And one of the Red Cross' own treatises defines "regularly constituted court" as used in Common Article 3 to mean "established and organized in accordance with the laws and procedures already in force in a country."

Inextricably intertwined with the question of regular constitution is the evaluation of the procedures governing the tribunal and whether they afford "all the judicial guarantees which are recognized as indispensable by civilized peoples." Like the phrase "regularly constituted court," this phrase is not defined in the text of the Geneva Conventions. But it must be understood to incorporate at least the barest of those trial protections that have been recognized by customary international law. Many of these are described in Article 75 of Protocol I to the Geneva Conventions of 1949, adopted in 1977 (Protocol I). Among the rights set forth in Article 75 is the "right to be tried in [one's] presence."

Common Article 3 obviously tolerates a great degree of flexibility in trying individuals captured during armed conflict; its requirements are general ones, crafted to accommodate a wide variety of legal systems. But requirements they are nonetheless. The commission that the President has convened to try Hamdan does not meet those requirements.

We have assumed, as we must, that the allegations made in the Government's charge against Hamdan are true. We have assumed, moreover, the truth of the message implicit in that charge—viz., that Hamdan is a dangerous individual whose beliefs, if acted upon, would cause great harm and even death to innocent civilians, and who would act upon those beliefs if given the opportunity. It bears emphasizing that Hamdan does not challenge, and we do not today address, the Government's power to detain him for the duration of active hostilities in order to prevent such harm. But in undertaking to try Hamdan and subject him to criminal punishment, the Executive is bound to comply with the Rule of Law that prevails in this jurisdiction.

Justice BREYER, with whom Justice KENNEDY, Justice SOUTER, and Justice GINSBURG join, concurring.

The dissenters say that today's decision would "sorely hamper the President's ability to confront and defeat a new and deadly enemy." They suggest that it undermines our Nation's ability to "preven[t] future attacks" of the grievous sort that we have already suffered. That claim leads me to state briefly what I believe the majority sets forth both explicitly and implicitly at greater length. The Court's conclusion ultimately rests upon a single ground: Congress has not issued the Executive a "blank check." Indeed, Congress has denied the President the legislative authority to create military commissions of the kind at issue here. Nothing prevents the President from returning to Congress to seek the authority he believes necessary.

Where, as here, no emergency prevents consultation with Congress, judicial insistence upon that consultation does not weaken our Nation's ability to deal with danger. To the contrary, that insistence strengthens the Nation's ability to determine—through democratic means—how best to do so. The Constitution places its faith in those democratic means. Our Court today simply does the same.

Justice KENNEDY concurring in part.

Military Commission Order No. 1, which governs the military commission established to try petitioner Salim Hamdan for war crimes, exceeds limits that certain statutes, duly enacted by Congress, have placed on the President's authority to convene military courts. This is not a case, then, where the Executive can assert some unilateral authority to fill a void left by congressional inaction. It is a case where Congress, in the proper exercise of its powers as an independent branch of government, and as part of a long tradition of legislative involvement in matters of military justice, has considered the subject of military tribunals and set limits on the President's authority. Where a statute provides the conditions for the exercise of governmental power, its requirements are the result of a deliberative and reflective process engaging both of the political branches. Respect for laws derived from the customary operation of the Executive and Legislative Branches gives some assurance of stability in time of crisis. The Constitution is best preserved by reliance on standards tested over time and insulated from the pressures of the moment.

These principles seem vindicated here, for a case that may be of extraordinary importance is resolved by ordinary rules. The rules of most relevance here are those pertaining to the authority of Congress and the interpretation of its enactments.

It seems appropriate to recite these rather fundamental points because the Court refers, as it should in its exposition of the case, to the requirement of the Geneva Conventions of 1949 that military tribunals be "regularly constituted" — a requirement that controls here, if for no other reason, because Congress requires that military commissions like the ones at issue conform to the "law of war." Whatever the substance and content of the term "regularly constituted" as interpreted in this and any later cases, there seems little doubt that it relies upon the importance of standards deliberated upon and chosen in advance of crisis, under a system where the single power of the Executive is checked by other constitutional mechanisms. All of which returns us to the point of beginning—that domestic statutes control this case. If Congress, after due consideration, deems it appropriate to change the controlling statutes, in conformance with the Constitution and other laws, it has the power and prerogative to do so.

In light of the conclusion that the military commission here is unauthorized under the UCMJ, I see no need to consider several further issues addressed in the plurality opinion by Justice Stevens and the dissent by Justice Thomas. First, I would not decide whether Common Article 3's standard—a "regularly constituted court affording all the judicial guarantees which are recognized as indispensable by civilized peoples,"— necessarily requires that the accused have the right to be present at all stages of a criminal trial. The evidentiary proceedings at Hamdan's trial have yet to commence, and it remains to be seen whether he will suffer any prejudicial exclusion.

There should be reluctance, furthermore, to reach unnecessarily the question whether, as the plurality seems to conclude, Article 75 of Protocol I to the Geneva Conventions is binding law notwithstanding the earlier decision by our Government not to accede to the Protocol. For all these reasons, and without detracting from the importance of the right of presence, I would rely on other deficiencies noted here and in the opinion by the Court—deficiencies that relate to the structure and procedure of the commission and that inevitably will affect the proceedings—as the basis for finding the military commissions lack authorization under 10 U.S.C. § 836 and fail to be regularly constituted under Common Article 3 and § 821.

I likewise see no need to address the validity of the conspiracy charge against Hamdan—an issue addressed at length in Justice Stevens' opinion and in Justice Thomas' dissent. In light of the conclusion that the military commissions at issue are unauthorized Congress may choose to provide further guidance in this area. Congress, not the Court, is the branch in the better position to undertake the "sensitive task of establishing a principle not inconsistent with the national interest or international justice."

Justice SCALIA, with whom Justice THOMAS and Justice ALITO join, dissenting.

On December 30, 2005, Congress enacted the Detainee Treatment Act (DTA). It unambiguously provides that, as of that date, "no court, justice, or judge" shall have jurisdiction to consider the habeas application of a Guantanamo Bay detainee. Notwithstanding this plain directive, the Court today concludes that, on what it calls the statute's most natural reading, every "court, justice, or judge" before whom such a habeas application was pending on December 30 has jurisdiction to hear, consider, and render judgment on it. This conclusion is patently erroneous. And even if it were not, the jurisdiction supposedly retained should, in an exercise of sound equitable discretion, not be exercised. [Justice Scalia then elaborated his argument that the Detainee Treatment Act should be seen as precluding the Court from having jurisdiction or reaching the merits of the case.]

Even if Congress had not clearly and constitutionally eliminated jurisdiction over this case, neither this Court nor the lower courts ought to exercise it. Traditionally, equitable principles govern both the exercise of habeas jurisdiction and the granting of the injunctive relief sought by petitioner. In light of Congress's provision of an alternate avenue for petitioner's claims in [the

Detainee Treatment Act] those equitable principles counsel that we abstain from exercising jurisdiction in this case.

Justice THOMAS dissenting.

For the reasons set forth in Justice Scalia's dissent, it is clear that this Court lacks jurisdiction to entertain petitioner's claims. The Court having concluded otherwise, it is appropriate to respond to the Court's resolution of the merits of petitioner's claims because its opinion openly flouts our well-established duty to respect the Executive's judgment in matters of military operations and foreign affairs. The Court's evident belief that it is qualified to pass on the "[m]ilitary necessity," of the Commander in Chief's decision to employ a particular form of force against our enemies is so antithetical to our constitutional structure that it simply cannot go unanswered. I respectfully dissent.

Our review of petitioner's claims arises in the context of the President's wartime exercise of his commander-in-chief authority in conjunction with the complete support of Congress. Accordingly, it is important to take measure of the respective roles the Constitution assigns to the three branches of our Government in the conduct of war.

As I explained in *Hamdi v. Rumsfeld* (2004), the structural advantages attendant to the Executive Branch—namely, the decisiveness, "activity, secrecy, and dispatch" that flow from the Executive's "unity," (quoting The Federalist No. 70, p. 472 (J. Cooke ed. 1961) (A.Hamilton)) led the Founders to conclude that the "President ha[s] primary responsibility—along with the necessary power—to protect the national security and to conduct the Nation's foreign relations." Consistent with this conclusion, the Constitution vests in the President "[t]he executive Power," Art. II, § 1, provides that he "shall be Commander in Chief" of the Armed Forces, § 2, and places in him the power to recognize foreign governments, § 3. This Court has observed that these provisions confer upon the President broad constitutional authority to protect the Nation's security in the manner he deems fit.

Congress, to be sure, has a substantial and essential role in both foreign affairs and national security. But "Congress cannot anticipate and legislate with regard to every possible action the President may find it necessary to take or every possible situation in which he might act," and "[s]uch failure of Congress . . . does not, 'especially . . . in the areas of foreign policy and national security,' imply 'congressional disapproval' of action taken by the Executive." Rather, in these domains, the fact that Congress has provided the President with broad authorities does not imply—and the Judicial Branch should not infer—that Congress intended to deprive him of particular powers not specifically enumerated.

When "the President acts pursuant to an express or implied authorization from Congress," his actions are "'supported by the strongest of presumptions and the widest latitude of judicial interpretation, and the burden of persuasion . . . rest[s] heavily upon any who might attack it.'" Accordingly, in the very context that we address today, this Court has concluded that "the detention and trial of petitioners—ordered by the President in the declared exercise of his powers as Commander in Chief of the Army in time of war and of grave public danger—are not to be set aside by the courts without the clear conviction that they are in conflict with the Constitution or laws of Congress constitutionally enacted." *Ex parte Quirin* (1942).

Under this framework, the President's decision to try Hamdan before a military commission for his involvement with al Qaeda is entitled to a heavy measure of deference. In the present conflict, Congress has authorized the President "to use all necessary and appropriate force against those nations, organizations, or persons he determines planned, authorized, committed, or aided the terrorist attacks that occurred on September 11, 2001 . . . in order to prevent any future acts of international terrorism against the United States by such nations, organizations or persons." As a plurality of the Court observed in Hamdi, the "capture, detention, and trial of unlawful combatants, by 'universal agreement and practice,' are 'important incident[s] of war,'" and are therefore "an exercise of the 'necessary and appropriate force' Congress has authorized the President to use." Hamdi's observation that military commissions are included within the AUMF's authorization is supported by this Court's previous recognition that "[a]n important incident to the conduct of war is the adoption of measures by the military commander, not only to repel and defeat the enemy, but to seize and subject to disciplinary measures those enemies who, in their attempt to thwart or impede our military effort, have violated the law of war."

Ultimately, the plurality's determination that Hamdan has not been charged with an offense triable before a military commission rests not upon any historical example or authority, but upon the plurality's raw judgment of the "inability on the Executive's part here to satisfy the most basic precondition . . . for establishment of military commissions: military necessity." This judgment starkly confirms that the plurality has appointed itself the ultimate arbiter of what is quintessentially a policy and military judgment, namely, the appropriate military measures to take against those who "aided the terrorist attacks that occurred on September 11, 2001." The plurality's suggestion that Hamdan's commission is illegitimate because it is not dispensing swift justice on the battlefield is unsupportable. Even a cursory review of the authorities confirms that law-of-war military commissions have wide-ranging jurisdiction to try offenses against the law of war in exigent and nonexigent circumstances alike.

Today a plurality of this Court would hold that conspiracy to massacre innocent civilians does not violate the laws of war. This determination is unsustainable. The judgment of the political branches that Hamdan, and others like him, must be held accountable before military commissions for their involvement with and membership in an unlawful organization dedicated to inflicting massive civilian casualties is supported by virtually every relevant authority, including all of the authorities invoked by the plurality today. It is also supported by the nature of the present conflict. We are not engaged in a traditional battle with a nation-state, but with a worldwide, hydra-headed enemy, who lurks in the shadows conspiring to reproduce the atrocities of September 11, 2001, and who has boasted of sending suicide bombers into civilian gatherings, has proudly distributed videotapes of beheadings of civilian workers, and has tortured and dismembered captured American soldiers. But according to the plurality, when our Armed Forces capture those who are plotting terrorist atrocities like the bombing of the Khobar Towers, the bombing of the U.S.S. Cole, and the attacks of September 11—even if their plots are advanced to the very brink of fulfillment—our military cannot charge those criminals with any offense against the laws of war. Instead, our troops must catch the terrorists "redhanded," ante, at 48, in the midst of the attack itself, in order to bring them to justice. Not only is this conclusion fundamentally inconsistent with the cardinal principal of the law of war, namely protecting non-combatants, but it would sorely hamper the President's ability to confront and defeat a new and deadly enemy.

Justice ALITO dissenting.

The holding of the Court, as I understand it, rests on the following reasoning. A military commission is lawful only if it is authorized by 10 U.S.C. § 821; this provision permits the use of a commission to try "offenders or offenses" that "by statute or by the law of war may be tried by" such a commission; because no statute provides that an offender such as petitioner or an offense such as the one with which he is charged may be tried by a military commission, he may be tried by military commission only if the trial is authorized by "the law of war"; the Geneva Conventions are part of the law of war; and Common Article 3 of the Conventions prohibits petitioner's trial because the commission before which he would be tried is not "a regularly constituted court." Third Geneva Convention, Art. 3, ¶ 1 (d) , Relative to the Treatment of Prisoners of War, Aug. 12, 1949. I disagree with this holding because petitioner's commission is "a regularly constituted court."

In sum, I believe that Common Article 3 is satisfied here because the military commissions (1) qualify as courts, (2) that were appointed and established in accordance with domestic law, and (3) any procedural improprieties that might occur in particular cases can be reviewed in those cases. [Justice Alito developed each of these points at length.]

Chapter 4

Limits on State Regulatory and Taxing Power

B. The Dormant Commerce Clause

3. The Contemporary Test for the Dormant Commerce Clause

The Court decided two dormant Commerce Clause cases during October Term 2004. One involved a law that was facially discriminatory and the other a law that was not discriminatory. Consistent with the Court's long-standing approach, the former was declared unconstitutional, while the latter was upheld.

c. Analysis if a Law Is Deemed Discriminatory (casebook, p. 411)

GRANHOLM v. HEALD
125 S. Ct. 1885 (2005)

Justice KENNEDY delivered the opinion of the Court.

These consolidated cases present challenges to state laws regulating the sale of wine from out-of-state wineries to consumers in Michigan and New York. The details and mechanics of the two regulatory schemes differ, but the object and effect of the laws are the same: to allow in-state wineries to sell wine directly to consumers in that State but to prohibit out-of-state wineries from doing so, or, at the least, to make direct sales impractical from an economic standpoint. It is evident that the object and design of the Michigan and New York statutes is to grant in-state wineries a competitive advantage over wineries located beyond the States' borders.

We hold that the laws in both States discriminate against interstate commerce in violation of the Commerce Clause, Art. I, § 8, cl. 3, and that the discrimination is neither authorized nor permitted by the Twenty-first Amendment.

I

Like many other States, Michigan and New York regulate the sale and importation of alcoholic beverages, including wine, through a three-tier distribution system. Separate licenses are required for producers, wholesalers, and retailers.

As relevant to today's cases, though, the three-tier system is, in broad terms and with refinements to be discussed, mandated by Michigan and New York only for sales from out-of-state wineries. In-state wineries, by contrast, can obtain a license for direct sales to consumers. The differential treatment between in-state and out-of-state wineries constitutes explicit discrimination against interstate commerce.

This discrimination substantially limits the direct sale of wine to consumers, an otherwise emerging and significant business. From 1994 to 1999, consumer spending on direct wine shipments doubled, reaching $500 million per year, or three percent of all wine sales. The expansion has been influenced by several related trends. First, the number of small wineries in the United States has significantly increased. By some estimates there are over 3,000 wineries in the country. At the same time, the wholesale market has consolidated. Between 1984 and 2002, the number of licensed wholesalers dropped from 1,600 to 600. The increasing winery-to-wholesaler ratio means that many small wineries do not produce enough wine or have sufficient consumer demand for their wine to make it economical for wholesalers to carry their products. This has led many small wineries to rely on direct shipping to reach new markets. Technological improvements, in particular the ability of wineries to sell wine over the Internet, have helped make direct shipments an attractive sales channel.

Approximately 26 States allow some direct shipping of wine, with various restrictions. Thirteen of these States have reciprocity laws, which allow direct shipment from wineries outside the State, provided the State of origin affords similar nondiscriminatory treatment. In many parts of the country, however, state laws that prohibit or severely restrict direct shipments deprive consumers of access to the direct market.

The wine producers in the cases before us are small wineries that rely on direct consumer sales as an important part of their businesses. Domaine Alfred, one of the plaintiffs in the Michigan suit, is a small winery located in San Luis Obispo, California. It produces 3,000 cases of wine per year. Domaine Alfred has received requests for its wine from Michigan consumers but cannot fill the orders because of the State's direct-shipment ban. Even if the winery could find a Michigan wholesaler to distribute its wine, the wholesaler's markup would render shipment through the three-tier system economically infeasible.

Under Michigan law, wine producers, as a general matter, must distribute their wine through wholesalers. There is, however, an exception for Michigan's approximately 40 in-state wineries, which are eligible for "wine maker" licenses that allow direct shipment to in-state consumers. Out-of-state wineries can apply for a $300 "outside seller of wine" license, but this license only allows them to sell to in-state wholesalers.

New York's licensing scheme is somewhat different. It channels most wine sales through the three-tier system, but it too makes exceptions for in-state wineries. As in Michigan, the result is to allow local wineries to make direct sales to consumers in New York on terms not available to out-of-state wineries.

We consolidated these cases and granted certiorari on the following question: " 'Does a State's regulatory scheme that permits in-state wineries directly to ship alcohol to consumers but restricts the ability of out-of-state wineries to do so violate the dormant Commerce Clause in light of § 2 of the Twenty-first Amendment?' "

II

A

Time and again this Court has held that, in all but the narrowest circumstances, state laws violate the Commerce Clause if they mandate "differential treatment of in-state and out-of-state economic interests that benefits the former and burdens the latter." This rule is essential to the foundations of the Union. The mere fact of nonresidence should not foreclose a producer in one State from access to markets in other States. States may not enact laws that burden out-of-state producers or shippers simply to give a competitive advantage to in-state businesses. This mandate "reflect[s] a central concern of the Framers that was an immediate reason for calling the Constitutional Convention: the conviction that in order to succeed, the new Union would have to avoid the tendencies toward economic Balkanization that had plagued relations among the Colonies and later among the States under the Articles of Confederation."

The rule prohibiting state discrimination against interstate commerce follows also from the principle that States should not be compelled to negotiate with each other regarding favored or disfavored status for their own citizens. States do not need, and may not attempt, to negotiate with other States regarding their mutual economic interests. Rivalries among the States are thus kept to a minimum, and a proliferation of trade zones is prevented.

Laws of the type at issue in the instant cases contradict these principles. They deprive citizens of their right to have access to the markets of other States on equal terms. The perceived necessity for reciprocal sale privileges risks generating the trade rivalries and animosities, the alliances and exclusivity, that the Constitution and, in particular, the Commerce Clause were designed to avoid. The current patchwork of laws—with some States banning direct shipments altogether, others doing so only for out-of-state wines, and still others requiring reciprocity—is essentially the product of an ongoing, low-level trade war. Allowing States to discriminate against out-of-state wine "invite[s] a multiplication of preferential trade areas destructive of the very purpose of the Commerce Clause."

B

The discriminatory character of the Michigan system is obvious. Michigan allows in-state wineries to ship directly to consumers, subject only to a licensing requirement. Out-of-state wineries, whether licensed or not, face a complete ban on direct shipment. The differential treatment requires all out-of-state wine, but not all in-state wine, to pass through an in-state wholesaler and retailer before reaching consumers. These two extra layers of overhead increase the cost of out-of-state wines to Michigan consumers. The cost differential, and in some cases the inability to secure a wholesaler for small shipments, can effectively bar small wineries from the Michigan market.

The New York regulatory scheme differs from Michigan's in that it does not ban direct shipments altogether. Out-of-state wineries are instead required to establish a distribution operation in New York in order to gain the privilege of direct shipment. The New York scheme grants in-state wineries access to the State's consumers on preferential terms. The suggestion of a limited exception for direct shipment from out-of-state wineries does nothing to eliminate the discriminatory nature of New York's regulations. In-state producers, with the applicable licenses, can ship directly to consumers from their wineries. Out-of-state wineries must open a branch office and warehouse in New York, additional steps that drive up the cost of their wine. For most wineries, the expense of establishing a bricks-and-mortar distribution operation in 1 State, let alone all 50, is prohibitive. It comes as no surprise that not a single out-of-state winery has availed itself of New York's direct-shipping privilege. We have "viewed with particular suspicion state statutes requiring business operations to be performed in the home State that could more efficiently be performed elsewhere." New York's in-state presence requirement runs contrary to our admonition that States cannot require an out-of-state firm "to become a resident in order to compete on equal terms."

III

State laws that discriminate against interstate commerce face "a virtually per se rule of invalidity." Philadelphia v. New Jersey (1978). The Michigan and New York laws by their own terms violate this proscription. The two States, however, contend their statutes are saved by § 2 of the Twenty-first Amendment, which provides: "The transportation or importation into any State, Territory, or possession of the United States for delivery or use therein of intoxicating liquors, in violation of the laws thereof, is hereby prohibited."

The States' position is inconsistent with our precedents and with the Twenty-first Amendment's history. Section 2 does not allow States to regulate the direct shipment of wine on terms that discriminate in favor of in-state producers.

A

Before 1919, the temperance movement fought to curb the sale of alcoholic beverages one State at a time. The movement made progress, and many States passed laws restricting or prohibiting the sale of alcohol. This Court upheld state laws banning the production and sale of alcoholic beverages, Mugler v. Kansas (1887), but was less solicitous of laws aimed at imports. In a series of cases before ratification of the Eighteenth Amendment the Court, relying on the Commerce Clause, invalidated a number of state liquor regulations.

These cases advanced two distinct principles. First, the Court held that the Commerce Clause prevented States from discriminating against imported liquor. Second, the Court held that the Commerce Clause prevented States from passing facially neutral laws that placed an impermissible burden on interstate commerce.

B

The ratification of the Eighteenth Amendment in 1919 provided a brief respite from the legal battles over the validity of state liquor regulations. With the ratification of the Twenty-first Amendment 14 years later, however, nationwide Prohibition came to an end. Section 1 of the Twenty-first Amendment repealed the Eighteenth Amendment. Section 2 of the Twenty-first Amendment is at issue here. Michigan and New York say the provision grants to the States the authority to discriminate against out-of-state goods. The history we have recited does not support this position. To the contrary, it provides strong support for the view that § 2 restored to the States the powers they had. The aim of the Twenty-first Amendment was to allow States to maintain an effective and uniform system for controlling liquor by regulating its transportation, importation, and use. The Amendment did not give States the authority to pass nonuniform laws in order to discriminate against out-of-state goods, a privilege they had not enjoyed at any earlier time. Our more recent cases, furthermore, confirm that the Twenty-first Amendment does not supersede other provisions of the Constitution and, in particular, does not displace the rule that States may not give a discriminatory preference to their own producers.

C

The modern § 2 cases fall into three categories. First, the Court has held that state laws that violate other provisions of the Constitution are not saved by the Twenty-first Amendment. The Court has applied this rule in the context of the First Amendment, 44 Liquormart, Inc. v. Rhode Island (1996); the Establishment Clause, Larkin v. Grendel's Den, Inc. (1982); the Equal Protection Clause, Craig v. Boren (1976); the Due Process Clause, Wisconsin v. Constantineau (1971); and the Import-Export Clause, Department of Revenue v. James B. Beam Distilling Co. (1964).

Second, the Court has held that § 2 does not abrogate Congress' Commerce Clause powers with regard to liquor. The argument that "the Twenty-first Amendment has somehow operated to 'repeal' the Commerce Clause" for alcoholic beverages has been rejected.

Finally, and most relevant to the issue at hand, the Court has held that state regulation of alcohol is limited by the nondiscrimination principle of the Commerce Clause. "When a state statute directly regulates or discriminates against interstate commerce, or when its effect is to favor in-state economic interests over out-of-state interests, we have generally struck down the statute without further inquiry."

IV

Our determination that the Michigan and New York direct-shipment laws are not authorized by the Twenty-first Amendment does not end the inquiry. We still must consider whether either State regime "advances a legitimate local purpose that cannot be adequately served by reasonable nondiscriminatory alternatives." The States offer two primary justifications for restricting direct shipments from out-of-state wineries: keeping alcohol out of the hands of minors and facilitating tax collection. We consider each in turn.

The States, aided by several amici, claim that allowing direct shipment from out-of-state wineries undermines their ability to police underage drinking. Minors, the States argue, have easy access to credit cards and the Internet and are likely to take advantage of direct wine shipments as a means of obtaining alcohol illegally. The States provide little evidence that the purchase of wine over the Internet by minors is a problem. Indeed, there is some evidence to the contrary. A recent study by the staff of the FTC found that the 26 States currently allowing direct shipments report no problems with minors' increased access to wine. This is not surprising for several reasons. First, minors are less likely to consume wine, as opposed to beer, wine coolers, and hard liquor. Second, minors who decide to disobey the law have more direct means of doing so. Third, direct shipping is an imperfect avenue of obtaining alcohol for minors who, in the words of the past president of the National Conference of State Liquor Administrators, " 'want instant gratification.' " Without concrete evidence that direct shipping of wine is likely to increase alcohol consumption by minors, we are left with the States' unsupported assertions. Under our precedents, which require the "clearest showing" to justify discriminatory state regulation, this is not enough.

Even were we to credit the States' largely unsupported claim that direct shipping of wine increases the risk of underage drinking, this would not justify regulations limiting only out-of-state direct shipments. As the wineries point out, minors are just as likely to order wine from in-state producers as from out-of-state ones.

The States' tax-collection justification is also insufficient. Increased direct shipping, whether originating in state or out of state, brings with it the potential for tax evasion. With regard to Michigan, however, the tax-collection argument is a diversion. That is because Michigan, unlike many other States, does not rely on wholesalers to collect taxes on wines imported from out-of-state. Instead, Michigan collects taxes directly from out-of-state wineries on all wine shipped to in-state wholesalers. If licensing and self-reporting provide adequate safeguards for wine distributed through the three-tier system, there is no reason to believe they will not suffice for direct shipments.

New York and its supporting parties also advance a tax-collection justification for the State's direct-shipment laws. In particular, New York could protect itself against lost tax revenue by requiring a permit as a condition of direct shipping. This is the approach taken by New York for in-state wineries. The State offers no reason to believe the system would prove ineffective for out-of-state wineries.

Licensees could be required to submit regular sales reports and to remit taxes. Indeed, various States use this approach for taxing direct interstate wine shipments, and report no problems with tax collection.

In summary, the States provide little concrete evidence for the sweeping assertion that they cannot police direct shipments by out-of-state wineries. Our Commerce Clause cases demand more than mere speculation to support discrimination against out-of-state goods. The "burden is on the State to show that 'the discrimination is demonstrably justified.' " The Court has upheld state regulations that discriminate against interstate commerce only after finding, based on concrete record evidence, that a State's nondiscriminatory alternatives will prove unworkable. See, e.g., Maine v. Taylor (1986). Michigan and New York have not satisfied this exacting standard.

V

States have broad power to regulate liquor under § 2 of the Twenty-first Amendment. This power, however, does not allow States to ban, or severely limit, the direct shipment of out-of-state wine while simultaneously authorizing direct shipment by in-state producers. If a State chooses to allow direct shipment of wine, it must do so on evenhanded terms. Without demonstrating the need for discrimination, New York and Michigan have enacted regulations that disadvantage out-of-state wine producers. Under our Commerce Clause jurisprudence, these regulations cannot stand.

Justice STEVENS, with whom Justice O'CONNOR joins, dissenting.

The New York and Michigan laws challenged in these cases would be patently invalid under well settled dormant Commerce Clause principles if they regulated sales of an ordinary article of commerce rather than wine. But ever since the adoption of the Eighteenth Amendment and the Twenty-first Amendment, our Constitution has placed commerce in alcoholic beverages in a special category. Section 2 of the Twenty-first Amendment expressly provides that "[t]he transportation or importation into any State, Territory, or possession of the United States for delivery or use therein of intoxicating liquors, in violation of the laws thereof, is hereby prohibited."

Today many Americans, particularly those members of the younger generations who make policy decisions, regard alcohol as an ordinary article of commerce, subject to substantially the same market and legal controls as other consumer products. That was definitely not the view of the generations that made policy in 1919 when the Eighteenth Amendment was ratified or in 1933 when it was repealed by the Twenty-first Amendment. On the contrary, the moral condemnation of the use of alcohol as a beverage represented not merely the convictions of our religious leaders, but the views of a sufficiently large majority of the population to warrant the rare exercise of the power to amend the Constitution on two occasions. The Eighteenth Amendment entirely prohibited commerce in "intoxicating liquors" for beverage purposes throughout the United States and the territories subject to its jurisdiction. While § 1 of the Twenty-first Amendment repealed the nationwide prohibition, § 2 gave the States the option to maintain equally comprehensive prohibitions in their respective jurisdictions.

In the years following the ratification of the Twenty-first Amendment, States adopted manifold laws regulating commerce in alcohol, and many of these laws were discriminatory. So-called "dry states" entirely prohibited such commerce; others prohibited the sale of alcohol on Sundays; others permitted the sale of beer and wine but not hard liquor; most created either state monopolies or distribution systems that gave discriminatory preferences to local retailers and distributors. The notion that discriminatory state laws violated the unwritten prohibition against balkanizing the American economy—while persuasive in contemporary times when alcohol is viewed as an ordinary article of commerce—would have seemed strange indeed to the millions of Americans who condemned the use of the "demon rum" in the 1920's and 1930's. Indeed, they expressly authorized the "balkanization" that today's decision condemns. Today's decision may represent sound economic policy and may be consistent with the policy choices of the contemporaries of Adam Smith who drafted our original Constitution; it is not, however, consistent with the policy choices made by those who amended our Constitution in 1919 and 1933.

My understanding (and recollection) of the historical context reinforces my conviction that the text of § 2 should be "broadly and colloquially interpreted." Indeed, the fact that the Twenty-first Amendment was the only Amendment in our history to have been ratified by the people in state conventions, rather than by state legislatures, provides further reason to give its terms their ordinary meaning. Because the New York and Michigan laws regulate the "transportation or importation" of "intoxicating liquors" for "delivery or use therein," they are exempt from dormant Commerce Clause scrutiny.

Justice THOMAS, with whom THE CHIEF JUSTICE, Justice STEVENS, and Justice O'CONNOR join, dissenting.

A century ago, this Court repeatedly invalidated, as inconsistent with the negative Commerce Clause, state liquor legislation that prevented out-of-state businesses from shipping liquor directly to a State's residents. The Webb-Kenyon Act and the Twenty-first Amendment cut off this intrusive review, as their text and history make clear and as this Court's early cases on the Twenty-first Amendment recognized. The Court today seizes back this power, based primarily on a historical argument that this Court decisively rejected long ago in State Bd. of Equalization of Cal. v. Young's Market Co. (1936). Because I would follow *Young's Market* and the language of both the statute that Congress enacted and the Amendment that the Nation ratified, rather than the Court's questionable reading of history and the "negative implications" of the Commerce Clause, I respectfully dissent.

I

The Court devotes much attention to the Twenty-first Amendment, yet little to the terms of the Webb-Kenyon Act. This is a mistake, because that Act's language displaces any negative Commerce Clause barrier to state regulation of liquor sales to in-state consumers.

The Webb-Kenyon Act immunizes from negative Commerce Clause review the state liquor laws that the Court holds are unconstitutional. The Act "prohibit [s]" any "shipment or transportation" of alcoholic beverages "into any State" when those beverages are "intended, by any person interested therein, to be received, possessed, sold, or in any manner used . . . in violation of any law of such State." State laws that regulate liquor imports in the manner described by the Act are exempt from judicial scrutiny under the negative Commerce Clause, as this Court has long held. The Webb-Kenyon Act's language, in other words, "prevent[s] the immunity characteristic of interstate commerce from being used to permit the receipt of liquor through such commerce in States contrary to their laws."

The Michigan and New York direct-shipment laws are within the Webb-Kenyon Act's terms and therefore do not run afoul of the negative Commerce Clause. Those laws restrict out-of-state wineries from shipping and selling wine directly to Michigan and New York consumers. Any winery that ships wine directly to a Michigan or New York consumer in violation of those state-law restrictions is a "person interested therein" "intend[ing]" to "s[ell]" wine "in violation of" Michigan and New York law, and thus comes within the terms of the Webb-Kenyon Act.

II

[T]he state laws the Court strikes down are lawful under the plain meaning of § 2 of the Twenty-first Amendment, as this Court's case law in the wake of the Amendment and the contemporaneous practice of the States reinforce.

The state laws at issue in these cases fall within § 2's broad terms. They prohibit wine manufacturers from "transport[ing] or import[ing]" wine directly to consumers in New York and Michigan "for delivery or use therein." Michigan law does so by requiring all out-of-state wine manufacturers to distribute wine through licensed in-state wholesalers. New York law does so by prohibiting out-of-state wineries from shipping wine directly to consumers unless they establish an in-state physical presence, something that in-state wineries naturally have. The Twenty-first Amendment prohibits out-of-state wineries from shipping wine into Michigan and New York in violation of these laws. In holding that the Constitution prohibits Michigan's and New York's laws, the majority turns the Amendment's text on its head.

Though the majority dismisses this Court's early Twenty-first Amendment case law, it relies on the reasoning, if not the holdings, of our more recent Twenty-first

Amendment cases. But the Court's later cases do not require the result the majority reaches. Moreover, I would resolve any conflict in this Court's precedents in favor of those cases most contemporaneous with the ratification of the Twenty-first Amendment.

[M]y interpretation of the Twenty-first Amendment would not free States to regulate liquor unhampered by other constitutional restraints, like the First Amendment and the Equal Protection Clause. As this Court explained in Craig v. Boren (1976), the text and history of the Twenty-first Amendment demonstrate that it displaces liquor's negative Commerce Clause immunity, not other constitutional provisions.

The Twenty-first Amendment and the Webb-Kenyon Act displaced the negative Commerce Clause as applied to regulation of liquor imports into a State. They require sustaining the constitutionality of Michigan's and New York's direct-shipment laws.

d. *Analysis if a Law Is Deemed Non-Discriminatory (casebook, p. 414)*

AMERICAN TRUCKING ASSOCIATIONS, INC. v. MICHIGAN PUBLIC SERVICE COMMISSION
125 S. Ct. 2419 (2005)

Justice BREYER delivered the opinion of the Court.

In this case, we consider whether a flat $100 fee that Michigan charges trucks engaging in intrastate commercial hauling violates the dormant Commerce Clause. We hold that it does not.

I

A subsection of Michigan's Motor Carrier Act imposes upon each motor carrier "for the administration of this act, an annual fee of $100.00 for each self-propelled motor vehicle operated by or on behalf of the motor carrier." The provision assesses the fee upon, and only upon, vehicles that engage in intrastate commercial operations—that is, on trucks that undertake point-to-point hauls between Michigan cities. Petitioners, USF Holland, Inc., a trucking company with trucks that engage in both interstate and intrastate hauling, and the American Trucking Associations, Inc. (ATA), asked the Michigan courts to invalidate the provision. Both petitioners told those courts that trucks that carry both interstate and intrastate loads engage in intrastate business less than trucks that confine their operations to the Great Lakes State. Hence, because Michigan's fee is flat, it discriminates against interstate carriers and imposes an unconstitutional burden upon interstate trade.

II

Our Constitution "was framed upon the theory that the peoples of the several states must sink or swim together." Thus, this Court has consistently held that the Constitution's express grant to Congress of the power to "regulate Commerce . . . among the several States," Art. I, § 8, cl. 3, contains "a further, negative command, known as the dormant Commerce Clause," that "create[s] an area of trade free from interference by the States." This negative command prevents a State from "jeopardizing the welfare of the Nation as a whole" by "plac[ing] burdens on the flow of commerce across its borders that commerce wholly within those borders would not bear."

Thus, we have found unconstitutional state regulations that unjustifiably discriminate on their face against out-of-state entities, see Philadelphia v. New Jersey (1978), or that impose burdens on interstate trade that are "clearly excessive in relation to the putative local benefits," Pike v. Bruce Church, Inc. (1970). We have held that States may not impose taxes that facially discriminate against interstate business and offer commercial advantage to local enterprises, that improperly apportion state assessments on transactions with out-of-state components, or that have the "inevitable effect [of] threaten[ing] the free movement of commerce by placing a financial barrier around the State."

Applying these principles and precedents, we find nothing in [the Michigan law] that offends the Commerce Clause. To begin with, Michigan imposes the flat $100 fee only upon intrastate transactions—that is, upon activities taking place exclusively within the State's borders. Section 478.2(1) does not facially discriminate against interstate or out-of-state activities or enterprises. The statute applies evenhandedly to all carriers that make domestic journeys. It does not reflect an effort to tax activity that takes place, in whole or in part, outside the State. Nothing in our case law suggests that such a neutral, locally focused fee or tax is inconsistent with the dormant Commerce Clause.

This legal vacuum is not surprising. States impose numerous flat fees upon local businesses and service providers, including, for example, upon insurers, auctioneers, ambulance operators, and hosts of others. The record, moreover, shows no special circumstance suggesting that Michigan's fee operates in practice as anything other than an unobjectionable exercise of the State's police power. To the contrary, as the Michigan Court of Appeals pointed out, the record contains little, if any, evidence that the $100 fee imposes any significant practical burden upon interstate trade.

Neither does the record show that the flat assessment unfairly discriminates against interstate truckers. The fee seeks to defray costs such as those of regulating "vehicular size and weight," of administering "insurance requirements," and of applying "safety standards." The bulk of such costs would seem more likely to vary per truck or per carrier than to vary per-mile traveled. And that fact means that a per-truck, rather than a per-mile, assessment is likely fair. Nothing in the record suggests the contrary.

Nor would an effort to switch the manner of fee assessment—from lump sum to, for example, miles traveled—be burden free. The record contains an affidavit, sworn by a Michigan Public Service Commission official, that states that to obtain the same revenue (about $3.5 million) through a per-mile fee would require the State to create a "data accumulation system" capable of separating out intrastate hauls and determining their length, and to develop related liability, billing, and auditing mechanisms. This affidavit, on its face, suggests that the game is unlikely to be worth the candle. While petitioners argue the contrary, they do not provide the details of their preferred alternative administrative system nor point to record evidence showing its practicality.

Justice THOMAS, concurring in the judgment.

I would affirm the judgment of the Michigan Court of Appeals because " '[t]he negative Commerce Clause has no basis in the text of the Constitution, makes little sense, and has proved virtually unworkable in application,' Camps Newfound/Owatonna, Inc. v. Town of Harrison (1997) (Thomas, J., dissenting), and, consequently, cannot serve as a basis for striking down a state statute."

Chapter 6

Economic Liberties

D. The Takings Clause

There were two important takings decisions during October Term 2004. First, in Lingle v. Chevron, U.S.A. Inc., the Court considered the test for regulatory takings and whether a government action must substantially advance a legitimate purpose in order to avoid being a taking. Second, in Kelo v. City of New London, the Court considered what is "public use" and whether a taking for purposes of economic development is for public use.

2. Is There a "Taking"? (casebook, p. 575)

The Court long has held that there are two types of takings: possessory and regulatory takings. As to regulatory takings, must the government's action "substantially advance" a legitimate government purpose in order to avoid being a taking?

LINGLE v. CHEVRON U.S.A. INC.
125 S. Ct. 2074 (2005)

Justice O'CONNOR delivered the opinion of the Court.

On occasion, a would-be doctrinal rule or test finds its way into our case law through simple repetition of a phrase—however fortuitously coined. A quarter century ago, in Agins v. City of Tiburon (1980), the Court declared that government regulation of private property "effects a taking if [such regulation] does not substantially advance legitimate state interests. . . . " Through reiteration in a half dozen or so decisions since *Agins*, this language has been ensconced in our Fifth Amendment takings jurisprudence.

In the case before us, the lower courts applied *Agins*' "substantially advances" formula to strike down a Hawaii statute that limits the rent that oil companies may charge to dealers who lease service stations owned by the companies. The lower courts held that the rent cap effects an uncompensated taking of private property in violation of the Fifth and Fourteenth Amendments because it does not substantially advance Hawaii's asserted interest in controlling retail gasoline prices. This case requires us to decide whether the "substantially advances" formula announced in *Agins* is an appropriate test for determining whether a regulation effects a Fifth Amendment taking. We conclude that it is not.

I

Gasoline is sold at retail in Hawaii from about 300 different service stations. About half of these stations are leased from oil companies by independent lessee-dealers, another 75 or so are owned and operated by "open" dealers, and the remainder are owned and operated by the oil companies. Chevron sells most of its product through 64 independent lessee-dealer stations. In a typical lessee-dealer arrangement, Chevron buys or leases land from a third party, builds a service station, and then leases the station to a dealer on a turnkey basis. Chevron charges the lessee-dealer a monthly rent, defined as a percentage of the dealer's margin on retail sales of gasoline and other goods. In addition, Chevron requires the lessee-dealer to enter into a supply contract, under which the dealer agrees to purchase from Chevron whatever is necessary to satisfy demand at the station for Chevron's product. Chevron unilaterally sets the wholesale price of its product.

The Hawaii Legislature enacted Act 257 in June 1997, apparently in response to concerns about the effects of market concentration on retail gasoline prices. The statute seeks to protect independent dealers by imposing certain restrictions on the ownership and leasing of service stations by oil companies. It prohibits oil companies from converting existing lessee-dealer stations to company-operated stations and from locating new company-operated stations in close proximity to existing dealer-operated stations. More importantly for present purposes, Act 257 limits the amount of rent that an oil company may charge a lessee-dealer to 15 percent of the dealer's gross profits from gasoline sales plus 15 percent of gross sales of products other than gasoline.

II

A

The Takings Clause of the Fifth Amendment, made applicable to the States through the Fourteenth, provides that private property shall not "be taken for public use, without just compensation." As its text makes plain, the Takings Clause "does not prohibit the taking of private property, but instead places a condition on the exercise of that power." In other words, it "is designed not to limit the governmental interference with property rights per se, but rather to secure compensation in the event of otherwise proper interference amounting to a taking."

Beginning with Pennsylvania Coal Co. v. Mahon (1922), the Court recognized that government regulation of private property may, in some instances, be so onerous that its effect is tantamount to a direct appropriation or ouster—and that such "regulatory takings" may be compensable under the Fifth Amendment.

Our precedents stake out two categories of regulatory action that generally will be deemed per se takings for Fifth Amendment purposes. First, where government requires an owner to suffer a permanent physical invasion of her property— however minor—it must provide just compensation. A second categorical rule applies to regulations that completely deprive an owner of "all economically beneficial us[e]" of her property.

Outside these two relatively narrow categories, regulatory takings challenges are governed by the standards set forth in Penn Central Transp. Co. v. New York City (1978). The Court in *Penn Central* acknowledged that it had hitherto been "unable to develop any 'set formula'" for evaluating regulatory takings claims, but identified "several factors that have particular significance." Primary among those factors are "[t]he economic impact of the regulation on the claimant and, particularly, the extent to which the regulation has interfered with distinct investment-backed expectations." In addition, the "character of the governmental action"—for instance whether it amounts to a physical invasion or instead merely affects property interests through "some public program adjusting the benefits and burdens of economic life to promote the common good"—may be relevant in discerning whether a taking has occurred. The *Penn Central* factors—though each has given rise to vexing subsidiary questions— have served as the principal guidelines for resolving regulatory takings claims that do not fall within the physical takings or *Lucas* rules.

B

In Agins v. City of Tiburon, a case involving a facial takings challenge to certain municipal zoning ordinances, the Court declared that "[t]he application of a general zoning law to particular property effects a taking if the ordinance does not substantially advance legitimate state interests or denies an owner economically viable use of his land." Because this statement is phrased in the disjunctive, *Agins*' "substantially advances" language has been read to announce a standalone regulatory takings test that is wholly independent of *Penn Central* or any other test. Indeed, the lower courts in this case struck down Hawaii's rent control statute as an "unconstitutional regulatory taking," based solely upon a finding that it does not substantially advance the State's asserted interest in controlling retail gasoline prices. Although a number of our takings precedents have recited the "substantially advances" formula minted in *Agins*, this is our first opportunity to consider its validity as a freestanding takings test. We conclude that this formula prescribes an inquiry in the nature of a due process, not a takings, test, and that it has no proper place in our takings jurisprudence.

There is no question that the "substantially advances" formula was derived from due process, not takings, precedents. Although *Agins*' reliance on due process precedents is understandable, the language the Court selected was regrettably imprecise. The "substantially advances" formula suggests a means-ends test: It asks, in essence, whether a regulation of private property is effective in achieving some legitimate public purpose. An inquiry of this nature has some logic in the context of a due process challenge, for a regulation that fails to serve any legitimate governmental objective may be so arbitrary or irrational that it runs afoul of the Due Process Clause. But such a test is not a valid method of discerning whether private property has been "taken" for purposes of the Fifth Amendment.

In stark contrast to the three regulatory takings tests discussed above, the "substantially advances" inquiry reveals nothing about the magnitude or character of the burden a particular regulation imposes upon private property rights. Nor does it provide any information about how any regulatory burden is distributed among property owners. In consequence, this test does not help to identify those regulations whose effects are functionally comparable to government appropriation or invasion of private property; it is tethered neither to the text of the Takings Clause nor to the basic justification for allowing regulatory actions to be challenged under the Clause.

Chevron appeals to the general principle that the Takings Clause is meant "'to bar Government from forcing some people alone to bear public burdens which, in all fairness and justice, should be borne by the public as a whole.'" But that appeal is clearly misplaced, for the reasons just indicated. A test that tells us nothing about the actual burden imposed on property rights, or how that burden is allocated cannot tell us when justice might require that the burden be spread among taxpayers through the payment of compensation. The owner of a property subject to a regulation that effectively serves a legitimate state interest may be just as singled out and just as burdened as the owner of a property subject to an ineffective regulation. It would make little sense to say that the second owner has suffered a taking while the first has not. Likewise, an ineffective regulation may not significantly burden property rights at all, and it may distribute any burden broadly and evenly among property owners. The notion that such a regulation nevertheless "takes" private property for public use merely by virtue of its ineffectiveness or foolishness is untenable.

Instead of addressing a challenged regulation's effect on private property, the "substantially advances" inquiry probes the regulation's underlying validity. But such an inquiry is logically prior to and distinct from the question whether a regulation effects a taking, for the Takings Clause presupposes that the government has acted in pursuit of a valid public purpose. The Clause expressly requires compensation where government takes private property "for public use." It does not bar government from interfering with property rights, but rather requires compensation "in the event of otherwise proper interference amounting to a taking." Conversely, if a government action is found to be impermissible—for instance because it fails to meet the "public use" requirement or is so arbitrary as to violate due process—that is the end of the inquiry. No amount of compensation can authorize such action.

Chevron's challenge to the Hawaii statute in this case illustrates the flaws in the "substantially advances" theory. To begin with, it is unclear how significantly Hawaii's rent cap actually burdens Chevron's property rights. The parties stipulated below that the cap would reduce Chevron's aggregate rental income on 11 of its 64 lessee-dealer stations by about $207,000 per year, but that Chevron nevertheless expects to receive a return on its investment in these stations that satisfies any constitutional standard. Moreover, Chevron asserted below, and the District Court found, that Chevron would recoup any reductions in its rental income by raising wholesale gasoline prices. In short, Chevron has not clearly argued—let alone established—that it has been singled out to bear any particularly severe regulatory burden. Rather, the gravamen of Chevron's claim is simply that Hawaii's rent cap will not actually serve the State's legitimate interest in protecting consumers against high gasoline prices. Whatever the merits of that claim, it does not sound under the Takings Clause. Chevron plainly does not seek compensation for a taking of its property for a legitimate public use, but rather an injunction against the enforcement of a regulation that it alleges to be fundamentally arbitrary and irrational.

Finally, the "substantially advances" formula is not only doctrinally untenable as a takings test—its application as such would also present serious practical difficulties. The *Agins* formula can be read to demand heightened means-ends review of virtually any regulation of private property. If so interpreted, it would require courts to scrutinize the efficacy of a vast array of state and federal regulations—a task for which courts are not well suited. Moreover, it would empower—and might often require—courts to substitute their predictive judgments for those of elected legislatures and expert agencies.

For the foregoing reasons, we conclude that the "substantially advances" formula announced in *Agins* is not a valid method of identifying regulatory takings for which the Fifth Amendment requires just compensation. Since Chevron argued only a "substantially advances" theory in support of its takings claim, it was not entitled to summary judgment on that claim.

III

We emphasize that our holding today—that the "substantially advances" formula is not a valid takings test—does not require us to disturb any of our prior holdings. To be sure, we applied a "substantially advances" inquiry in *Agins* itself. But in no case have we found a compensable taking based on such an inquiry. Indeed, in most of the cases reciting the "substantially advances" formula, the Court has merely assumed its validity when referring to it in dicta.

We hold that the "substantially advances" formula is not a valid takings test, and indeed conclude that it has no proper place in our takings jurisprudence. In so doing, we reaffirm that a plaintiff seeking to challenge a government regulation as an uncompensated taking of private property may proceed under one of the other theories discussed above—by alleging a "physical" taking, a *Lucas*-type "total regulatory taking," a *Penn Central* taking, or a land-use exaction violating the standards set forth in *Nollan* and *Dolan*. Because Chevron argued only a "substantially advances" theory in support of its takings claim, it was not entitled to summary judgment on that claim.

Justice KENNEDY, concurring.

This separate writing is to note that today's decision does not foreclose the possibility that a regulation might be so arbitrary or irrational as to violate due process. The failure of a regulation to accomplish a stated or obvious objective would be relevant to that inquiry. Chevron voluntarily dismissed its due process claim without prejudice, however, and we have no occasion to consider whether Act 257 of the 1997 Hawaii Session Laws "represents one of the rare instances in which even such a permissive standard has been violated." With these observations, I join the opinion of the Court.

3.   Is It for "Public Use"? (casebook, p. 609)

The Court's decision in Kelo v. City of New London was among the most controversial of the year. In reading the decision, it is important to focus on whether the ruling changes the law concerning what is "public use" (and, if so, how).

KELO v. CITY OF NEW LONDON
125 S. Ct. 2655 (2005)

Justice STEVENS delivered the opinion of the Court.

In 2000, the city of New London approved a development plan that, in the words of the Supreme Court of Connecticut, was "projected to create in excess of 1,000 jobs, to increase tax and other revenues, and to revitalize an economically distressed city, including its downtown and waterfront areas." In assembling the land needed for this project, the city's development agent has purchased property from willing sellers and proposes to use the power of eminent domain to acquire the remainder of the property from unwilling owners in exchange for just compensation. The question presented is whether the city's proposed disposition of this property qualifies as a "public use" within the meaning of the Takings Clause of the Fifth Amendment to the Constitution.

I

The city of New London (hereinafter City) sits at the junction of the Thames River and the Long Island Sound in southeastern Connecticut. Decades of economic decline led a state agency in 1990 to designate the City a "distressed municipality." In 1996, the Federal Government closed the Naval Undersea Warfare Center, which had been located in the Fort Trumbull area of the City and had employed over 1,500 people. In 1998, the City's unemployment rate was nearly double that of the State, and its population of just under 24,000 residents was at its lowest since 1920.

These conditions prompted state and local officials to target New London, and particularly its Fort Trumbull area, for economic revitalization. To this end, respondent New London Development Corporation (NLDC), a private nonprofit entity established some years earlier to assist the City in planning economic development, was reactivated. In January 1998, the State authorized a $5.35 million bond issue to support the NLDC's planning activities and a $10 million bond issue toward the creation of a Fort Trumbull State Park. In February, the pharmaceutical company Pfizer Inc. announced that it would build a $300 million research facility on a site immediately adjacent to Fort Trumbull; local planners hoped that Pfizer would draw new business to the area, thereby serving as a catalyst to the area's rejuvenation. After receiving initial approval from the city council, the NLDC continued its planning activities and held a series of neighborhood meetings to educate the public about the process.

The city council approved the plan in January 2000, and designated the NLDC as its development agent in charge of implementation. The city council also authorized the NLDC to purchase property or to acquire property by exercising eminent domain in the City's name. The NLDC successfully negotiated the purchase of most of the real estate in the 90-acre area, but its negotiations with petitioners failed. As a consequence, in November 2000, the NLDC initiated the condemnation proceedings that gave rise to this case.

II

Petitioner Susette Kelo has lived in the Fort Trumbull area since 1997. She has made extensive improvements to her house, which she prizes for its water view. Petitioner Wilhelmina Dery was born in her Fort Trumbull house in 1918 and has lived there her entire life. Her husband Charles (also a petitioner) has lived in the house since they married some 60 years ago. In all, the nine petitioners own 15 properties in Fort Trumbull. There is no allegation that any of these properties is blighted or otherwise in poor condition; rather, they were condemned only because they happen to be located in the development area.

III

Two polar propositions are perfectly clear. On the one hand, it has long been accepted that the sovereign may not take the property of A for the sole purpose of transferring it to another private party B, even though A is paid just compensation. On the other hand, it is equally clear that a State may transfer property from one private party to another if future "use by the public" is the purpose of the taking; the condemnation of land for a railroad with common-carrier duties is a familiar example. Neither of these propositions, however, determines the disposition of this case.

As for the first proposition, the City would no doubt be forbidden from taking petitioners' land for the purpose of conferring a private benefit on a particular private party. Nor would the City be allowed to take property under the mere pretext of a public purpose, when its actual purpose was to bestow a private benefit. The takings before us, however, would be executed pursuant to a "carefully considered" development plan. The trial judge and all the members of the Supreme Court of Connecticut agreed that there was no evidence of an illegitimate purpose in this case.

On the other hand, this is not a case in which the City is planning to open the condemned land—at least not in its entirety—to use by the general public. Nor will the private lessees of the land in any sense be required to operate like common carriers, making their services available to all comers. But although such a projected use would be sufficient to satisfy the public use requirement, this "Court long ago rejected any literal requirement that condemned property be put into use for the general public." Indeed, while many state courts in the mid-19th century endorsed "use by the public" as the proper definition of public use, that narrow view steadily eroded over time. Not only was the "use by the public" test difficult to administer (e.g., what proportion of the public need have access to the property? at what price?), but it proved to be impractical given the diverse and always evolving needs of society. Accordingly, when this Court began applying the Fifth Amendment to the States at the close of the 19th century, it embraced the broader and more natural interpretation of public use as "public purpose." Thus, in a case upholding a mining company's use of an aerial bucket line to transport ore over property it did not own, Justice Holmes' opinion for the Court stressed "the inadequacy of use by the general public as a universal test." Strickley v. Highland Boy Gold Mining Co. (1906). We have repeatedly and consistently rejected that narrow test ever since.

The disposition of this case therefore turns on the question whether the City's development plan serves a "public purpose." Without exception, our cases have defined that concept broadly, reflecting our longstanding policy of deference to legislative judgments in this field.

In Berman v. Parker (1954), this Court upheld a redevelopment plan targeting a blighted area of Washington, D.C., in which most of the housing for the area's 5,000 inhabitants was beyond repair. Under the plan, the area would be condemned and part of it utilized for the construction of streets, schools, and other public facilities. The remainder of the land would be leased or sold to private parties for the purpose of redevelopment, including the construction of low-cost housing. The owner of a department store located in the area challenged the condemnation, pointing out that his store was not itself blighted and arguing that the creation of a "better balanced, more attractive community" was not a valid public use. Writing for a unanimous Court, Justice Douglas refused to evaluate this claim in isolation, deferring instead to the legislative and agency judgment that the area "must be planned as a whole" for the plan to be successful. The Court explained that "community redevelopment programs need not, by force of the Constitution, be on a piecemeal basis—lot by lot, building by building." The public use underlying the taking was unequivocally affirmed.

In Hawaii Housing Authority v. Midkiff (1984), the Court considered a Hawaii statute whereby fee title was taken from lessors and transferred to lessees (for just compensation) in order to reduce the concentration of land ownership. We unanimously upheld the statute and rejected the Ninth Circuit's view that it was "a naked attempt on the part of the state of Hawaii to take the property of A and transfer it to B solely for B's private use and benefit." Reaffirming *Berman*'s deferential approach to legislative judgments in this field, we concluded that the State's purpose of eliminating the "social and economic evils of a land oligopoly" qualified as a valid public use. Our opinion also rejected the contention that the mere fact that the State immediately transferred the properties to private individuals upon condemnation somehow diminished the public character of the taking. "[I]t is only the taking's purpose, and not its mechanics," we explained, that matters in determining public use.

In that same Term we decided another public use case that arose in a purely economic context. In Ruckelshaus v. Monsanto Co. (1984), the Court dealt with provisions of the Federal Insecticide, Fungicide, and Rodenticide Act under which the Environmental Protection Agency could consider the data (including trade secrets) submitted by a prior pesticide applicant in evaluating a subsequent application, so long as the second applicant paid just compensation for the data. We acknowledged that the "most direct beneficiaries" of these provisions were the subsequent applicants, but we nevertheless upheld the statute under Berman and *Midkiff*. We found sufficient Congress' belief that sparing applicants the cost of time-consuming research eliminated a significant barrier to entry in the pesticide market and thereby enhanced competition.

Viewed as a whole, our jurisprudence has recognized that the needs of society have varied between different parts of the Nation, just as they have evolved over time in response to changed circumstances. Our earliest cases in particular embodied a strong theme of federalism, emphasizing the "great respect" that we owe to state legislatures and state courts in discerning local public needs. For more than a century, our public use jurisprudence has wisely eschewed rigid formulas and intrusive scrutiny in favor of affording legislatures broad latitude in determining what public needs justify the use of the takings power.

IV

Those who govern the City were not confronted with the need to remove blight in the Fort Trumbull area, but their determination that the area was sufficiently distressed to justify a program of economic rejuvenation is entitled to our deference. The City has carefully formulated an economic development plan that it believes will provide appreciable benefits to the community, including—but by no means limited to—new jobs and increased tax revenue. As with other exercises in urban planning and development, the City is endeavoring to coordinate a variety of commercial, residential, and recreational uses of land, with the hope that they will form a whole greater than the sum of its parts. To effectuate this plan, the City has invoked a state statute that specifically authorizes the use of eminent domain to promote economic development. Given the comprehensive character of the plan, the thorough deliberation that preceded its adoption, and the limited scope of our review, it is appropriate for us, as it was in *Berman*, to resolve the challenges of the individual owners, not on a piecemeal basis, but rather in light of the entire plan. Because that plan unquestionably serves a public purpose, the takings challenged here satisfy the public use requirement of the Fifth Amendment.

To avoid this result, petitioners urge us to adopt a new bright-line rule that economic development does not qualify as a public use. Putting aside the unpersuasive suggestion that the City's plan will provide only purely economic benefits, neither precedent nor logic supports petitioners' proposal. Promoting economic development is a traditional and long accepted function of government. There is, moreover, no principled way of distinguishing economic development from the other public purposes that we have recognized. In our cases upholding takings that facilitated agriculture and mining, for example, we emphasized the importance of those industries to the welfare of the States in question. It would be incongruous to hold that the City's interest in the economic benefits to be derived from the development of the Fort Trumbull area has less of a public character than any of those other interests. Clearly, there is no basis for exempting economic development from our traditionally broad understanding of public purpose.

Petitioners contend that using eminent domain for economic development impermissibly blurs the boundary between public and private takings. Again, our cases foreclose this objection. Quite simply, the government's pursuit of a public purpose will often benefit individual private parties.

It is further argued that without a bright-line rule nothing would stop a city from transferring citizen A's property to citizen B for the sole reason that citizen B will put the property to a more productive use and thus pay more taxes. Such a one-to-one transfer of property, executed outside the confines of an integrated development plan, is not presented in this case. While such an unusual exercise of government power would certainly raise a suspicion that a private purpose was afoot, the hypothetical cases posited by petitioners can be confronted if and when they arise. They do not warrant the crafting of an artificial restriction on the concept of public use.

Alternatively, petitioners maintain that for takings of this kind we should require a "reasonable certainty" that the expected public benefits will actually accrue. Such a rule, however, would represent an even greater departure from our precedent. "When the legislature's purpose is legitimate and its means are not irrational, our cases make clear that empirical debates over the wisdom of takings—no less than debates over the wisdom of other kinds of socioeconomic legislation—are not to be carried out in the federal courts."

In affirming the City's authority to take petitioners' properties, we do not minimize the hardship that condemnations may entail, notwithstanding the payment of just compensation. We emphasize that nothing in our opinion precludes any State from placing further restrictions on its exercise of the takings power. Indeed, many States already impose "public use" requirements that are stricter than the federal baseline. Some of these requirements have been established as a matter of state constitutional law, while others are expressed in state eminent domain statutes that carefully limit the grounds upon which takings may be exercised. As the submissions of the parties and their amici make clear, the necessity and wisdom of using eminent domain to promote economic development are certainly matters of legitimate public debate. This Court's authority, however, extends only to determining whether the City's proposed condemnations are for a "public use" within the meaning of the Fifth Amendment to the Federal Constitution. Because over a century of our case law interpreting that provision dictates an affirmative answer to that question, we may not grant petitioners the relief that they seek.

Justice KENNEDY, concurring.

I join the opinion for the Court and add these further observations.This Court has declared that a taking should be upheld as consistent with the Public Use Clause, U.S. Const., Amdt. 5., as long as it is "rationally related to a conceivable public purpose." Hawaii Housing Authority v. Midkiff (1984); see also Berman v. Parker (1954). This deferential standard of review echoes the rational-basis test used to review economic regulation under the Due Process and Equal Protection Clauses. The determination that a rational-basis standard of review is appropriate does not, however, alter the fact that transfers intended to confer benefits on particular, favored private entities, and with only incidental or pretextual public benefits, are forbidden by the Public Use Clause.

A court applying rational-basis review under the Public Use Clause should strike down a taking that, by a clear showing, is intended to favor a particular private party, with only incidental or pretextual public benefits, just as a court applying rational-basis review under the Equal Protection Clause must strike down a government classification that is clearly intended to injure a particular class of private parties, with only incidental or pretextual public justifications.

A court confronted with a plausible accusation of impermissible favoritism to private parties should treat the objection as a serious one and review the record to see if it has merit, though with the presumption that the government's actions were reasonable and intended to serve a public purpose. Here, the trial court conducted a careful and extensive inquiry.

Petitioners and their amici argue that any taking justified by the promotion of economic development must be treated by the courts as per se invalid, or at least presumptively invalid. Petitioners overstate the need for such a rule, however, by making the incorrect assumption that review under *Berman* and *Midkiff* imposes no meaningful judicial limits on the government's power to condemn any property it likes. A broad per se rule or a strong presumption of invalidity, furthermore, would prohibit a large number of government takings that have the purpose and expected effect of conferring substantial benefits on the public at large and so do not offend the Public Use Clause.

My agreement with the Court that a presumption of invalidity is not warranted for economic development takings in general, or for the particular takings at issue in this case, does not foreclose the possibility that a more stringent standard of review than that announced in *Berman* and *Midkiff* might be appropriate for a more narrowly drawn category of takings. There may be private transfers in which the risk of undetected impermissible favoritism of private parties is so acute that a presumption (rebuttable or otherwise) of invalidity is warranted under the Public Use Clause. This demanding level of scrutiny, however, is not required simply because the purpose of the taking is economic development.

This is not the occasion for conjecture as to what sort of cases might justify a more demanding standard, but it is appropriate to underscore aspects of the instant case that convince me no departure from *Berman* and *Midkiff* is appropriate here. This taking occurred in the context of a comprehensive development plan meant to address a serious city-wide depression, and the projected economic benefits of the project cannot be characterized as de minimus. The identity of most of the private beneficiaries were unknown at the time the city formulated its plans. The city complied with elaborate procedural requirements that facilitate review of the record and inquiry into the city's purposes. In sum, while there may be categories of cases in which the transfers are so suspicious, or the procedures employed so prone to abuse, or the purported benefits are so trivial or implausible, that courts should presume an impermissible private purpose, no such circumstances are present in this case.

Justice O'CONNOR, with whom THE CHIEF JUSTICE, Justice SCALIA, and Justice THOMAS join, dissenting.

Over two centuries ago, just after the Bill of Rights was ratified, Justice Chase wrote: "An ACT of the Legislature (for I cannot call it a law) contrary to the great first principles of the social compact, cannot be considered a rightful exercise of legislative authority . . . . A few instances will suffice to explain what I mean . . . . [A] law that takes property from A. and gives it to B: It is against all reason and justice, for a people to entrust a Legislature with SUCH powers; and, therefore, it cannot be presumed that they have done it." Calder v. Bull (1798).

Today the Court abandons this long-held, basic limitation on government power. Under the banner of economic development, all private property is now vulnerable to being taken and transferred to another private owner, so long as it might be upgraded—i.e., given to an owner who will use it in a way that the legislature deems more beneficial to the public—in the process. To reason, as the Court does, that the incidental public benefits resulting from the subsequent ordinary use of private property render economic development takings "for public use" is to wash out any distinction between private and public use of property— and thereby effectively to delete the words "for public use" from the Takings Clause of the Fifth Amendment. Accordingly I respectfully dissent.

The public use requirement, in turn, imposes a more basic limitation, circumscribing the very scope of the eminent domain power: Government may compel an individual to forfeit her property for the public's use, but not for the benefit of another private person. This requirement promotes fairness as well as security. Where is the line between "public" and "private" property use? We give considerable deference to legislatures' determinations about what governmental activities will advantage the public. But were the political branches the sole arbiters of the public-private distinction, the Public Use Clause would amount to little more than hortatory fluff. An external, judicial check on how the public use requirement is interpreted, however limited, is necessary if this constraint on government power is to retain any meaning.

Our cases have generally identified three categories of takings that comply with the public use requirement, though it is in the nature of things that the boundaries between these categories are not always firm. Two are relatively straightforward and uncontroversial. First, the sovereign may transfer private property to public ownership—such as for a road, a hospital, or a military base. Second, the sovereign may transfer private property to private parties, often common carriers, who make the property available for the public's use—such as with a railroad, a public utility, or a stadium. But "public ownership" and "use-by-the-public" are sometimes too constricting and impractical ways to define the scope of the Public Use Clause. Thus we have allowed that, in certain circumstances and to meet certain exigencies, takings that serve a public purpose also satisfy the Constitution even if the property is destined for subsequent private use. See, e.g., Berman v. Parker (1954); Hawaii Housing Authority v. Midkiff (1984).

This case returns us for the first time in over 20 years to the hard question of when a purportedly "public purpose" taking meets the public use requirement. It presents an issue of first impression: Are economic development takings constitutional? I would hold that they are not.

Here New London does not claim that Susette Kelo's and Wilhelmina Dery's well-maintained homes are the source of any social harm. Indeed, it could not so claim without adopting the absurd argument that any single-family home that might be razed to make way for an apartment building, or any church that might be replaced with a retail store, or any small business that might be more lucrative if it were instead part of a national franchise, is inherently harmful to society and thus within the government's power to condemn.

In moving away from our decisions sanctioning the condemnation of harmful property use, the Court today significantly expands the meaning of public use. It holds that the sovereign may take private property currently put to ordinary private use, and give it over for new, ordinary private use, so long as the new use is predicted to generate some secondary benefit for the public—such as increased tax revenue, more jobs, maybe even aesthetic pleasure. But nearly any lawful use of real private property can be said to generate some incidental benefit to the public. Thus, if predicted (or even guaranteed) positive side-effects are enough to render transfer from one private party to another constitutional, then the words "for public use" do not realistically exclude any takings, and thus do not exert any constraint on the eminent domain power.

Even if there were a practical way to isolate the motives behind a given taking, the gesture toward a purpose test is theoretically flawed. If it is true that incidental public benefits from new private use are enough to ensure the "public purpose" in a taking, why should it matter, as far as the Fifth Amendment is concerned, what inspired the taking in the first place? How much the government does or does not desire to benefit a favored private party has no bearing on whether an economic development taking will or will not generate secondary benefit for the public. And whatever the reason for a given condemnation, the effect is the same from the constitutional perspective—private property is forcibly relinquished to new private ownership.

A second proposed limitation is implicit in the Court's opinion. The logic of today's decision is that eminent domain may only be used to upgrade—not downgrade—property. At best this makes the Public Use Clause redundant with the Due Process Clause, which already prohibits irrational government action. The Court rightfully admits, however, that the judiciary cannot get bogged down in predictive judgments about whether the public will actually be better off after a property transfer. In any event, this constraint has no realistic import. For who among us can say she already makes the most productive or attractive possible use of her property? The specter of condemnation hangs over all property. Nothing is to prevent the State from replacing any Motel 6 with a Ritz-Carlton, any home with a shopping mall, or any farm with a factory.

Any property may now be taken for the benefit of another private party, but the fallout from this decision will not be random. The beneficiaries are likely to be those citizens with disproportionate influence and power in the political process, including large corporations and development firms. As for the victims, the government now has license to transfer property from those with fewer resources to those with more. The Founders cannot have intended this perverse result. "[T]hat alone is a just government," wrote James Madison, "which impartially secures to every man, whatever is his own."

Justice THOMAS, dissenting.

Long ago, William Blackstone wrote that "the law of the land . . . postpone[s] even public necessity to the sacred and inviolable rights of private property." The Framers embodied that principle in the Constitution, allowing the government to take property not for "public necessity," but instead for "public use." Defying this understanding, the Court replaces the Public Use Clause with a "'[P]ublic [P]urpose'" Clause (or perhaps the "Diverse and Always Evolving Needs of Society" Clause), a restriction that is satisfied, the Court instructs, so long as the purpose is "legitimate" and the means "not irrational." This deferential shift in phraseology enables the Court to hold, against all common sense, that a costly urban-renewal project whose stated purpose is a vague promise of new jobs and increased tax revenue, but which is also suspiciously agreeable to the Pfizer Corporation, is for a "public use."

I cannot agree. If such "economic development" takings are for a "public use," any taking is, and the Court has erased the Public Use Clause from our Constitution, as Justice O'Connor powerfully argues in dissent. I do not believe that this Court can eliminate liberties expressly enumerated in the Constitution and therefore join her dissenting opinion.

Regrettably, however, the Court's error runs deeper than this. Today's decision is simply the latest in a string of our cases construing the Public Use Clause to be a virtual nullity, without the slightest nod to its original meaning. In my view, the Public Use Clause, originally understood, is a meaningful limit on the government's eminent domain power. Our cases have strayed from the Clause's original meaning, and I would reconsider them.

There is no justification, however, for affording almost insurmountable deference to legislative conclusions that a use serves a "public use." To begin with, a court owes no deference to a legislature's judgment concerning the quintessentially legal question of whether the government owns, or the public has a legal right to use, the taken property. Even under the "public purpose" interpretation, moreover, it is most implausible that the Framers intended to defer to legislatures as to what satisfies the Public Use Clause, uniquely among all the express provisions of the Bill of Rights. We would not defer to a legislature's determination of the various circumstances that establish, for example, when a search of a home would be reasonable, or when a convicted double-murderer may be shackled during a sentencing proceeding without on-the-record findings, or when state law creates a property interest protected by the Due Process Clause.

Still worse, it is backwards to adopt a searching standard of constitutional review for nontraditional property interests, such as welfare benefits, while deferring to the legislature's determination as to what constitutes a public use when it exercises the power of eminent domain, and thereby invades individuals' traditional rights in real property.

The consequences of today's decision are not difficult to predict, and promise to be harmful. So-called "urban renewal" programs provide some compensation for the properties they take, but no compensation is possible for the subjective value of these lands to the individuals displaced and the indignity inflicted by uprooting them from their homes. Allowing the government to take property solely for public purposes is bad enough, but extending the concept of public purpose to encompass any economically beneficial goal guarantees that these losses will fall disproportionately on poor communities. Those communities are not only systematically less likely to put their lands to the highest and best social use, but are also the least politically powerful. If ever there were justification for intrusive judicial review of constitutional provisions that protect "discrete and insular minorities," United States v. Carolene Products Co. (1938), surely that principle would apply with great force to the powerless groups and individuals the Public Use Clause protects. The deferential standard this Court has adopted for the Public Use Clause is therefore deeply perverse. It encourages "those citizens with disproportionate influence and power in the political process, including large corporations and development firms" to victimize the weak.

The Court relies almost exclusively on this Court's prior cases to derive today's far-reaching, and dangerous, result. But the principles this Court should employ to dispose of this case are found in the Public Use Clause itself, not in Justice Peckham's high opinion of reclamation laws. When faced with a clash of constitutional principle and a line of unreasoned cases wholly divorced from the text, history, and structure of our founding document, we should not hesitate to resolve the tension in favor of the Constitution's original meaning. For the reasons I have given, and for the reasons given in Justice O'Connor's dissent, the conflict of principle raised by this boundless use of the eminent domain power should be resolved in petitioners' favor. I would reverse the judgment of the Connecticut Supreme Court.

Chapter 7

Equal Protection

C. Classifications Based on Race and National Origin

3. Proving the Existence of a Race or National Origin Classification (casebook, p. 653)

The Supreme Court long has held that laws requiring separation of the races are a form of race discrimination that must meet strict scrutiny. Is this also so in prisons? That is the focus of Johnson v. California. It is important to note that the Court does not decide the constitutionality of the California prison regulation, but only announces the legal test and then remands the case for its application.

JOHNSON v. CALIFORNIA
125 S. Ct. 1141 (2005)

Justice O'CONNOR delivered the opinion of the Court.

The California Department of Corrections (CDC) has an unwritten policy of racially segregating prisoners in double cells in reception centers for up to 60 days each time they enter a new correctional facility. We consider whether strict scrutiny is the proper standard of review for an equal protection challenge to that policy.

I

A

CDC institutions house all new male inmates and all male inmates transferred from other state facilities in reception centers for up to 60 days upon their arrival. During that time, prison officials evaluate the inmates to determine their ultimate placement. Double-cell assignments in the reception centers are based on a number of factors, predominantly race. In fact, the CDC has admitted that the chances of an inmate being assigned a cellmate of another race are "'[p]retty close'" to zero percent. The CDC further subdivides prisoners within each racial group.

Thus, Japanese-Americans are housed separately from Chinese-Americans, and Northern California Hispanics are separated from Southern California Hispanics.

The CDC's asserted rationale for this practice is that it is necessary to prevent violence caused by racial gangs. It cites numerous incidents of racial violence in CDC facilities and identifies five major prison gangs in the State: Mexican Mafia, Nuestra Familia, Black Guerrilla Family, Aryan Brotherhood, and Nazi Low Riders. The CDC also notes that prison-gang culture is violent and murderous. An associate warden testified that if race were not considered in making initial housing assignments, she is certain there would be racial conflict in the cells and in the yard. Other prison officials also expressed their belief that violence and conflict would result if prisoners were not segregated. The CDC claims that it must therefore segregate all inmates while it determines whether they pose a danger to others.

With the exception of the double cells in reception areas, the rest of the state prison facilities—dining areas, yards, and cells—are fully integrated. After the initial 60-day period, prisoners are allowed to choose their own cellmates. The CDC usually grants inmate requests to be housed together, unless there are security reasons for denying them.

B

Garrison Johnson is an African-American inmate in the custody of the CDC. He has been incarcerated since 1987 and, during that time, has been housed at a number of California prison facilities. Upon his arrival at Folsom prison in 1987, and each time he was transferred to a new facility thereafter, Johnson was double-celled with another African-American inmate.

Johnson filed a complaint pro se in the United States District Court for the Central District of California on February 24, 1995, alleging that the CDC's reception-center housing policy violated his right to equal protection under the Fourteenth Amendment by assigning him cellmates on the basis of his race.

II

A

We have held that "*all* racial classifications [imposed by government] . . . must be analyzed by a reviewing court under strict scrutiny." Adarand Constructors, Inc. v. Peña (1995) (emphasis added). Under strict scrutiny, the government has the burden of proving that racial classifications "are narrowly tailored measures that further compelling governmental interests." We have insisted on strict scrutiny in every context, even for so-called "benign" racial classifications, such as race-conscious university admissions policies, see Grutter v. Bollinger (2003), race-based preferences in government contracts, and race-based districting intended to improve minority representation, Shaw v. Reno (1993).

The reasons for strict scrutiny are familiar. Racial classifications raise special fears that they are motivated by an invidious purpose. Thus, we have admonished time and again that, "[a]bsent searching judicial inquiry into the justification for such race-based measures, there is simply no way of determining . . . what classifications are in fact motivated by illegitimate notions of racial inferiority or simple racial politics." Richmond v. J. A. Croson Co. (1989) (plurality opinion). We therefore apply strict scrutiny to all racial classifications to "'smoke out' illegitimate uses of race by assuring that [government] is pursuing a goal important enough to warrant use of a highly suspect tool."

The CDC claims that its policy should be exempt from our categorical rule because it is "neutral"—that is, it "neither benefits nor burdens one group or individual more than any other group or individual." In other words, strict scrutiny should not apply because all prisoners are "equally" segregated. The CDC's argument ignores our repeated command that "racial classifications receive close scrutiny even when they may be said to burden or benefit the races equally." Indeed, we rejected the notion that separate can ever be equal— or "neutral"—50 years ago in Brown v. Board of Education (1954), and we refuse to resurrect it today.

We have previously applied a heightened standard of review in evaluating racial segregation in prisons. In Lee v. Washington (1968) (per curiam), we upheld a three-judge court's decision striking down Alabama's policy of segregation in its prisons.

The need for strict scrutiny is no less important here, where prison officials cite racial violence as the reason for their policy. As we have recognized in the past, racial classifications "threaten to stigmatize individuals by reason of their membership in a racial group and to incite racial hostility." Indeed, by insisting that inmates be housed only with other inmates of the same race, it is possible that prison officials will breed further hostility among prisoners and reinforce racial and ethnic divisions. By perpetuating the notion that race matters most, racial segregation of inmates "may exacerbate the very patterns of [violence that it is] said to counteract."

The CDC's policy is unwritten. Although California claimed at oral argument that two other States follow a similar policy, this assertion was unsubstantiated, and we are unable to confirm or deny its accuracy. Virtually all other States and the Federal Government manage their prison systems without reliance on racial segregation. Federal regulations governing the Federal Bureau of Prisons (BOP) expressly prohibit racial segregation. The United States contends that racial integration actually "leads to less violence in BOP's institutions and better prepares inmates for re-entry into society." Indeed, the United States argues, based on its experience with the BOP, that it is possible to address "concerns of prison security through individualized consideration without the use of racial segregation, unless warranted as a necessary and temporary response to a race riot or other serious threat of race-related violence." As to transferees, in particular, whom the CDC has already evaluated at least once, it is not clear why more individualized determinations are not possible.

Because the CDC's policy is an express racial classification, it is "immediately suspect." We therefore hold that the Court of Appeals erred when it failed to apply strict scrutiny to the CDC's policy and to require the CDC to demonstrate that its policy is narrowly tailored to serve a compelling state interest.

B

The CDC invites us to make an exception to the rule that strict scrutiny applies to all racial classifications, and instead to apply the deferential standard of review articulated in Turner v. Safley (1987), because its segregation policy applies only in the prison context. We decline the invitation. In *Turner*, we considered a claim by Missouri prisoners that regulations restricting inmate marriages and inmate-to-inmate correspondence were unconstitutional. We rejected the prisoners' argument that the regulations should be subject to strict scrutiny, asking instead whether the regulation that burdened the prisoners' fundamental rights was "reasonably related" to "legitimate penological interests."

We have never applied *Turner* to racial classifications. *Turner* itself did not involve any racial classification, and it cast no doubt on *Lee*. We think this unsurprising, as we have applied *Turner*'s reasonable-relationship test only to rights that are "inconsistent with proper incarceration." This is because certain privileges and rights must necessarily be limited in the prison context. Thus, for example, we have relied on *Turner* in addressing First Amendment challenges to prison regulations, including restrictions on freedom of association; limits on inmate correspondence; restrictions on inmates' access to courts; restrictions on receipt of subscription publications; and work rules limiting prisoners' attendance at religious services. We have also applied *Turner* to some due process claims, such as involuntary medication of mentally ill prisoners, and restrictions on the right to marry.

The right not to be discriminated against based on one's race is not susceptible to the logic of *Turner*. It is not a right that need necessarily be compromised for the sake of proper prison administration. On the contrary, compliance with the Fourteenth Amendment's ban on racial discrimination is not only consistent with proper prison administration, but also bolsters the legitimacy of the entire criminal justice system. Race discrimination is "especially pernicious in the administration of justice." And public respect for our system of justice is undermined when the system discriminates based on race. When government officials are permitted to use race as a proxy for gang membership and violence without demonstrating a compelling government interest and proving that their means are narrowly tailored, society as a whole suffers.

In the prison context, when the government's power is at its apex, we think that searching judicial review of racial classifications is necessary to guard against invidious discrimination. Granting the CDC an exemption from the rule that strict scrutiny applies to all racial classifications would undermine our "unceasing efforts to eradicate racial prejudice from our criminal justice system." McCleskey v. Kemp (1987).

The CDC argues that "[d]eference to the particular expertise of prison officials in the difficult task of managing daily prison operations" requires a more relaxed standard of review for its segregation policy. But we have refused to defer to state officials' judgments on race in other areas where those officials traditionally exercise substantial discretion. For example, we have held that, despite the broad discretion given to prosecutors when they use their peremptory challenges, using those challenges to strike jurors on the basis of their race is impermissible. Similarly, in the redistricting context, despite the traditional deference given to States when they design their electoral districts, we have subjected redistricting plans to strict scrutiny when States draw district lines based predominantly on race.

We did not relax the standard of review for racial classifications in prison in *Lee*, and we refuse to do so today. Rather, we explicitly reaffirm what we implicitly held in *Lee*: The "necessities of prison security and discipline" are a compelling government interest justifying only those uses of race that are narrowly tailored to address those necessities.

Justice Thomas would subject race-based policies in prisons to *Turner*'s deferential standard of review because, in his view, judgments about whether race-based policies are necessary "are better left in the first instance to the officials who run our Nation's prisons." But *Turner* is too lenient a standard to ferret out invidious uses of race. *Turner* requires only that the policy be "reasonably related" to "legitimate penological interests." *Turner* would allow prison officials to use race-based policies even when there are race-neutral means to accomplish the same goal, and even when the race-based policy does not in practice advance that goal.

For example, in Justice Thomas' world, prison officials could segregate visiting areas on the ground that racial mixing would cause unrest in the racially charged prison atmosphere. Indeed, under Justice Thomas' view, there is no obvious limit to permissible segregation in prisons. It is not readily apparent why, if segregation in reception centers is justified, segregation in the dining halls, yards, and general housing areas is not also permissible. Any of these areas could be the potential site of racial violence. If Justice Thomas' approach were to carry the day, even the blanket segregation policy struck down in *Lee* might stand a chance of survival if prison officials simply asserted that it was necessary to prison management. We therefore reject the *Turner* standard for racial classifications in prisons because it would make rank discrimination too easy to defend.

The CDC protests that strict scrutiny will handcuff prison administrators and render them unable to address legitimate problems of race-based violence in prisons. Not so. Strict scrutiny is not "strict in theory, but fatal in fact." Strict scrutiny does not preclude the ability of prison officials to address the compelling interest in prison safety. Prison administrators, however, will have to demonstrate that any race-based policies are narrowly tailored to that end.

The fact that strict scrutiny applies "says nothing about the ultimate validity of any particular law; that determination is the job of the court applying strict scrutiny." At this juncture, no such determination has been made. On remand, the CDC will have the burden of demonstrating that its policy is narrowly tailored with regard to new inmates as well as transferees. Prisons are dangerous places, and the special circumstances they present may justify racial classifications in some contexts. Such circumstances can be considered in applying strict scrutiny, which is designed to take relevant differences into account.

We do not decide whether the CDC's policy violates the Equal Protection Clause. We hold only that strict scrutiny is the proper standard of review and remand the case to allow the Court of Appeals for the Ninth Circuit, or the District Court, to apply it in the first instance.

Justice STEVENS, dissenting.

In my judgment a state policy of segregating prisoners by race during the first 60 days of their incarceration, as well as the first 60 days after their transfer from one facility to another, violates the Equal Protection Clause of the Fourteenth Amendment. The California Department of Corrections (CDC) has had an ample opportunity to justify its policy during the course of this litigation, but has utterly failed to do so whether judged under strict scrutiny or the more deferential standard set out in Turner v. Safley (1987). The CDC had no incentive in the proceedings below to withhold evidence supporting its policy; nor has the CDC made any offer of proof to suggest that a remand for further factual development would serve any purpose other than to postpone the inevitable. I therefore agree with the submission of the United States as amicus curiae that the Court should hold the policy unconstitutional on the current record.

The CDC's segregation policy is based on a conclusive presumption that housing inmates of different races together creates an unacceptable risk of racial violence. Under the policy's logic, an inmate's race is a proxy for gang membership, and gang membership is a proxy for violence. The CDC, however, has offered scant empirical evidence or expert opinion to justify this use of race under even a minimal level of constitutional scrutiny. The presumption underlying the policy is undoubtedly overbroad. The CDC has made no effort to prove what fraction of new or transferred inmates are members of race-based gangs, nor has it shown more generally that interracial violence is disproportionately greater than intraracial violence in its prisons. Proclivity toward racial violence unquestionably varies from inmate to inmate, yet the CDC applies its blunderbuss policy to all new and transferred inmates housed in double cells regardless of their criminal histories or records of previous incarceration. Under the CDC's policy, for example, two car thieves of different races—neither of whom has any history of gang involvement, or of violence, for that matter— would be barred from being housed together during their first two months of prison. This result derives from the CDC's inflexible judgment that such integrated living conditions are simply too dangerous. This Court has never countenanced such racial prophylaxis.

Given the inherent indignity of segregation and its shameful historical connotations, one might assume that the CDC came to its policy only as a last resort. Distressingly, this is not so: There is no evidence that the CDC has ever experimented with, or even carefully considered, race-neutral methods of achieving its goals. That the policy is unwritten reflects, I think, the evident lack of deliberation that preceded its creation.

Specifically, the CDC has failed to explain why it could not, as an alternative to automatic segregation, rely on an individualized assessment of each inmate's risk of violence when assigning him to a cell in a reception center. The Federal Bureau of Prisons and other state systems do so without any apparent difficulty. For inmates who are being transferred from one facility to another—who represent approximately 85% of those subject to the segregation policy—the CDC can simply examine their prison records to determine if they have any known gang affiliations or if they have ever engaged in or threatened racial violence. For example, the CDC has had an opportunity to observe the petitioner for almost 20 years; surely the CDC could have determined his placement without subjecting him to a period of segregation. For new inmates, assignments can be based on their presentence reports, which contain information about offense conduct, criminal record, and personal history—including any available information about gang affiliations.

Justice THOMAS, with whom Justice SCALIA joins, dissenting.

The questions presented in this case require us to resolve two conflicting lines of precedent. On the one hand, as the Court stresses, this Court has said that "'all racial classifications reviewable under the Equal Protection Clause must be strictly scrutinized.'" Gratz v. Bollinger (2003). On the other, this Court has no less categorically said that "the [relaxed] standard of review we adopted in Turner [v. Safley (1987)] applies to *all* circumstances in which the needs of prison administration implicate constitutional rights." Washington v. Harper (1990) (emphasis added).

Emphasizing the former line of cases, the majority resolves the conflict in favor of strict scrutiny. I disagree. The Constitution has always demanded less within the prison walls. Time and again, even when faced with constitutional rights no less "fundamental" than the right to be free from state-sponsored racial discrimination, we have deferred to the reasonable judgments of officials experienced in running this Nation's prisons. There is good reason for such deference in this case. California oversees roughly 160,000 inmates, in prisons that have been a breeding ground for some of the most violent prison gangs in America—all of them organized along racial lines. In that atmosphere, California racially segregates a portion of its inmates, in a part of its prisons, for brief periods of up to 60 days, until the State can arrange permanent housing. The majority is concerned with sparing inmates the indignity and stigma of racial discrimination. California is concerned with their safety and saving their lives. I respectfully dissent.

The majority decides this case without addressing the problems that racial violence poses for wardens, guards, and inmates throughout the federal and state prison systems. But that is the core of California's justification for its policy: It maintains that, if it does not racially separate new cellmates thrown together in close confines during their initial admission or transfer, violence will erupt. The dangers California seeks to prevent are real.

The problem of prison gangs is not unique to California, but California has a history like no other. There are at least five major gangs in this country—the Aryan Brotherhood, the Black Guerrilla Family, the Mexican Mafia, La Nuestra Familia, and the Texas Syndicate—all of which originated in California's prisons. Unsurprisingly, then, California has the largest number of gang-related inmates of any correctional system in the country, including the Federal Government.

As their very names suggest, prison gangs like the Aryan Brotherhood and the Black Guerrilla Family organize themselves along racial lines, and these gangs perpetuate hate and violence. Interracial murders and assaults among inmates perpetrated by these gangs are common. And, again, that brutality is particularly severe in California's prisons.

It is against this backdrop of pervasive racial violence that California racially segregates inmates in the reception centers' double cells, for brief periods of up to 60 days, until such time as the State can assign permanent housing. Viewed in that context and in light of the four factors enunciated in *Turner*, California's policy is constitutional: The CDC's policy is reasonably related to a legitimate penological interest; alternative means of exercising the restricted right remain open to inmates; racially integrating double cells might negatively impact prison inmates, staff, and administrators; and there are no obvious, easy alternatives to the CDC's policy.

The majority offers various other reasons for applying strict scrutiny. None is persuasive. The majority's main reason is that *"Turner's* reasonable-relationship test [applies] only to rights that are 'inconsistent with proper incarceration.'" This inconsistency-with-proper-prison-administration test begs the question at the heart of this case. For a court to know whether any particular right is inconsistent with proper prison administration, it must have some implicit notion of what a proper prison ought to look like and how it ought to be administered. But the very issue in this case is whether such second-guessing is permissible.

The majority's test eviscerates *Turner*. Inquiring whether a given right is consistent with "proper prison administration" calls for precisely the sort of judgments that *Turner* said courts were ill equipped to make. In none of the cases in which the Court deferred to the judgments of prison officials under *Turner* did it examine whether "proper" prison security and discipline permitted greater speech or associational rights, expanded access to the courts, broader freedom from bodily restraint, or additional free exercise rights. The Court has steadfastly refused to undertake the threshold standard-of-review inquiry that *Turner* settled, and that the majority today resurrects. And with good reason: As *Turner* pointed out, these judgments are better left in the first instance to the officials who run our Nation's prisons, not to the judges who run its courts.

In place of the Court's usual deference, the majority gives conclusive force to its own guesswork about "proper" prison administration. It hypothesizes that California's policy might incite, rather than diminish, racial hostility. The majority's speculations are implausible. New arrivals have a strong interest in promptly convincing other inmates of their willingness to use violent force. In any event, the majority's guesswork falls far short of the compelling showing needed to overcome the deference we owe to prison administrators.

Petitioner Garrison Johnson challenges not permanent, but temporary, segregation of only a portion of California's prisons. Of the 17 years Johnson has been incarcerated, California has assigned him a cellmate of the same race for no more than a year (and probably more like four months); Johnson has had black cellmates during the other 16 years, but by his own choice. Nothing in the record demonstrates that if Johnson (or any other prisoner) requested to be housed with a person of a different race, it would be denied (though Johnson's gang affiliation with the Crips might stand in his way). Moreover, Johnson concedes that California's prisons are racially violent places, and that he lives in fear of being attacked because of his race. Perhaps on remand the CDC's policy will survive strict scrutiny, but in the event that it does not, Johnson may well have won a Pyrrhic victory.

Chapter 8

Fundamental Rights Under Due Process and Equal Protecion

D. Constitutional Protection for Reproductive Autonomy

3. The Right to Abortion

e. Parental Notice and Consent Requirements (casebook, p. 901)

In *Ayotte v. Planned Parenthood of Northern New England,* the Court considered the constitutionality of a state law requiring parental notification for abortions for unemancipated minors. The United States Court of Appeals for the First Circuit invalidated the law because of a lack of an exception permitting doctors to perform abortions without parental notification or judicial approval where the health of the minor warranted it. The Supreme Court did not decide the constitutionality of the statute, but instead remanded the case to see if the lower courts could interpret it narrowly to avoid the constitutional issues.

AYOTTE v. PLANNED PARENTHOOD
OF NORTHERN NEW ENGLAND
126 S. Ct. 961 (2006)

Justice O'CONNOR delivered the opinion of the Court.

We do not revisit our abortion precedents today, but rather address a question of remedy: If enforcing a statute that regulates access to abortion would be unconstitutional in medical emergencies, what is the appropriate judicial response? We hold that invalidating the statute entirely is not always necessary or justified, for lower courts may be able to render narrower declaratory and injunctive relief.

I

In 2003, New Hampshire enacted the Parental Notification Prior to Abortion Act. The Act prohibits physicians from performing an abortion on a pregnant minor (or a woman for whom a guardian or conservator has been appointed) until 48 hours after written notice of the pending abortion is delivered to her parent or guardian. Notice may be delivered personally or by certified mail. Violations of the Act are subject to criminal and civil penalties.

The Act allows for three circumstances in which a physician may perform an abortion without notifying the minor's parent. First, notice is not required if "[t]he attending abortion provider certifies in the pregnant minor's record that the abortion is necessary to prevent the minor's death and there is insufficient time to provide the required notice." Second, a person entitled to receive notice may certify that he or she has already been notified. Finally, a minor may petition a judge to authorize her physician to perform an abortion without parental notification. The judge must so authorize if he or she finds that the minor is mature and capable of giving informed consent, or that an abortion without notification is in the minor's best interests. These judicial bypass proceedings "shall be confidential and shall be given precedence over other pending matters so that the court may reach a decision promptly and without delay," and access to the courts "shall be afforded [to the] pregnant minor 24 hours a day, 7 days a week." The trial and appellate courts must each rule on bypass petitions within seven days.

The Act does not explicitly permit a physician to perform an abortion in a medical emergency without parental notification.

II

As the case comes to us, three propositions—two legal and one factual—are established. First, States unquestionably have the right to require parental involvement when a minor considers terminating her pregnancy, because of their "strong and legitimate interest in the welfare of [their] young citizens, whose immaturity, inexperience, and lack of judgment may sometimes impair their ability to exercise their rights wisely." Accordingly, we have long upheld state parental involvement statutes like the Act before us, and we cast no doubt on those holdings today.

Second, New Hampshire does not dispute, and our precedents hold, that a State may not restrict access to abortions that are "'necessary, in appropriate medical judgment, for preservation of the life or health of the mother.'"

Third, New Hampshire has not taken real issue with the factual basis of this litigation: In some very small percentage of cases, pregnant minors, like adult women, need immediate abortions to avert serious and often irreversible damage to their health.

New Hampshire has maintained that in most if not all cases, the Act's judicial bypass and the State's "competing harms" statutes should protect both physician and patient when a minor needs an immediate abortion. But the District Court and Court of Appeals found neither of these provisions to protect minors' health reliably in all emergencies. And New Hampshire has conceded that, under our cases, it would be unconstitutional to apply the Act in a manner that subjects minors to significant health risks.

III

We turn to the question of remedy: When a statute restricting access to abortion may be applied in a manner that harms women's health, what is the appropriate relief? Generally speaking, when confronting a constitutional flaw in a statute, we try to limit the solution to the problem. We prefer, for example, to enjoin only the unconstitutional applications of a statute while leaving other applications in force, or to sever its problematic portions while leaving the remainder intact.

Three interrelated principles inform our approach to remedies. First, we try not to nullify more of a legislature's work than is necessary, for we know that "[a] ruling of unconstitutionality frustrates the intent of the elected representatives of the people." It is axiomatic that a "statute may be invalid as applied to one state of facts and yet valid as applied to another." Accordingly, the "normal rule" is that "partial, rather than facial, invalidation is the required course," such that a "statute may . . . be declared invalid to the extent that it reaches too far, but otherwise left intact."

Second, mindful that our constitutional mandate and institutional competence are limited, we restrain ourselves from "rewrit[ing] state law to conform it to constitutional requirements" even as we strive to salvage it. Our ability to devise a judicial remedy that does not entail quintessentially legislative work often depends on how clearly we have already articulated the background constitutional rules at issue and how easily we can articulate the remedy. But making distinctions in a murky constitutional context, or where line-drawing is inherently complex, may call for a "far more serious invasion of the legislative domain" than we ought to undertake.

Third, the touchstone for any decision about remedy is legislative intent, for a court cannot "use its remedial powers to circumvent the intent of the legislature." After finding an application or portion of a statute unconstitutional, we must next ask: Would the legislature have preferred what is left of its statute to no statute at all? All the while, we are wary of legislatures who would rely on our intervention, for "[i]t would certainly be dangerous if the legislature could set a net large enough to catch all possible offenders, and leave it to the courts to step inside" to announce to whom the statute may be applied. "This would, to some extent, substitute the judicial for the legislative department of the government."

In this case, the courts below chose the most blunt remedy—permanently enjoining the enforcement of New Hampshire's parental notification law and thereby invalidating it entirely. That is understandable, for we, too, have previously invalidated an abortion statute in its entirety because of the same constitutional flaw. In *Stenberg*, we addressed a Nebraska law banning so-called "partial birth abortion" unless the procedure was necessary to save the pregnant woman's life. We held Nebraska's law unconstitutional because it lacked a health exception. But the parties in *Stenberg* did not ask for, and we did not contemplate, relief more finely drawn.

In the case that is before us, however, we agree with New Hampshire that the lower courts need not have invalidated the law wholesale. Respondents, too, recognize the possibility of a modest remedy: They pleaded for any relief "just and proper," and conceded at oral argument that carefully crafted injunctive relief may resolve this case. Only a few applications of New Hampshire's parental notification statute would present a constitutional problem. So long as they are faithful to legislative intent, then, in this case the lower courts can issue a declaratory judgment and an injunction prohibiting the statute's unconstitutional application.

There is some dispute as to whether New Hampshire's legislature intended the statute to be susceptible to such a remedy. New Hampshire notes that the Act contains a severability clause providing that "[i]f any provision of this subdivision or the application thereof to any person or circumstance is held invalid, such invalidity shall not affect the provisions or applications of this subdivision which can be given effect without the invalid provisions or applications." Respondents, on the other hand, contend that New Hampshire legislators preferred no statute at all to a statute enjoined in the way we have described. Because this is an open question, we remand for the lower courts to determine legislative intent in the first instance.

Either an injunction prohibiting unconstitutional applications or a holding that consistency with legislative intent requires invalidating the statute in toto should obviate any concern about the Act's life exception. We therefore need not pass on the lower courts' alternative holding. Finally, if the Act does survive in part on remand, the Court of Appeals should address respondents' separate objection to the judicial bypass' confidentiality provision.

L. Procedural Due Process (casebook, p. 1006)

1. What Is a Deprivation?

There were two important procedural due process cases in October Term 2004. They were in different contexts and raised different issues. In DeShaney v. Winnebago County Department of Social Services (1989) (casebook, p. 1011), the Court held that generally the government has no duty to protect people from privately inflicted harms. In Town of Castle Rock v. Gonzales, excerpted below, the Court considered whether state law, and a restraining order pursuant to it, might be used to create a duty to provide protection as a property right.

In Wilkinson v. Austin, which appears after *Castle Rock*, the Court considered whether placing a prisoner in a "Supermax" facility, with 23 hours a day of solitary confinement, is a deprivation of liberty, and if so, what due process requires.

TOWN OF CASTLE ROCK v. GONZALES
125 S. Ct. 2796 (2005)

Justice SCALIA delivered the opinion of the Court.

We decide in this case whether an individual who has obtained a state-law restraining order has a constitutionally protected property interest in having the police enforce the restraining order when they have probable cause to believe it has been violated.

I

The horrible facts of this case are contained in the complaint that respondent Jessica Gonzales filed in Federal District Court. (Because the case comes to us on appeal from a dismissal of the complaint, we assume its allegations are true.) Respondent alleges that petitioner, the town of Castle Rock, Colorado, violated the Due Process Clause of the Fourteenth Amendment to the United States Constitution when its police officers, acting pursuant to official policy or custom, failed to respond properly to her repeated reports that her estranged husband was violating the terms of a restraining order.

The restraining order had been issued by a state trial court several weeks earlier in conjunction with respondent's divorce proceedings. The original form order, issued on May 21, 1999, and served on respondent's husband on June 4, 1999, commanded him not to "molest or disturb the peace of [respondent] or of any child," and to remain at least 100 yards from the family home at all times. The bottom of the pre-printed form noted that the reverse side contained "IMPOR-TANT NOTICES FOR RESTRAINED PARTIES AND LAW ENFORCEMENT OFFICIALS." the preprinted text on the back of the form included the following "WARNING":

A KNOWING VIOLATION OF A RESTRAINING ORDER IS A CRIME. . . . A VIOLATION WILL ALSO CONSTITUTE CONTEMPT OF COURT. YOU MAY BE ARRESTED WITHOUT NOTICE IF A LAW ENFORCEMENT OFFICER HAS PROBABLE CAUSE TO BELIEVE THAT YOU HAVE KNOWINGLY VI-OLATED THIS ORDER.

The preprinted text on the back of the form also included a "NOTICE TO LAW ENFORCEMENT OFFICIALS," which read in part:

YOU SHALL USE EVERY REASONABLE MEANS TO ENFORCE THIS RESTRAINING ORDER. YOU SHALL ARREST, OR, IF AN ARREST WOULD BE IMPRACTICAL UNDER THE CIRCUMSTANCES, SEEK A WARRANT FOR THE ARREST OF THE RESTRAINED PERSON WHEN YOU HAVE INFORMA-TION AMOUNTING TO PROBABLE CAUSE THAT THE RESTRAINED PER-SON HAS VIOLATED OR ATTEMPTED TO VIOLATE ANY PROVISION OF THIS ORDER AND THE RESTRAINED PERSON HAS BEEN PROPERLY SERVED WITH A COPY OF THIS ORDER OR HAS RECEIVED ACTUAL NOTICE OF THE EXISTENCE OF THIS ORDER.

On June 4, 1999, the state trial court modified the terms of the restraining order and made it permanent. The modified order gave respondent's husband the right to spend time with his three daughters (ages 10, 9, and 7) on alternate weekends, for two weeks during the summer, and, "'upon reasonable notice,'" for a midweek dinner visit "'arranged by the parties'"; the modified order also allowed him to visit the home to collect the children for such "parenting time."

According to the complaint, at about 5 or 5:30 p.m. on Tuesday, June 22, 1999, respondent's husband took the three daughters while they were playing outside the family home. No advance arrangements had been made for him to see the daughters that evening. When respondent noticed the children were missing, she suspected her husband had taken them. At about 7:30 p.m., she called the Castle Rock Police Department, which dispatched two officers. The complaint continues: "When [the officers] arrived ..., she showed them a copy of the TRO and requested that it be enforced and the three children be returned to her immediately. [The officers] stated that there was nothing they could do about the TRO and suggested that [respondent] call the Police Department again if the three children did not return home by 10:00 p.m."

At approximately 8:30 p.m., respondent talked to her husband on his cellular telephone. He told her "he had the three children [at an] amusement park in Denver." She called the police again and asked them to "have someone check for" her husband or his vehicle at the amusement park and "put out an [all points bulletin]" for her husband, but the officer with whom she spoke "refused to do so," again telling her to "wait until 10:00 p.m. and see if" her husband returned the girls.

At approximately 10:10 p.m., respondent called the police and said her children were still missing, but she was now told to wait until midnight. She called at midnight and told the dispatcher her children were still missing. She went to her husband's apartment and, finding nobody there, called the police at 12:10 a.m.; she was told to wait for an officer to arrive. When none came, she went to the police station at 12:50 a.m. and submitted an incident report. The officer who took the report "made no reasonable effort to enforce the TRO or locate the three children. Instead, he went to dinner."

At approximately 3:20 a.m., respondent's husband arrived at the police station and opened fire with a semiautomatic handgun he had purchased earlier that evening. Police shot back, killing him. Inside the cab of his pickup truck, they found the bodies of all three daughters, whom he had already murdered.

On the basis of the foregoing factual allegations, respondent brought an action claiming that the town violated the Due Process Clause because its police department had "an official policy or custom of failing to respond properly to complaints of restraining order violations" and "tolerate[d] the non-enforcement of restraining orders by its police officers." The complaint also alleged that the town's actions "were taken either willfully, recklessly or with such gross negligence as to indicate wanton disregard and deliberate indifference to" respondent's civil rights.

II

The Fourteenth Amendment to the United States Constitution provides that a State shall not "deprive any person of life, liberty, or property, without due process of law." Amdt. 14, § 1. In 42 U.S.C. § 1983, Congress has created a federal cause of action for "the deprivation of any rights, privileges, or immunities secured by the Constitution and laws." Respondent claims the benefit of this provision on the ground that she had a property interest in police enforcement of the restraining order against her husband; and that the town deprived her of this property without due process by having a policy that tolerated nonenforcement of restraining orders.

As the Court of Appeals recognized, we left a similar question unanswered in DeShaney v. Winnebago County Dept. of Social Servs. (1989), another case with "undeniably tragic" facts: Local child-protection officials had failed to protect a young boy from beatings by his father that left him severely brain damaged. We held that the so-called "substantive" component of the Due Process Clause does not "requir[e] the State to protect the life, liberty, and property of its citizens against invasion by private actors."

The procedural component of the Due Process Clause does not protect everything that might be described as a "benefit": "To have a property interest in a benefit, a person clearly must have more than an abstract need or desire" and "more than a unilateral expectation of it. He must, instead, have a legitimate claim of entitlement to it." Board of Regents of State Colleges v. Roth (1972). Such entitlements are "'of course, . . . not created by the Constitution. Rather, they are created and their dimensions are defined by existing rules or understandings that stem from an independent source such as state law.'" Paul v. Davis (1976).

A

Our cases recognize that a benefit is not a protected entitlement if government officials may grant or deny it in their discretion. The Court of Appeals in this case determined that Colorado law created an entitlement to enforcement of the restraining order because the "court-issued restraining order . . . specifically dictated that its terms must be enforced" and a "state statute command[ed]" enforcement of the order when certain objective conditions were met (probable cause to believe that the order had been violated and that the object of the order had received notice of its existence).

B

The critical language in the restraining order came not from any part of the order itself (which was signed by the state-court trial judge and directed to the restrained party, respondent's husband), but from the preprinted notice to law-enforcement personnel that appeared on the back of the order. That notice effectively restated the statutory provision describing "peace officers' duties" related to the crime of violation of a restraining order. We do not believe that these provisions of Colorado law truly made enforcement of restraining orders mandatory. A well established tradition of police discretion has long coexisted with apparently mandatory arrest statutes.

"In each and every state there are long-standing statutes that, by their terms, seem to preclude nonenforcement by the police. . . . However, for a number of reasons, including their legislative history, insufficient resources, and sheer physical impossibility, it has been recognized that such statutes cannot be interpreted literally. . . .[T]hey clearly do not mean that a police officer may not lawfully decline to make an arrest. As to third parties in these states, the full-enforcement statutes simply have no effect, and their significance is further diminished." 1 ABA Standards for Criminal Justice (2d ed.1980).

The deep-rooted nature of law-enforcement discretion, even in the presence of seemingly mandatory legislative commands, is illustrated by Chicago v. Morales (1999), which involved an ordinance that said a police officer "'shall order'" persons to disperse in certain circumstances. This Court rejected out of hand the possibility that "the mandatory language of the ordinance . . . afford [ed] the police no discretion." It is, the Court proclaimed, simply "common sense that all police officers must use some discretion in deciding when and where to enforce city ordinances."

Against that backdrop, a true mandate of police action would require some stronger indication from the Colorado Legislature than "shall use every reasonable means to enforce a restraining order" (or even "shall arrest . . . or . . . seek a warrant"). That language is not perceptibly more mandatory than the Colorado statute which has long told municipal chiefs of police that they "shall pursue and arrest any person fleeing from justice in any part of the state" and that they "shall apprehend any person in the act of committing any offense . . . and, forthwith and without any warrant, bring such person before a . . . competent authority for examination and trial." It is hard to imagine that a Colorado peace officer would not have some discretion to determine that—despite probable cause to believe a restraining order has been violated—the circumstances of the violation or the competing duties of that officer or his agency counsel decisively against enforcement in a particular instance. The practical necessity for discretion is particularly apparent in a case such as this one, where the suspected violator is not actually present and his whereabouts are unknown.

The dissent correctly points out that, in the specific context of domestic violence, mandatory-arrest statutes have been found in some States to be more mandatory than traditional mandatory-arrest statutes. Even in the domestic-violence context, however, it is unclear how the mandatory-arrest paradigm applies to cases in which the offender is not present to be arrested.

Respondent does not specify the precise means of enforcement that the Colorado restraining-order statute assertedly mandated—whether her interest lay in having police arrest her husband, having them seek a warrant for his arrest, or having them "use every reasonable means, up to and including arrest, to enforce the order's terms." Such indeterminacy is not the hallmark of a duty that is mandatory. Nor can someone be safely deemed "entitled" to something when the identity of the alleged entitlement is vague.

Even if the statute could be said to have made enforcement of restraining orders "mandatory" because of the domestic-violence context of the underlying statute, that would not necessarily mean that state law gave respondent an entitlement to enforcement of the mandate. Making the actions of government employees obligatory can serve various legitimate ends other than the conferral of a benefit on a specific class of people. The serving of public rather than private ends is the normal course of the criminal law because criminal acts, "besides the injury [they do] to individuals, . . . strike at the very being of society; which cannot possibly subsist, where actions of this sort are suffered to escape with impunity." This principle underlies, for example, a Colorado district attorney's discretion to prosecute a domestic assault, even though the victim withdraws her charge.

C

Even if we were to think otherwise concerning the creation of an entitlement by Colorado, it is by no means clear that an individual entitlement to enforcement of a restraining order could constitute a "property" interest for purposes of the Due Process Clause. Such a right would not, of course, resemble any traditional conception of property. Although that alone does not disqualify it from due process protection, as *Roth* and its progeny show, the right to have a restraining order enforced does not "have some ascertainable monetary value," as even our "*Roth*-type property-as-entitlement" cases have implicitly required.

Perhaps most radically, the alleged property interest here arises incidentally, not out of some new species of government benefit or service, but out of a function that government actors have always performed—to wit, arresting people who they have probable cause to believe have committed a criminal offense.

III

We conclude, therefore, that respondent did not, for purposes of the Due Process Clause, have a property interest in police enforcement of the restraining order against her husband. In light of today's decision and that in *DeShaney*, the benefit that a third party may receive from having someone else arrested for a crime generally does not trigger protections under the Due Process Clause, neither in its procedural nor in its "substantive" manifestations. This result reflects our continuing reluctance to treat the Fourteenth Amendment as "'a font of tort law,'" Parratt v. Taylor (1981), but it does not mean States are powerless to provide victims with personally enforceable remedies. Although the framers of the Fourteenth Amendment and the Civil Rights Act of 1871 did not create a system by which police departments are generally held financially accountable for crimes that better policing might have prevented, the people of Colorado are free to craft such a system under state law.

Justice SOUTER, with whom Justice BREYER joins, concurring.

I agree with the Court that Jessica Gonzales has shown no violation of an interest protected by the Fourteenth Amendment's Due Process Clause, and I join the Court's opinion.

"Ms. Gonzales alleges that . . . she was denied the process laid out in the statute. The police did not consider her request in a timely fashion, but instead repeatedly required her to call the station over several hours. The statute promised a process by which her restraining order would be given vitality through careful and prompt consideration of an enforcement request. . . . Denial of that process drained all of the value from her property interest in the restraining order." The argument is unconventional because the state-law benefit for which it claims federal procedural protection is itself a variety of procedural regulation, a set of rules to be followed by officers exercising the State's executive power: use all reasonable means to enforce, arrest upon demonstrable probable cause, get a warrant, and so on.

When her argument is understood as unconventional in this sense, a further reason appears for rejecting its call to apply *Roth*, a reason that would apply even if the statutory mandates to the police were absolute, leaving the police with no discretion when the beneficiary of a protective order insists upon its enforcement. The Due Process Clause extends procedural protection to guard against unfair deprivation by state officials of substantive state-law property rights or entitlements; the federal process protects the property created by state law. But Gonzales claims a property interest in a state-mandated process in and of itself. This argument is at odds with the rule that "[p]rocess is not an end in itself. Its constitutional purpose is to protect a substantive interest to which the individual has a legitimate claim of entitlement."

Just as a State cannot diminish a property right, once conferred, by attaching less than generous procedure to its deprivation, neither does a State create a property right merely by ordaining beneficial procedure unconnected to some articulable substantive guarantee. This is not to say that state rules of executive procedure may not provide significant reasons to infer an articulable property right meant to be protected; but it is to say that we have not identified property with procedure as such. State rules of executive procedure, however important, may be nothing more than rules of executive procedure.

Thus, in every instance of property recognized by this Court as calling for federal procedural protection, the property has been distinguishable from the procedural obligations imposed on state officials to protect it. [T]he property interest recognized in our cases has always existed apart from state procedural protection before the Court has recognized a constitutional claim to protection by federal process. To accede to Gonzales's argument would therefore work a sea change in the scope of federal due process, for she seeks federal process as a substitute simply for state process. There is no articulable distinction between the object of Gonzales's asserted entitlement and the process she desires in order to protect her entitlement; both amount to certain steps to be taken by the police to protect her family and herself. Gonzales's claim would thus take us beyond *Roth* or any other recognized theory of Fourteenth Amendment due process, by collapsing the distinction between property protected and the process that protects it, and would federalize every mandatory state-law direction to executive officers whose performance on the job can be vitally significant to individuals affected.

Justice STEVENS, with whom Justice GINSBURG joins, dissenting.

The issue presented to us is much narrower than is suggested by the far-ranging arguments of the parties and their amici. Neither the tragic facts of the case, nor the importance of according proper deference to law enforcement professionals, should divert our attention from that issue. That issue is whether the restraining order entered by the Colorado trial court on June 4, 1999, created a "property" interest that is protected from arbitrary deprivation by the Due Process Clause of the Fourteenth Amendment.

It is perfectly clear, on the one hand, that neither the Federal Constitution itself, nor any federal statute, granted respondent or her children any individual entitlement to police protection. See DeShaney v. Winnebago County Dept. of Social Servs. (1989). Nor, I assume, does any Colorado statute create any such entitlement for the ordinary citizen. On the other hand, it is equally clear that federal law imposes no impediment to the creation of such an entitlement by Colorado law. Respondent certainly could have entered into a contract with a private security firm, obligating the firm to provide protection to respondent's family; respondent's interest in such a contract would unquestionably constitute "property" within the meaning of the Due Process Clause. If a Colorado statute enacted for her benefit, or a valid order entered by a Colorado judge, created the functional equivalent of such a private contract by granting respondent an entitlement to mandatory individual protection by the local police force, that state-created right would also qualify as "property" entitled to constitutional protection.

I do not understand the majority to rule out the foregoing propositions, although it does express doubts. Moreover, the majority does not contest that if respondent did have a cognizable property interest in this case, the deprivation of that interest violated due process. As the Court notes, respondent has alleged that she presented the police with a copy of the restraining order issued by the Colorado court and requested that it be enforced. In response, she contends, the officers effectively ignored her. If these allegations are true, a federal statute, 42 U.S.C. § 1983, provides her with a remedy against the petitioner, even if Colorado law does not.

The central question in this case is therefore whether, as a matter of Colorado law, respondent had a right to police assistance comparable to the right she would have possessed to any other service the government or a private firm might have undertaken to provide.

Even if the Court had good reason to doubt the Court of Appeals' determination of state law, it would, in my judgment, be a far wiser course to certify the question to the Colorado Supreme Court. Powerful considerations support certification in this case. First, principles of federalism and comity favor giving a State's high court the opportunity to answer important questions of state law, particularly when those questions implicate uniquely local matters such as law enforcement and might well require the weighing of policy considerations for their correct resolution. Second, by certifying a potentially dispositive state-law issue, the Court would adhere to its wise policy of avoiding the unnecessary adjudication of difficult questions of constitutional law. Third, certification would promote both judicial economy and fairness to the parties. After all, the Colorado Supreme Court is the ultimate authority on the meaning of Colorado law, and if in later litigation it should disagree with this Court's provisional state-law holding, our efforts will have been wasted and respondent will have been deprived of the opportunity to have her claims heard under the authoritative view of Colorado law. The unique facts of this case only serve to emphasize the importance of employing a procedure that will provide the correct answer to the central question of state law.

Three flaws in the Court's rather superficial analysis of the merits highlight the unwisdom of its decision to answer the state-law question de novo. First, the Court places undue weight on the various statutes throughout the country that seemingly mandate police enforcement but are generally understood to preserve police discretion. As a result, the Court gives short shrift to the unique case of "mandatory arrest" statutes in the domestic violence context; States passed a wave of these statutes in the 1980's and 1990's with the unmistakable goal of eliminating police discretion in this area. Second, the Court's formalistic analysis fails to take seriously the fact that the Colorado statute at issue in this case was enacted for the benefit of the narrow class of persons who are beneficiaries of domestic restraining orders, and that the order at issue in this case was specifically intended to provide protection to respondent and her children. Finally, the Court is simply wrong to assert that a citizen's interest in the government's commitment to provide police enforcement in certain defined circumstances does not resemble any "traditional conception of property"; in fact, a citizen's property interest in such a commitment is just as concrete and worthy of protection as her interest in any other important service the government or a private firm has undertaken to provide.

Given that Colorado law has quite clearly eliminated the police's discretion to deny enforcement, respondent is correct that she had much more than a "unilateral expectation" that the restraining order would be enforced; rather, she had a "legitimate claim of entitlement" to enforcement. Recognizing respondent's property interest in the enforcement of her restraining order is fully consistent with our precedent. This Court has "made clear that the property interests protected by procedural due process extend well beyond actual ownership of real estate, chattels, or money." The "types of interests protected as 'property' are varied and, as often as not, intangible, 'relating to the whole domain of social and economic fact.'" Police enforcement of a restraining order is a government service that is no less concrete and no less valuable than other government services, such as education.

The relative novelty of recognizing this type of property interest is explained by the relative novelty of the domestic violence statutes creating a mandatory arrest duty; before this innovation, the unfettered discretion that characterized police enforcement defeated any citizen's "legitimate claim of entitlement" to this service. Novel or not, respondent's claim finds strong support in the principles that underlie our due process jurisprudence. In this case, Colorado law guaranteed the provision of a certain service, in certain defined circumstances, to a certain class of beneficiaries, and respondent reasonably relied on that guarantee. As we observed in *Roth*, "[i]t is a purpose of the ancient institution of property to protect those claims upon which people rely in their daily lives, reliance that must not be arbitrarily undermined." Surely, if respondent had contracted with a private security firm to provide her and her daughters with protection from her husband, it would be apparent that she possessed a property interest in such a contract. Here, Colorado undertook a comparable obligation, and respondent—with restraining order in hand—justifiably relied on that undertaking. Respondent's claim of entitlement to this promised service is no less legitimate than the other claims our cases have upheld, and no less concrete than a hypothetical agreement with a private firm. The fact that it is based on a statutory enactment and a judicial order entered for her special protection, rather than on a formal contract, does not provide a principled basis for refusing to consider it "property" worthy of constitutional protection.

Because respondent had a property interest in the enforcement of the restraining order, state officials could not deprive her of that interest without observing fair procedures. Her description of the police behavior in this case and the department's callous policy of failing to respond properly to reports of restraining order violations clearly alleges a due process violation. At the very least, due process requires that the relevant state decisionmaker listen to the claimant and then apply the relevant criteria in reaching his decision.

2. Is It a Deprivation of "Life, Liberty, or Property"?

Liberty Interests for Prisoners (casebook, p. 1032)

In *Wilkinson v. Austin*, below, the Court considered whether prisoners placed in "super-max" facilities are deprived of liberty and, if so, whether the state's procedures are sufficient to meet due process.

WILKINSON v. AUSTIN
125 S. Ct. 2384 (2005)

Justice KENNEDY delivered the opinion of the Court

This case involves the process by which Ohio classifies prisoners for placement at its highest security prison, known as a "Supermax" facility. Supermax facilities are maximum-security prisons with highly restrictive conditions, designed to segregate the most dangerous prisoners from the general prison population. We must consider what process the Fourteenth Amendment to the United States Constitution requires Ohio to afford to inmates before assigning them to Supermax. We hold that the procedures Ohio has adopted provide sufficient procedural protection to comply with due process requirements.

I

The use of Supermax prisons has increased over the last 20 years, in part as a response to the rise in prison gangs and prison violence. About 30 States now operate Supermax prisons, in addition to the two operated by the Federal Government. In 1998, Ohio opened its only Supermax facility, the Ohio State Penitentiary (OSP), after a riot in one of its maximum-security prisons. OSP has the capacity to house up to 504 inmates in single-inmate cells and is designed to "separate the most predatory and dangerous prisoners from the rest of the . . . general [prison] population."

Conditions at OSP are more restrictive than any other form of incarceration in Ohio, including conditions on its death row or in its administrative control units. In the OSP almost every aspect of an inmate's life is controlled and monitored. Inmates must remain in their cells, which measure 7 by 14 feet, for 23 hours per day. A light remains on in the cell at all times, though it is sometimes dimmed, and an inmate who attempts to shield the light to sleep is subject to further discipline. During the one hour per day that an inmate may leave his cell, access is limited to one of two indoor recreation cells.

Incarceration at OSP is synonymous with extreme isolation. In contrast to any other Ohio prison, including any segregation unit, OSP cells have solid metal doors with metal strips along their sides and bottoms which prevent conversation or communication with other inmates. All meals are taken alone in the inmate's cell instead of in a common eating area. Opportunities for visitation are rare and in all events are conducted through glass walls. It is fair to say OSP inmates are deprived of almost any environmental or sensory stimuli and of almost all human contact.

Aside from the severity of the conditions, placement at OSP is for an indefinite period of time, limited only by an inmate's sentence. For an inmate serving a life sentence, there is no indication how long he may be incarcerated at OSP once assigned there. Inmates otherwise eligible for parole lose their eligibility while incarcerated at OSP.

Placement at OSP is determined in the following manner: Upon entering the prison system, all Ohio inmates are assigned a numerical security classification from level 1 through level 5, with 1 the lowest security risk and 5 the highest. The initial security classification is based on numerous factors (e.g., the nature of the underlying offense, criminal history, or gang affiliation) but is subject to modification at any time during the inmate's prison term if, for instance, he engages in misconduct or is deemed a security risk. Level 5 inmates are placed in OSP, and levels 1 through 4 inmates are placed at lower security facilities throughout the State.

Ohio concedes that when OSP first became operational, the procedures used to assign inmates to the facility were inconsistent and undefined. For a time, no official policy governing placement was in effect. Haphazard placements were not uncommon, and some individuals who did not pose high-security risks were designated, nonetheless, for OSP. In an effort to establish guidelines for the selection and classification of inmates suitable for OSP, Ohio issued Department of Rehabilitation and Correction Policy 111-07 (Aug. 31, 1998). This policy has been revised at various points but relevant here are two versions: the "Old Policy" and the "New Policy." The New Policy provided more guidance regarding the factors to be considered in placement decisions and afforded inmates more procedural protection against erroneous placement at OSP.

Although the record is not altogether clear regarding the precise manner in which the New Policy operates, we construe it based on the policy's text, the accompanying forms, and the parties' representations at oral argument and in their briefs. The New Policy appears to operate as follows: A classification review for OSP placement can occur either (1) upon entry into the prison system if the inmate was convicted of certain offenses, e.g., organized crime, or (2) during the term of incarceration if an inmate engages in specified conduct, e.g., leads a prison gang. The review process begins when a prison official prepares a "Security Designation Long Form." This three-page form details matters such as the inmate's recent violence, escape attempts, gang affiliation, underlying offense, and other pertinent details. A three-member Classification Committee (Committee) convenes to review the proposed classification and to hold a hearing. At least 48 hours before the hearing, the inmate is provided with written notice summarizing the conduct or offense triggering the review. At the time of notice, the inmate also has access to the Long Form, which details why the review was initiated. The inmate may attend the hearing, may "offer any pertinent information, explanation and/or objections to [OSP] placement," and may submit a written statement. He may not call witnesses.

If the Committee does not recommend OSP placement, the process terminates. If the Committee does recommend OSP placement, it documents the decision on a "Classification Committee Report" (CCR), setting forth "the nature of the threat the inmate presents and the committee's reasons for the recommendation," as well as a summary of any information presented at the hearing. The Committee sends the completed CCR to the warden of the prison where the inmate is housed or, in the case of an inmate just entering the prison system, to another designated official.

If, after reviewing the CCR, the warden (or the designated official) disagrees and concludes that OSP is inappropriate, the process terminates and the inmate is not placed in OSP. If the warden agrees, he indicates his approval on the CCR, provides his reasons, and forwards the annotated CCR to the Bureau of Classification (Bureau) for a final decision. The annotated CCR is served upon the inmate, notifying him of the Classification Committee's and warden's recommendations and reasons. The inmate has 15 days to file any objections with the Bureau of Classification.

After the 15-day period, the Bureau of Classification reviews the CCR and makes a final determination. If it concludes OSP placement is inappropriate, the process terminates. If the Bureau approves the warden's recommendation, the inmate is transferred to OSP. The Bureau's chief notes the reasons for the decision on the CCR, and the CCR is again provided to the inmate.

Inmates assigned to OSP receive another review within 30 days of their arrival. That review is conducted by a designated OSP staff member, who examines the inmate's file. If the OSP staff member deems the inmate inappropriately placed, he prepares a written recommendation to the OSP warden that the inmate be transferred to a lower security institution. If the OSP warden concurs, he forwards that transfer recommendation to the Bureau of Classification for appropriate action. If the inmate is deemed properly placed, he remains in OSP and his placement is reviewed on at least an annual basis according to the initial three-tier classification review process outlined above.

[II]

Withdrawing from the position taken in the Court of Appeals, Ohio in its briefs to this Court conceded that the inmates have a liberty interest in avoiding assignment at OSP. The United States, supporting Ohio as amicus curiae, disagrees with Ohio's concession and argues that the inmates have no liberty interest in avoiding assignment to a prison facility with more restrictive conditions of confinement. At oral argument Ohio initially adhered to its earlier concession, but when pressed, the State backtracked. We need reach the question of what process is due only if the inmates establish a constitutionally protected liberty interest, so it is appropriate to address this threshold question at the outset.

The Fourteenth Amendment's Due Process Clause protects persons against deprivations of life, liberty, or property; and those who seek to invoke its procedural protection must establish that one of these interests is at stake. A liberty interest may arise from the Constitution itself, by reason of guarantees implicit in the word "liberty," or it may arise from an expectation or interest created by state laws or policies. We have held that the Constitution itself does not give rise to a liberty interest in avoiding transfer to more adverse conditions of confinement. Meachum v. Fano (1976) (no liberty interest arising from Due

Process Clause itself in transfer from low-to maximum-security prison because "[c]onfinement in any of the State's institutions is within the normal limits or range of custody which the conviction has authorized the State to impose"). We have also held, however, that a liberty interest in avoiding particular conditions of confinement may arise from state policies or regulations, subject to the important limitations set forth in Sandin v. Conner (1995).

After *Sandin*, it is clear that the touchstone of the inquiry into the existence of a protected, state-created liberty interest in avoiding restrictive conditions of confinement is not the language of regulations regarding those conditions but the nature of those conditions themselves "in relation to the ordinary incidents of prison life." The *Sandin* standard requires us to determine if assignment to OSP "imposes atypical and significant hardship on the inmate in relation to the ordinary incidents of prison life." In *Sandin*'s wake the Courts of Appeals have not reached consistent conclusions for identifying the baseline from which to measure what is atypical and significant in any particular prison system. We need not resolve the issue here, however, for we are satisfied that assignment to OSP imposes an atypical and significant hardship under any plausible baseline.

For an inmate placed in OSP, almost all human contact is prohibited, even to the point that conversation is not permitted from cell to cell; the light, though it may be dimmed, is on for 24 hours; exercise is for 1 hour per day, but only in a small indoor room. Save perhaps for the especially severe limitations on all human contact, these conditions likely would apply to most solitary confinement facilities, but here there are two added components. First is the duration. Unlike the 30-day placement in *Sandin*, placement at OSP is indefinite and, after an initial 30-day review, is reviewed just annually. Second is that placement disqualifies an otherwise eligible inmate for parole consideration. While any of these conditions standing alone might not be sufficient to create a liberty interest, taken together they impose an atypical and significant hardship within the correctional context. It follows that respondents have a liberty interest in avoiding assignment to OSP.

OSP's harsh conditions may well be necessary and appropriate in light of the danger that high-risk inmates pose both to prison officials and to other prisoners. That necessity, however, does not diminish our conclusion that the conditions give rise to a liberty interest in their avoidance.

[III]

A liberty interest having been established, we turn to the question of what process is due an inmate whom Ohio seeks to place in OSP. Because the requirements of due process are "flexible and cal[l] for such procedural protections as the particular situation demands," Morrissey v. Brewer (1972), we generally have declined to establish rigid rules and instead have embraced a framework to evaluate the sufficiency of particular procedures. The framework, established in Mathews v. Eldridge (1976), requires consideration of three distinct factors:

"First, the private interest that will be affected by the official action; second, the risk of an erroneous deprivation of such interest through the procedures used, and the probable value, if any, of additional or substitute procedural safeguards; and finally, the Government's interest, including the function involved and the fiscal and administrative burdens that the additional or substitute procedural requirement would entail."

Applying the three factors set forth in *Mathews*, we find Ohio's New Policy provides a sufficient level of process. We first consider the significance of the inmate's interest in avoiding erroneous placement at OSP. Prisoners held in lawful confinement have their liberty curtailed by definition, so the procedural protections to which they are entitled are more limited than in cases where the right at stake is the right to be free from confinement at all. The private interest at stake here, while more than minimal, must be evaluated, nonetheless, within the context of the prison system and its attendant curtailment of liberties.

The second factor addresses the risk of an erroneous placement under the procedures in place, and the probable value, if any, of additional or alternative procedural safeguards. The New Policy provides that an inmate must receive notice of the factual basis leading to consideration for OSP placement and a fair opportunity for rebuttal. Our procedural due process cases have consistently observed that these are among the most important procedural mechanisms for purposes of avoiding erroneous deprivations. Requiring officials to provide a brief summary of the factual basis for the classification review and allowing the inmate a rebuttal opportunity safeguards against the inmate's being mistaken for another or singled out for insufficient reason. In addition to having the opportunity to be heard at the Classification Committee stage, Ohio also invites the inmate to submit objections prior to the final level of review. This second opportunity further reduces the possibility of an erroneous deprivation.

Although a subsequent reviewer may overturn an affirmative recommendation for OSP placement, the reverse is not true; if one reviewer declines to recommend OSP placement, the process terminates. This avoids one of problems apparently present under the Old Policy, where, even if two levels of reviewers recommended against placement, a later reviewer could overturn their recommendation without explanation.

If the recommendation is OSP placement, Ohio requires that the decision-maker provide a short statement of reasons. This requirement guards against arbitrary decisionmaking while also providing the inmate a basis for objection before the next decisionmaker or in a subsequent classification review. The statement also serves as a guide for future behavior.

As we have noted, Ohio provides multiple levels of review for any decision recommending OSP placement, with power to overturn the recommendation at each level. In addition to these safeguards, Ohio further reduces the risk of erroneous placement by providing for a placement review within 30 days of an inmate's initial assignment to OSP.

The third *Mathews* factor addresses the State's interest. In the context of prison management, and in the specific circumstances of this case, this interest is a dominant consideration. Ohio has responsibility for imprisoning nearly 44,000 inmates. The State's first obligation must be to ensure the safety of guards and prison personnel, the public, and the prisoners themselves.

Prison security, imperiled by the brutal reality of prison gangs, provides the backdrop of the State's interest. Clandestine, organized, fueled by race-based hostility, and committed to fear and violence as a means of disciplining their own members and their rivals, gangs seek nothing less than to control prison life and to extend their power outside prison walls. Murder of an inmate, a guard, or one of their family members on the outside is a common form of gang discipline and control, as well as a condition for membership in some gangs.

The problem of scarce resources is another component of the State's interest. The cost of keeping a single prisoner in one of Ohio's ordinary maximum-security prisons is $34,167 per year, and the cost to maintain each inmate at OSP is $49,007 per year. We can assume that Ohio, or any other penal system, faced with costs like these will find it difficult to fund more effective education and vocational assistance programs to improve the lives of the prisoners. It follows that courts must give substantial deference to prison management decisions before mandating additional expenditures for elaborate procedural safeguards when correctional officials conclude that a prisoner has engaged in disruptive behavior.

The State's interest must be understood against this background. Were Ohio to allow an inmate to call witnesses or provide other attributes of an adversary hearing before ordering transfer to OSP, both the State's immediate objective of controlling the prisoner and its greater objective of controlling the prison could be defeated. This problem, moreover, is not alleviated by providing an exemption for witnesses who pose a hazard, for nothing in the record indicates simple mechanisms exist to determine when witnesses may be called without fear of reprisal. The danger to witnesses, and the difficulty in obtaining their cooperation, make the probable value of an adversary-type hearing doubtful in comparison to its obvious costs.

A balance of the *Mathews* factors yields the conclusion that Ohio's New Policy is adequate to safeguard an inmate's liberty interest in not being assigned to OSP. Prolonged confinement in Supermax may be the State's only option for the control of some inmates, and claims alleging violation of the Eighth Amendment's prohibition of cruel and unusual punishments were resolved, or withdrawn, by settlement in an early phase of this case. Here, any claim of excessive punishment in individual circumstances is not before us.

3.   What Procedures Are Required? (casebook, p. 1037)

In *Jones v. Flowers*, below, the Court considered what type of notice is required before the government sells a person's property. In a 5-4 decision with Chief Justice Roberts writing the majority opinion, joined by Justices Stevens, Souter, Ginsburg, and Breyer, the Court held that notice requires more than sending a letter by certified mail and publishing a notice in a newspaper.

JONES v. FLOWERS
126 S. Ct. 1708 (2006)

Chief Justice ROBERTS delivered the opinion of the Court.

Before a State may take property and sell it for unpaid taxes, the Due Process Clause of the Fourteenth Amendment requires the government to provide the owner "notice and opportunity for hearing appropriate to the nature of the case." We granted certiorari to determine whether, when notice of a tax sale is mailed to the owner and returned undelivered, the government must take additional reasonable steps to provide notice before taking the owner's property.

I

In 1967, petitioner Gary Jones purchased a house at 717 North Bryan Street in Little Rock, Arkansas. He lived in the house with his wife until they separated in 1993. Jones then moved into an apartment in Little Rock, and his wife continued to live in the North Bryan Street house. Jones paid his mortgage each month for 30 years, and the mortgage company paid Jones' property taxes. After Jones paid off his mortgage in 1997, the property taxes went unpaid, and the property was certified as delinquent.

In April 2000, respondent Mark Wilcox, the Commissioner of State Lands (Commissioner), attempted to notify Jones of his tax delinquency, and his right to redeem the property, by mailing a certified letter to Jones at the North Bryan Street address. The packet of information stated that unless Jones redeemed the property, it would be subject to public sale two years later on April 17, 2002. Nobody was home to sign for the letter, and nobody appeared at the post office to retrieve the letter within the next 15 days. The post office returned the unopened packet to the Commissioner marked "unclaimed."

Two years later, and just a few weeks before the public sale, the Commissioner published a notice of public sale in the Arkansas Democrat Gazette. No bids were submitted, which permitted the State to negotiate a private sale of the property. Several months later, respondent Linda Flowers submitted a purchase offer. The Commissioner mailed another certified letter to Jones at the North Bryan Street address, attempting to notify him that his house would be sold to Flowers if he did not pay his taxes. Like the first letter, the second was also returned to the Commissioner marked "unclaimed". Flowers purchased the house, which the parties stipulated in the trial court had a fair market value of $80,000, for $21,042.15. Immediately after the 30-day period for postsale redemption passed, Flowers had an unlawful detainer notice delivered to the property. The notice was served on Jones' daughter, who contacted Jones and notified him of the tax sale.

Jones filed a lawsuit in Arkansas state court against the Commissioner and Flowers, alleging that the Commissioner's failure to provide notice of the tax sale and of Jones' right to redeem resulted in the taking of his property without due process.

We granted certiorari, to resolve a conflict among the Circuits and State Supreme Courts concerning whether the Due Process Clause requires the government to take additional reasonable steps to notify a property owner when notice of a tax sale is returned undelivered. We hold that when mailed notice of a tax sale is returned unclaimed, the State must take additional reasonable steps to attempt to provide notice to the property owner before selling his property, if it is practicable to do so. Under the circumstances presented here, additional reasonable steps were available to the State.

II

A

Due process does not require that a property owner receive actual notice before the government may take his property. Rather, we have stated that due process requires the government to provide "notice reasonably calculated, under all the circumstances, to apprise interested parties of the pendency of the action and afford them an opportunity to present their objections." The Commissioner argues that once the State provided notice reasonably calculated to apprise Jones of the impending tax sale by mailing him a certified letter, due process was satisfied. The Arkansas statutory scheme is reasonably calculated to provide notice, the Commissioner continues, because it provides for notice by certified mail to an address that the property owner is responsible for keeping up to date. The Commissioner notes this Court's ample precedent condoning notice by mail, and adds that the Arkansas scheme exceeds constitutional requirements by requiring the Commissioner to use certified mail.

It is true that this Court has deemed notice constitutionally sufficient if it was reasonably calculated to reach the intended recipient when sent. In each of these cases, the government attempted to provide notice and heard nothing back indicating that anything had gone awry, and we stated that "[t]he reasonableness and hence the constitutional validity of [the] chosen method may be defended on the ground that it is in itself reasonably certain to inform those affected." But we have never addressed whether due process entails further responsibility when the government becomes aware prior to the taking that its attempt at notice has failed.

We do not think that a person who actually desired to inform a real property owner of an impending tax sale of a house he owns would do nothing when a certified letter sent to the owner is returned unclaimed. If the Commissioner prepared a stack of letters to mail to delinquent taxpayers, handed them to the postman, and then watched as the departing postman accidentally dropped the letters down a storm drain, one would certainly expect the Commissioner's office to prepare a new stack of letters and send them again. No one "desirous of actually informing" the owners would simply shrug his shoulders as the letters disappeared and say "I tried." Failure to follow up would be unreasonable, despite the fact that the letters were reasonably calculated to reach their intended recipients when delivered to the postman.

By the same token, when a letter is returned by the post office, the sender will ordinarily attempt to resend it, if it is practicable to do so. This is especially true when, as here, the subject matter of the letter concerns such an important and irreversible prospect as the loss of a house. Although the State may have made a reasonable calculation of how to reach Jones, it had good reason to suspect when the notice was returned that Jones was "no better off than if the notice had never been sent." Deciding to take no further action is not what someone "desirous of actually informing" Jones would do; such a person would take further reasonable steps if any were available.

The Commissioner has three further arguments for why reasonable followup measures were not required in this case. First, notice was sent to an address that Jones provided and had a legal obligation to keep updated. Second, "after failing to receive a property tax bill and pay property taxes, a property holder is on inquiry—notice that his property is subject to governmental taking." Third, Jones was obliged to ensure that those in whose hands he left his property would alert him if it was in jeopardy. None of these contentions relieves the State of its constitutional obligation to provide adequate notice.

The Commissioner does not argue that Jones' failure to comply with a statutory obligation to keep his address updated forfeits his right to constitutionally sufficient notice, and we agree. Although Ark.Code Ann. § 26-35-705 provides strong support for the Commissioner's argument that mailing a certified letter to Jones at 717 North Bryan Street was reasonably calculated to reach him, it does not alter the reasonableness of the Commissioner's position that he must do nothing more when the notice is promptly returned "unclaimed."

As for the Commissioner's inquiry notice argument, the common knowledge that property may become subject to government taking when taxes are not paid does not excuse the government from complying with its constitutional obligation of notice before taking private property. We have previously stated the opposite: An interested party's "knowledge of delinquency in the payment of taxes is not equivalent to notice that a tax sale is pending."

Finally, the Commissioner reminds us that the State can assume an owner leaves his property in the hands of one who will inform him if his interest is in jeopardy. An occupant, however, is not charged with acting as the owner's agent in all respects, and it is quite a leap from Justice Jackson's examples to conclude that it is an obligation of tenancy to follow up with certified mail of unknown content addressed to the owner. In fact, the State makes it impossible for the occupant to learn why the Commissioner is writing the owner, because an occupant cannot call for a certified letter without first obtaining the owner's signature. For all the occupant knows, the Commissioner of State Lands might write to certain residents about a variety of matters he finds important, such as state parks or highway construction; it would by no means be obvious to an occupant observing a certified mail slip from the Commissioner that the owner is in danger of losing his property. In any event, there is no record evidence that notices of attempted delivery were left at 717 North Bryan Street.

Mr. Jones should have been more diligent with respect to his property, no question. People must pay their taxes, and the government may hold citizens accountable for tax delinquency by taking their property. But before forcing a citizen to satisfy his debt by forfeiting his property, due process requires the government to provide adequate notice of the impending taking.

We think there were several reasonable steps the State could have taken. What steps are reasonable in response to new information depends upon what the new information reveals. The return of the certified letter marked "unclaimed" meant either that Jones still lived at 717 North Bryan Street, but was not home when the postman called and did not retrieve the letter at the post office, or that Jones no longer resided at that address. One reasonable step primarily addressed to the former possibility would be for the State to resend the notice by regular mail, so that a signature was not required. The Commissioner says that use of certified mail makes actual notice more likely, because requiring the recipient's signature protects against misdelivery. But that is only true, of course, when someone is home to sign for the letter, or to inform the mail carrier that he has arrived at the wrong address. Otherwise, "[c]ertified mail is dispatched and handled in transit as ordinary mail," and the use of certified mail might make actual notice less likely in some cases—the letter cannot be left like regular mail to be examined at the end of the day, and it can only be retrieved from the post office for a specified period of time. Following up with regular mail might also increase the chances of actual notice to Jones if—as it turned out—he had moved. Even occupants who ignored certified mail notice slips addressed to the owner (if any had been left) might scrawl the owner's new address on the notice packet and leave it for the postman to retrieve, or notify Jones directly.

Other reasonable followup measures, directed at the possibility that Jones had moved as well as that he had simply not retrieved the certified letter, would have been to post notice on the front door, or to address otherwise undeliverable mail to "occupant." Most States that explicitly outline additional procedures in their tax sale statutes require just such steps. Either approach would increase the likelihood that the owner would be notified that he was about to lose his property, given the failure of a letter deliverable only to the owner in person. That is clear in the case of an owner who still resided at the premises. It is also true in the case of an owner who has moved: Occupants who might disregard a certified mail slip not addressed to them are less likely to ignore posted notice, and a letter addressed to them (even as "occupant") might be opened and read. In either case, there is a significant chance the occupants will alert the owner, if only because a change in ownership could well affect their own occupancy. In fact, Jones first learned of the State's effort to sell his house when he was alerted by one of the occupants—his daughter—after she was served with an unlawful detainer notice.

There is no reason to suppose that the State will ever be less than fully zealous in its efforts to secure the tax revenue it needs. The same cannot be said for the State's efforts to ensure that its citizens receive proper notice before the

State takes action against them. In this case, the State is exerting extraordinary power against a property owner—taking and selling a house he owns. It is not too much to insist that the State do a bit more to attempt to let him know about it when the notice letter addressed to him is returned unclaimed. The Commissioner's effort to provide notice to Jones of an impending tax sale of his house was insufficient to satisfy due process given the circumstances of this case.

Justice ALITO took no part in the consideration or decision of this case.

Justice THOMAS, with whom Justice SCALIA and Justice KENNEDY join, dissenting.

Adopting petitioner's arguments, the Court holds today that "when mailed notice of a tax sale is returned unclaimed, the State must take additional reasonable steps to attempt to provide notice to the property owner before selling his property, if it is practicable to do so." Because, under this Court's precedents, the State's notice methods clearly satisfy the requirements of the Due Process Clause, I respectfully dissent.

I

The methods of notice employed by Arkansas were reasonably calculated to inform petitioner of proceedings affecting his property interest and thus satisfy the requirements of the Due Process Clause. The State mailed a notice by certified letter to the address provided by petitioner. The certified letter was returned to the State marked "unclaimed" after three attempts to deliver it. The State then published a notice of public sale containing redemption information in the Arkansas Democrat Gazette newspaper. After Flowers submitted a purchase offer, the State sent yet another certified letter to petitioner at his record address. That letter, too, was returned to the State marked "unclaimed" after three delivery attempts.

Arkansas' attempts to contact petitioner by certified mail at his "record address," without more, satisfy due process. Because the notices were sent to the address provided by petitioner himself, the State had an especially sound basis for determining that notice would reach him. Moreover, Arkansas exceeded the constitutional minimum by additionally publishing notice in a local newspaper. Due process requires nothing more—and certainly not here, where petitioner had a statutory duty to pay his taxes and to report any change of address to the state taxing authority.

My conclusion that Arkansas' notice methods satisfy due process is reinforced by the well-established presumption that individuals, especially those owning property, act in their own interest. Recognizing that "[i]t is the part of common prudence for all those who have any interest in [a thing], to guard that interest by persons who are in a situation to protect it," this Court has concluded that "[t]he ways of an owner with tangible property are such that he usually arranges means to learn of any direct attack upon his possessory or proprietary rights." Consistent with this observation, Arkansas was free to "indulge the assumption" that petitioner had either provided the State taxing authority with a correct and up-to-date mailing address—as required by state law—"or that he left some caretaker under a duty to let him know that [his property was] being jeopardized."

II

The Court's proposed methods, aside from being constitutionally unnecessary, are also burdensome, impractical, and no more likely to effect notice than the methods actually employed by the State.

In Arkansas, approximately 18,000 parcels of delinquent real estate are certified annually. Under the Court's rule, the State will bear the burden of locating thousands of delinquent property owners. These administrative burdens are not compelled by the Due Process Clause. Here, Arkansas has determined that its law requiring property owners to maintain a current address with the state taxing authority, in conjunction with its authorization to send property notices to the record address, is an efficient and fair way to administer its tax collection system. The Court's decision today forecloses such a reasonable system and burdens the State with inefficiencies caused by delinquent taxpayers.

Moreover, the Court's proposed methods are no more reasonably calculated to achieve notice than the methods employed by the State here. Regular mail is hardly foolproof; indeed, it is arguably less effective than certified mail. Certified mail is tracked, delivery attempts are recorded, actual delivery is logged, and notices are posted to alert someone at the residence that certified mail is being held at a local post office. By creating a record, these features give parties grounds for defending or challenging notice. By contrast, regular mail is untraceable; there is no record of either delivery or receipt. Had the State used regular mail, petitioner would presumably argue that it should have sent notice by certified mail because it creates a paper trail.

The meaning of the Constitution should not turn on the antics of tax evaders and scofflaws. Nor is the self-created conundrum in which petitioner finds himself a legitimate ground for imposing additional constitutional obligations on the State. The State's attempts to notify petitioner by certified mail at the address that he provided and, additionally, by publishing notice in a local newspaper satisfy due process.

Chapter 9

First Amendment: Freedom of Expression

B. Free Speech Methodology

4. What Is an Infringement of Freedom of Speech?

Compelled Speech (casebook, p. 1129)

In the last two years, the Supreme Court has decided two cases concerning compelled speech. In *Iohanns v. Livestock Marketing Association*, below, the Court considered whether forcing beef producers to fund generic advertising is a violation of the First Amendment. In concluding that there was not a violation of the First Amendment, Justice Scalia emphasized that this is government speech and the government may tax, even selectively, to fund this. After this case, it is worth considering whether there are any limits on the government's ability to tax some to advertise or advance messages—even messages that those taxed disagree with.

In *Rumsfeld v. Forum for Academic and Institutional Rights*, also below, the Court rejected a challenge to a federal law that requires universities receiving federal funds to allow military recruiters equal access to campus facilities. The law was adopted because many law schools refused to allow military recruiters access to career services facilities because of policies preventing employers from recruiting on campus if they discriminate based on race, gender, religion, or sexual orientation. A federal statute bars gays and lesbians from the military. The Court rejected challenges based on compelled speech and association.

JOHANNS v. LIVESTOCK MARKETING ASSOCIATION
125 S. Ct. 2055 (2005)

Justice SCALIA delivered the opinion of the Court

We consider whether a federal program that finances generic advertising to promote an agricultural product violates the First Amendment. [T]he dispositive question is whether the generic advertising at issue is the Government's own speech and therefore is exempt from First Amendment scrutiny.

I.

The Beef Promotion and Research Act of 1985 (Beef Act or Act), announces a federal policy of promoting the marketing and consumption of "beef and beef products," using funds raised by an assessment on cattle sales and importation. The Secretary is to impose a $1-per-head assessment (or "checkoff") on all sales or importation of cattle and a comparable assessment on imported beef products. And the assessment is to be used to fund beef-related projects, including promotional campaigns, designed by the Operating Committee and approved by the Secretary.

Respondents are two associations whose members collect and pay the checkoff, and several individuals who raise and sell cattle subject to the checkoff. Respondents noted that the advertising promotes beef as a generic commodity, which, they contended, impedes their efforts to promote the superiority of American beef, grain-fed beef, or certified Angus or Hereford beef.

II

We have sustained First Amendment challenges to allegedly compelled expression in two categories of cases: true "compelled speech" cases, in which an individual is obliged personally to express a message he disagrees with, imposed by the government; and "compelled subsidy" cases, in which an individual is required by the government to subsidize a message he disagrees with, expressed by a private entity. We have not heretofore considered the First Amendment consequences of government-compelled subsidy of the government's own speech.

In all of the cases invalidating exactions to subsidize speech, the speech was, or was presumed to be, that of an entity other than the government itself. Our compelled-subsidy cases have consistently respected the principle that "[c]ompelled support of a private association is fundamentally different from compelled support of government." "Compelled support of government"— even those programs of government one does not approve—is of course perfectly constitutional, as every taxpayer must attest. And some government programs involve, or entirely consist of, advocating a position. "The government, as a general rule, may support valid programs and policies by taxes or other exactions binding on protesting parties. Within this broader principle it seems inevitable that funds raised by the government will be spent for speech and other expression to advocate and defend its own policies." We have generally assumed, though not yet squarely held, that compelled funding of government speech does not alone raise First Amendment concerns.

III

Respondents do not seriously dispute these principles, nor do they contend that, as a general matter, their First Amendment challenge requires them to show only that their checkoff dollars pay for speech with which they disagree. Rather, they assert that the challenged promotional campaigns differ dispositively from the type of government speech that, our cases suggest, is not susceptible to First Amendment challenge. They point to the role of the Beef Board and its Operating Committee in designing the promotional campaigns, and to the use of a mandatory assessment on beef producers to fund the advertising. We consider each in turn.

A

The Secretary of Agriculture does not write ad copy himself. Rather, the Beef Board's promotional campaigns are designed by the Beef Board's Operating Committee, only half of whose members are Beef Board members appointed by the Secretary. (All members of the Operating Committee are subject to *removal* by the Secretary.) Respondents contend that speech whose content is effectively controlled by a nongovernmental entity—the Operating Committee—cannot be considered "government speech." We need not address this contention, because we reject its premise: The message of the promotional campaigns is effectively controlled by the Federal Government itself.

The message set out in the beef promotions is from beginning to end the message established by the Federal Government. Congress has directed the implementation of a "coordinated program" of promotion, "including paid advertising, to advance the image and desirability of beef and beef products." Congress and the Secretary have also specified, in general terms, what the promotional campaigns shall contain (campaigns "shall . . . take into account" different types of beef products), and what they shall not (campaigns shall not, without prior approval, refer "to a brand or trade name of any beef product"). Thus, Congress and the Secretary have set out the overarching message and some of its elements, and they have left the development of the remaining details to an entity whose members are answerable to the Secretary (and in some cases appointed by him as well).

Moreover, the record demonstrates that the Secretary exercises final approval authority over every word used in every promotional campaign. All proposed promotional messages are reviewed by Department officials both for substance and for wording, and some proposals are rejected or rewritten by the Department. Nor is the Secretary's role limited to final approval or rejection: officials of the Department also attend and participate in the open meetings at which proposals are developed. When, as here, the government sets the overall message to be communicated and approves every word that is disseminated, it is not precluded from relying on the government-speech doctrine merely because it solicits assistance from nongovernmental sources in developing specific messages.

B

Respondents also contend that the beef program does not qualify as "government speech" because it is funded by a targeted assessment on beef producers, rather than by general revenues. This funding mechanism, they argue, has two relevant effects: it gives control over the beef program not to politically accountable legislators, but to a narrow interest group that will pay no heed to respondents' dissenting views, and it creates the perception that the advertisements speak for beef producers such as respondents.

We reject the first point. The compelled-*subsidy* analysis is altogether unaffected by whether the funds for the promotions are raised by general taxes or through a targeted assessment. Citizens may challenge compelled support of private speech, but have no First Amendment right not to fund government speech. And that is no less true when the funding is achieved through targeted assessments devoted exclusively to the program to which the assessed citizens object.

Some of our cases have justified compelled funding of government speech by pointing out that government speech is subject to democratic accountability. But our references to "traditional political controls" do not signify that the First Amendment duplicates the Appropriations Clause, or that every instance of government speech must be funded by a line item in an appropriations bill. Here, the beef advertisements are subject to political safeguards more than adequate to set them apart from private messages. The program is authorized and the basic message prescribed by federal statute, and specific requirements for the promotions' content are imposed by federal regulations promulgated after notice and comment. The Secretary of Agriculture, a politically accountable official, oversees the program, appoints and dismisses the key personnel, and retains absolute veto power over the advertisements' content, right down to the wording. And Congress, of course, retains oversight authority, not to mention the ability to reform the program at any time. No more is required.

As to the second point, respondents' argument proceeds as follows: They contend that crediting the advertising to "America's Beef Producers" impermissibly uses not only their money but also their seeming endorsement to promote a message with which they do not agree. Communications cannot be "government speech," they argue, if they are attributed to someone other than the government; and the person to whom they are attributed, when he is, by compulsory funding, made the unwilling instrument of communication, may raise a First Amendment objection.

We need not determine the validity of this argument—which relates to compelled *speech* rather than compelled *subsidy*—with regard to respondents' facial challenge. Since neither the Beef Act nor the Beef Order requires attribution, neither can be the cause of any possible First Amendment harm.

On some set of facts, this second theory might (again, we express no view on the point) form the basis for an as-applied challenge—if it were established, that is, that individual beef advertisements were attributed to respondents. The record, however, includes only a stipulated sampling of these promotional materials, and none of the exemplars provides any support for this attribution theory except for the tagline identifying the funding. Respondents apparently presented no other evidence of attribution at trial, and the District Court made no factual findings on the point.

Justice THOMAS, concurring.

I join the Court's opinion. I continue to believe that "[a]ny regulation that compels the funding of advertising must be subjected to the most stringent First Amendment scrutiny." At the same time, I recognize that this principle must be qualified where the regulation compels the funding of speech that is the government's own. It cannot be that all taxpayers have a First Amendment objection to taxpayer-funded government speech, even if the funded speech is not "germane" to some broader regulatory program. Like the Court, I see no analytical distinction between "pure" government speech funded from general tax revenues and from speech funded from targeted exactions; the practice of using targeted taxes to fund government operations, such as excise taxes, dates from the founding.

Still, if the advertisements associated their generic pro-beef message with either the individual or organization respondents, then respondents would have a valid as-applied First Amendment challenge. The government may not, consistent with the First Amendment, associate individuals or organizations involuntarily with speech by attributing an unwanted message to them, whether or not those individuals fund the speech, and whether or not the message is under the government's control. This principle follows not only from our cases establishing that the government may not compel individuals to convey messages with which they disagree, but also from our expressive-association cases, which prohibit the government from coercively associating individuals or groups with unwanted messages. The present record, however, does not show that the advertisements objectively associate their message with any individual respondent.

Justice SOUTER, with whom Justice STEVENS and Justice KENNEDY join, dissenting.

The Beef Promotion and Research Act of 1985, known as the Beef Act, taxes cattle sold in or imported into the United States at one dollar a head. Much of the revenue is spent urging people to eat beef, as in advertisements with the slogan, "Beef. It's What's for Dinner." Respondent taxpayers object to the tax because they disagree with the advertisements' content, which they see as a generic message that "beef is good." This message, the ranchers say, ignores the fact that not all beef is the same; the ads fail to distinguish, for example, the American ranchers' grain-fed beef from the grass-fed beef predominant in the imports, which the Americans consider inferior.

[T]he Government argues here that the beef advertising is its own speech, exempting it from the First Amendment bar against extracting special subsidies from those unwilling to underwrite an objectionable message.

The Court accepts the defense unwisely. The error is not that government speech can never justify compelling a subsidy, but that a compelled subsidy should not be justifiable by speech unless the government must put that speech forward as its own. Otherwise there is no check whatever on government's power to compel special speech subsidies. I take the view that if government relies on the government-speech doctrine to compel specific groups to fund speech with targeted taxes, it must make itself politically accountable by indicating that the content actually is a government message, not just the statement of one self-interested group the government is currently willing to invest with power. Sometimes, as in these very cases, government can make an effective disclosure only by explicitly labeling the speech as its own. Because the Beef Act fails to require the Government to show its hand, I would affirm the judgment of the Court of Appeals holding the Act unconstitutional, and I respectfully dissent from the Court's decision to condone this compelled subsidy.

RUMSFELD v. FORUM FOR ACADEMIC AND INSTITUTIONAL RIGHTS, INC.
126 S. Ct. 1297 (2006)

Chief Justice ROBERTS delivered the opinion of the Court.

When law schools began restricting the access of military recruiters to their students because of disagreement with the Government's policy on homosexuals in the military, Congress responded by enacting the Solomon Amendment. See 10 U.S.C.A. § 983. That provision specifies that if any part of an institution of higher education denies military recruiters access equal to that provided other recruiters, the entire institution would lose certain federal funds. The law schools responded by suing, alleging that the Solomon Amendment infringed their First Amendment freedoms of speech and association. The District Court disagreed but was reversed by a divided panel of the Court of Appeals for the Third Circuit, which ordered the District Court to enter a preliminary injunction against enforcement of the Solomon Amendment.

I

Respondent Forum for Academic and Institutional Rights, Inc. (FAIR), is an association of law schools and law faculties. They would like to restrict military recruiting on their campuses because they object to the policy Congress has adopted with respect to homosexuals in the military. See 10 U.S.C. § 654.[2] The Solomon Amendment, however, forces institutions to choose between enforcing their nondiscrimination policy against military recruiters in this way and continuing to receive specified federal funding.

---

2. Under this policy, a person generally may not serve in the Armed Forces if he has engaged in homosexual acts, stated that he is a homosexual, or married a person of the same sex. Respondents do not challenge that policy in this litigation. [Footnote by Court]

II

The Solomon Amendment denies federal funding to an institution of higher education that "has a policy or practice . . . that either prohibits, or in effect prevents" the
military "from gaining access to campuses, or access to students . . . on campuses,
for purposes of military recruiting in a manner that is at least equal in quality and
scope to the access to campuses and to students that is provided to any other
employer." 10 U.S.C.A. § 983(b). The statute provides an exception for an institution with "a longstanding policy of pacifism based on historical religious
affiliation." The Government and FAIR agree on what this statute requires: In
order for a law school and its university to receive federal funding, the law school
must offer military recruiters the same access to its campus and students that it
provides to the nonmilitary recruiter receiving the most favorable access.

III

The Constitution grants Congress the power to "provide for the common Defence,"
"[t]o raise and support Armies," and "[t]o provide and maintain a Navy." Art. I,
§ 8, cls. 1, 12-13. Congress' power in this area "is broad and sweeping," and there is
no dispute in this case that it includes the authority to require campus access for
military recruiters. That is, of course, unless Congress exceeds constitutional
limitations on its power in enacting such legislation. But the fact that legislation
that raises armies is subject to First Amendment constraints does not mean that we
ignore the purpose of this legislation when determining its constitutionality; as we
[have] recognized"judicial deference . . . is at its apogee" when Congress legis-
lates under its authority to raise and support armies. Id., at 70.

Although Congress has broad authority to legislate on matters of military recruiting, it nonetheless chose to secure campus access for military recruiters indirectly,
through its Spending Clause power. The Solomon Amendment gives universities a
choice: Either allow military recruiters the same access to students afforded any
other recruiter or forgo certain federal funds. Congress' decision to proceed indirectly does not reduce the deference given to Congress in the area of military affairs.
Congress' choice to promote its goal by creating a funding condition deserves at
least as deferential treatment as if Congress had imposed a mandate on universities.

This case does not require us to determine when a condition placed on
university funding goes beyond the "reasonable" choice and becomes an
unconstitutional condition. It is clear that a funding condition cannot be unconstitutional if it could be constitutionally imposed directly. Because the First
Amendment would not prevent Congress from directly imposing the Solomon
Amendment's access requirement, the statute does not place an unconstitutional
condition on the receipt of federal funds.

A

The Solomon Amendment neither limits what law schools may say nor
requires them to say anything. Law schools remain free under the statute to

express whatever views they may have on the military's congressionally mandated employment policy, all the while retaining eligibility for federal funds. As a general matter, the Solomon Amendment regulates conduct, not speech. It affects what law schools must do — afford equal access to military recruiters — not what they may or may not say.

Nevertheless, the Third Circuit concluded that the Solomon Amendment violates law schools' freedom of speech in a number of ways. First, in assisting military recruiters, law schools provide some services, such as sending e-mails and distributing flyers, that clearly involve speech. The Court of Appeals held that in supplying these services law schools are unconstitutionally compelled to speak the Government's message. Second, military recruiters are, to some extent, speaking while they are on campus. The Court of Appeals held that, by forcing law schools to permit the military on campus to express its message, the Solomon Amendment unconstitutionally requires law schools to host or accommodate the military's speech. Third, although the Court of Appeals thought that the Solomon Amendment regulated speech, it held in the alternative that, if the statute regulates conduct, this conduct is expressive and regulating it unconstitutionally infringes law schools' right to engage in expressive conduct. We consider each issue in turn.

1

Some of this Court's leading First Amendment precedents have established the principle that freedom of speech prohibits the government from telling people what they must say. In *West Virginia Bd. of Ed. v. Barnette* (1943), we held unconstitutional a state law requiring schoolchildren to recite the Pledge of Allegiance and to salute the flag. And in *Wooley v. Maynard* (1977), we held unconstitutional another that required New Hampshire motorists to display the state motto—"Live Free or Die"—on their license plates.

The Solomon Amendment does not require any similar expression by law schools. Nonetheless, recruiting assistance provided by the schools often includes elements of speech. For example, schools may send e-mails or post notices on bulletin boards on an employer's behalf. Law schools offering such services to other recruiters must also send e-mails and post notices on behalf of the military to comply with the Solomon Amendment. As FAIR points out, these compelled statements of fact ("The U.S. Army recruiter will meet interested students in Room 123 at 11 a.m."), like compelled statements of opinion, are subject to First Amendment scrutiny.

This sort of recruiting assistance, however, is a far cry from the compelled speech in *Barnette* and *Wooley*. The Solomon Amendment, unlike the laws at issue in those cases, does not dictate the content of the speech at all, which is only "compelled" if, and to the extent, the school provides such speech for other recruiters. There is nothing in this case approaching a government-mandated pledge or motto that the school must endorse.

The compelled speech to which the law schools point is plainly incidental to the Solomon Amendment's regulation of conduct, and "it has never been deemed an abridgment of freedom of speech or press to make a course of conduct illegal merely because the conduct was in part initiated, evidenced, or carried out by means of language, either spoken, written, or printed." Congress, for example, can prohibit employers from discriminating in hiring on the basis of race. The fact that this will require an employer to take down a sign reading "White Applicants Only" hardly means that the law should be analyzed as one regulating the employer's speech rather than conduct. Compelling a law school that sends scheduling e-mails for other recruiters to send one for a military recruiter is simply not the same as forcing a student to pledge allegiance, or forcing a Jehovah's Witness to display the motto "Live Free or Die," and it trivializes the freedom protected in *Barnette* and *Wooley* to suggest that it is.

2

Our compelled-speech cases are not limited to the situation in which an individual must personally speak the government's message. We have also in a number of instances limited the government's ability to force one speaker to host or accommodate another speaker's message. See *Hurley v. Irish-American Gay, Lesbian and Bisexual Group of Boston, Inc.* (1995) (state law cannot require a parade to include a group whose message the parade's organizer does not wish to send); *Pacific Gas & Elec. Co. v. Public Util. Comm'n of Cal.* (1986) (state agency cannot require a utility company to include a third-party newsletter in its billing envelope); *Miami Herald Publishing Co. v. Tornillo* (right-of-reply statute violates editors' right to determine the content of their newspapers). Relying on these precedents, the Third Circuit concluded that the Solomon Amendment unconstitutionally compels law schools to accommodate the military's message "[b]y requiring schools to include military recruiters in the interviews and recruiting receptions the schools arrange."

The compelled-speech violation in each of our prior cases, however, resulted from the fact that the complaining speaker's own message was affected by the speech it was forced to accommodate. The expressive nature of a parade was central to our holding in *Hurley*. We concluded that because "every participating unit affects the message conveyed by the [parade's] private organizers," a law dictating that a particular group must be included in the parade "alter[s] the expressive content of th[e] parade." As a result, we held that the State's public accommodation law, as applied to a private parade, "violates the fundamental rule of protection under the First Amendment, that a speaker has the autonomy to choose the content of his own message."

In this case, accommodating the military's message does not affect the law schools' speech, because the schools are not speaking when they host interviews and recruiting receptions. Unlike a parade organizer's choice of parade contingents, a law school's decision to allow recruiters on campus is not inherently expressive. Law schools facilitate recruiting to assist their students in obtaining jobs. A law school's recruiting services lack the expressive quality of a parade, a newsletter, or the editorial page of a newspaper; its accommodation of a military recruiter's message is not compelled speech because the accommodation does not sufficiently interfere with any message of the school.

The schools respond that if they treat military and nonmilitary recruiters alike in order to comply with the Solomon Amendment, they could be viewed as sending the message that they see nothing wrong with the military's policies, when they do. We rejected a similar argument in *PruneYard Shopping Center v. Robins* (1980). In that case, we upheld a state law requiring a shopping center owner to allow certain expressive activities by others on its property. We explained that there was little likelihood that the views of those engaging in the expressive activities would be identified with the owner, who remained free to disassociate himself from those views and who was "not . . . being compelled to affirm [a] belief in any governmentally prescribed position or view."

The same is true here. Nothing about recruiting suggests that law schools agree with any speech by recruiters, and nothing in the Solomon Amendment restricts what the law schools may say about the military's policies.

3

Having rejected the view that the Solomon Amendment impermissibly regulates speech, we must still consider whether the expressive nature of the conduct regulated by the statute brings that conduct within the First Amendment's protection. [W]e have extended First Amendment protection only to conduct that is inherently expressive. In *Texas v. Johnson* (1989), for example, we held that burning the American flag was sufficiently expressive to warrant First Amendment protection.

Unlike flag burning, the conduct regulated by the Solomon Amendment is not inherently expressive. Prior to the adoption of the Solomon Amendment's equal-access requirement, law schools "expressed" their disagreement with the military by treating military recruiters differently from other recruiters. But these actions were expressive only because the law schools accompanied their conduct with speech explaining it. For example, the point of requiring military interviews to be conducted on the undergraduate campus is not "overwhelmingly apparent." An observer who sees military recruiters interviewing away from the law school has no way of knowing whether the law school is expressing its disapproval of the military, all the law school's interview rooms are full, or the military recruiters decided for reasons of their own that they would rather interview someplace else. The expressive component of a law school's actions is not created by the conduct itself but by the speech that accompanies it. The fact that such explanatory speech is necessary is strong evidence that the conduct at issue here is not so inherently expressive that it warrants protection. If combining speech and conduct were enough to create expressive conduct, a regulated party could always transform conduct into "speech" simply by talking about it.

B

The Solomon Amendment does not violate law schools' freedom of speech, but the First Amendment's protection extends beyond the right to speak. We have recognized a First Amendment right to associate for the purpose of speaking, which we have termed a "right of expressive association." See, e.g., *Boy Scouts of America v. Dale* (2000). The reason we have extended First Amendment protection in this way is clear: The right to speak is often exercised most effectively by combining one's voice with the voices of others. If the government were free to restrict individuals' ability to join together and speak, it could essentially silence views that the First Amendment is intended to protect.

FAIR argues that the Solomon Amendment violates law schools' freedom of expressive association. According to FAIR, law schools' ability to express their message that discrimination on the basis of sexual orientation is wrong is significantly affected by the presence of military recruiters on campus and the schools' obligation to assist them.

The Solomon Amendment, however, does not similarly affect a law school's associational rights. To comply with the statute, law schools must allow military recruiters on campus and assist them in whatever way the school chooses to assist other employers. Law schools therefore "associate" with military recruiters in the sense that they interact with them. But recruiters are not part of the law school. Recruiters are, by definition, outsiders who come onto campus for the limited purpose of trying to hire students—not to become members of the school's expressive association. This distinction is critical. Unlike the public accommodations law in *Dale*, the Solomon Amendment does not force a law school "to accept members it does not desire." The law schools say that allowing military recruiters equal access impairs their own expression by requiring them to associate with the recruiters, but just as saying conduct is undertaken for expressive purposes cannot make it symbolic speech, so too a speaker cannot "erect a shield" against laws requiring access "simply by asserting" that mere association "would impair its message."

The Solomon Amendment has no similar effect on a law school's associational rights. Students and faculty are free to associate to voice their disapproval of the military's message; nothing about the statute affects the composition of the group by making group membership less desirable. The Solomon Amendment therefore does not violate a law school's First Amendment rights. A military recruiter's mere presence on campus does not violate a law school's right to associate, regardless of how repugnant the law school considers the recruiter's message.

In this case, FAIR has attempted to stretch a number of First Amendment doctrines well beyond the sort of activities these doctrines protect. The law schools object to having to treat military recruiters like other recruiters, but that regulation of conduct does not violate the First Amendment. To the extent that the Solomon Amendment incidentally affects expression, the law schools' effort to cast themselves as just like the schoolchildren in *Barnette*, the parade organizers in *Hurley*, and the Boy Scouts in *Dale* plainly overstates the expressive nature of their activity and the impact of the Solomon Amendment on it, while exaggerating the reach of our First Amendment precedents.

C. Types of Unprotected and Less Protected Speech

6. Conduct that Communicates

v. The Continuing Distinction Between Contributions and Expenditures (casebook, p. 1332)

In the October 2005 Term, the Supreme Court considered two cases concerning regulation of campaign spending. In *Wisconsin Right to Life, Inc. v. Federal Election Commission*, 125 S.Ct. 1016 (2006), the Court held that "as applied" challenges may be considered against the Bipartisan Campaign Finance Reform Act. In *McConnell v. Federal Election Commission* (casebook p. 1336), the Court upheld the constitutionality of the Act. In *Wisconsin Right to Life*, the Court said that this earlier decision did not preclude the possibility of an argument that the law was unconstitutional as applied in a particular instance. In a brief per curium opinion, the Court remanded the case for further consideration.

The more important campaign finance case was *Randall v. Sorrell*, below. Although the Court was very fragmented, the following clearly emerged: A majority of the Justices accept the *Buckley* framework (restrictions on contributions in election campaigns are allowed, but restrictions on expenditures are unconstitutional); and restrictions on contributions violate the First Amendment if they are too low. Justice Breyer's plurality opinion articulated reasons for finding the limit in this case to be too low. Because this is the first case ever to invalidate contributions as being too low, it undoubtedly will lead to challenges to many campaign finance laws around the country.

RANDALL v. SORRELL
126 S. Ct. 2479 (2006)

Justice BREYER announced the judgment of the Court, and delivered an opinion in which THE CHIEF JUSTICE joins, and in which Justice ALITO joins except as to Parts II-B-1 and II-B-2.

We here consider the constitutionality of a Vermont campaign finance statute that limits both (1) the amounts that candidates for state office may spend on their campaigns (expenditure limitations) and (2) the amounts that individuals, organizations, and political parties may contribute to those campaigns (contribution limitations). We hold that both sets of limitations are inconsistent with the First Amendment. Well-established precedent makes clear that the expenditure limits violate the First Amendment. *Buckley v. Valeo* (1976) (per curiam). The contribution limits are unconstitutional because in their specific details (involving low maximum levels and other restrictions) they fail to satisfy the First Amendment's requirement of careful tailoring. That is to say, they impose burdens upon First Amendment interests that (when viewed in light of the statute's legitimate objectives) are disproportionately severe.

I

Prior to 1997, Vermont's campaign finance law imposed no limit upon the amount a candidate for state office could spend. It did, however, impose limits upon the amounts that individuals, corporations, and political committees could contribute to the campaign of such a candidate.

In 1997, Vermont enacted a more stringent campaign finance law, Pub. Act No. 64, the statute at issue here. Act 64, which took effect immediately after the 1998 elections, imposes mandatory expenditure limits on the total amount a candidate for state office can spend during a "two-year general election cycle," i.e., the primary plus the general election, in approximately the following amounts: governor, $300,000; lieutenant governor, $100,000; other statewide offices, $45,000; state senator, $4,000 (plus an additional $2,500 for each additional seat in the district); state representative (two-member district), $3,000; and state representative (single member district), $2,000. These limits are adjusted for inflation in odd-numbered years based on the Consumer Price Index. Incumbents seeking reelection to statewide office may spend no more than 85% of the above amounts, and incumbents seeking reelection to the State Senate or House may spend no more than 90% of the above amounts. The Act defines "[e]xpenditure" broadly to mean the "payment, disbursement, distribution, advance, deposit, loan or gift of money or anything of value, paid or promised to be paid, for the purpose of influencing an election, advocating a position on a public question, or supporting or opposing one or more candidates."

Act 64 also imposes strict contribution limits. The amount any single individual can contribute to the campaign of a candidate for state office during a "two-year general election cycle" is limited as follows: governor, lieutenant governor, and other statewide offices, $400; state senator, $300; and state representative, $200. § 2805(a). Unlike its expenditure limits, Act 64's contribution limits are not indexed for inflation.

A political committee is subject to these same limits. Ibid. So is a political party, defined broadly to include "any subsidiary, branch or local unit" of a party, as well as any "national or regional affiliates" of a party (taken separately or together). Thus, for example, the statute treats the local, state, and national affiliates of the Democratic Party as if they were a single entity and limits their total contribution to a single candidate's campaign for governor (during the primary and the general election together) to $400.

The Act also imposes a limit of $2,000 upon the amount any individual can give to a political party during a 2-year general election cycle. The Act defines "contribution" broadly in approximately the same way it defines "expenditure."

II

We turn first to the Act's expenditure limits. Do those limits violate the First Amendment's free speech guarantees? In *Buckley v. Valeo*, the Court considered the constitutionality of the Federal Election Campaign Act of 1971 (FECA), a statute that, much like the Act before us, imposed both expenditure and contribution limitations on campaigns for public office. The Court, while upholding FECA's contribution limitations as constitutional, held that the statute's expenditure limitations violated the First Amendment. Over the last 30 years, in considering the constitutionality of a host of different campaign finance statutes, this Court has repeatedly adhered to *Buckley's* constraints, including those on expenditure limits.

The respondents recognize that, in respect to expenditure limits, *Buckley* appears to be a controlling—and unfavorable—precedent. They seek to overcome that precedent in two ways. First, they ask us in effect to overrule *Buckley*. Post- *Buckley* experience, they believe, has shown that contribution limits (and disclosure requirements) alone cannot effectively deter corruption or its appearance; hence experience has undermined an assumption underlying that case. Indeed, the respondents have devoted several pages of their briefs to attacking *Buckley's* holding on expenditure limits.

Second, in the alternative, they ask us to limit the scope of *Buckley* significantly by distinguishing *Buckley* from the present case. They advance as a ground for distinction a justification for expenditure limitations that, they say, *Buckley* did not consider, namely that such limits help to protect candidates from spending too much time raising money rather than devoting that time to campaigning among ordinary voters. We find neither argument persuasive.

The Court has often recognized the "fundamental importance" of stare decisis, the basic legal principle that commands judicial respect for a court's earlier decisions and the rules of law they embody. The Court has pointed out that stare decisis "promotes the evenhanded, predictable, and consistent development of legal principles, fosters reliance on judicial decisions, and contributes to the actual and perceived integrity of the judicial process." Stare decisis thereby avoids the instability and unfairness that accompany disruption of settled legal expectations. For this reason, the rule of law demands that adhering to our prior case law be the norm. Departure from precedent is exceptional, and requires "special justification." This is especially true where, as here, the principle has become settled through iteration and reiteration over a long period of time.

We can find here no such special justification that would require us to overrule *Buckley*. Subsequent case law has not made *Buckley* a legal anomaly or otherwise undermined its basic legal principles. We cannot find in the respondents' claims any demonstration that circumstances have changed so radically as to undermine *Buckley's* critical factual assumptions. The respondents have not shown, for example, any dramatic increase in corruption or its appearance in Vermont; nor have they shown that expenditure limits are the only way to attack that problem. At the same time, *Buckley* has promoted considerable reliance. Congress and state legislatures have used *Buckley* when drafting campaign finance laws. And, as we have said, this Court has followed *Buckley*, upholding and applying its reasoning in later cases. Overruling *Buckley* now would dramatically undermine this reliance on our settled precedent.

For all these reasons, we find this a case that fits the stare decisis norm. And we do not perceive the strong justification that would be necessary to warrant overruling so well established a precedent. We consequently decline the respondents' invitation to reconsider *Buckley*.

The respondents also ask us to distinguish these cases from *Buckley*. But we can find no significant basis for that distinction. Act 64's expenditure limits are not substantially different from those at issue in *Buckley*. In both instances the limits consist of a dollar cap imposed upon a candidate's expenditures. Nor is Vermont's primary justification for imposing its expenditure limits significantly different from Congress' rationale for the *Buckley* limits: preventing corruption and its appearance.

The sole basis on which the respondents seek to distinguish *Buckley* concerns a further supporting justification. They argue that expenditure limits are necessary in order to reduce the amount of time candidates must spend raising money. Increased campaign costs, together with the fear of a better-funded opponent, mean that, without expenditure limits, a candidate must spend too much time raising money instead of meeting the voters and engaging in public debate.

In our view, it is highly unlikely that fuller consideration of this time protection rationale would have changed *Buckley's* result. The *Buckley* Court was aware of the connection between expenditure limits and a reduction in fundraising time. In a section of the opinion dealing with FECA's public financing provisions, it wrote that Congress was trying to "free candidates from the rigors of fundraising." And, in any event, the connection between high campaign expenditures and increased fundraising demands seems perfectly obvious. Under these circumstances, the respondents' argument amounts to no more than an invitation so to limit Buckley's holding as effectively to overrule it. For the reasons set forth above, we decline that invitation as well. And, given Buckley's continued authority, we must conclude that Act 64's expenditure limits violate the First Amendment.

III

We turn now to a more complex question, namely the constitutionality of Act 64's contribution limits. The parties, while accepting *Buckley's* approach, dispute whether, despite *Buckley's* general approval of statutes that limit campaign contributions, Act 64's contribution limits are so severe that in the circumstances its particular limits violate the First Amendment.

Following *Buckley*, we must determine whether Act 64's contribution limits prevent candidates from "amassing the resources necessary for effective [campaign] advocacy," whether they magnify the advantages of incumbency to the point where they put challengers to a significant disadvantage; in a word, whether they are too low and too strict to survive First Amendment scrutiny. In answering these questions, we recognize, as *Buckley* stated, that we have "no scalpel to probe" each possible contribution level. We cannot determine with any degree of exactitude the precise restriction necessary to carry out the statute's legitimate objectives. In practice, the legislature is better equipped to make such empirical judgments, as legislators have "particular expertise" in matters related to the costs and nature of running for office. Thus ordinarily we have deferred to the legislature's determination of such matters.

Nonetheless, as *Buckley* acknowledged, we must recognize the existence of some lower bound. At some point the constitutional risks to the democratic electoral process become too great. After all, the interests underlying contribution limits, preventing corruption and the appearance of corruption, "directly implicate the integrity of our electoral process." Yet that rationale does not simply mean "the lower the limit, the better." That is because contribution limits that are too low can also harm the electoral process by preventing challengers from mounting effective campaigns against incumbent officeholders, thereby reducing democratic accountability. Thus, we see no alternative to the exercise of independent judicial judgment as a statute reaches those outer limits. And, where there is strong indication in a particular case, i.e., danger signs, that such risks exist (both present in kind and likely serious in degree), courts, including appellate courts, must review the record independently and carefully with an eye toward assessing the statute's "tailoring," that is, toward assessing the proportionality of the restrictions.

We find those danger signs present here. As compared with the contribution limits upheld by the Court in the past, and with those in force in other States, Act 64's limits are sufficiently low as to generate suspicion that they are not closely drawn. The Act sets its limits per election cycle, which includes both a primary and a general election. Thus, in a gubernatorial race with both primary and final election contests, the Act's contribution limit amounts to $200 per election per candidate (with significantly lower limits for contributions to candidates for State Senate and House of Representatives.) These limits apply both to contributions from individuals and to contributions from political parties, whether made in cash or in expenditures coordinated (or presumed to be coordinated) with the candidate.

In sum, Act 64's contribution limits are substantially lower than both the limits we have previously upheld and comparable limits in other States. These are danger signs that Act 64's contribution limits may fall outside tolerable First Amendment limits. We consequently must examine the record independently and carefully to determine whether Act 64's contribution limits are "closely drawn" to match the State's interests.

C

Our examination of the record convinces us that, from a constitutional perspective, Act 64's contribution limits are too restrictive. We reach this conclusion based not merely on the low dollar amounts of the limits themselves, but also on the statute's effect on political parties and on volunteer activity in Vermont elections. Taken together, Act 64's substantial restrictions on the ability of candidates to raise the funds necessary to run a competitive election, on the ability of political parties to help their candidates get elected, and on the ability of individual citizens to volunteer their time to campaigns show that the Act is not closely drawn to meet its objectives. In particular, five factors together lead us to this decision.

First, the record suggests, though it does not conclusively prove, that Act 64's contribution limits will significantly restrict the amount of funding available for challengers to run competitive campaigns.

Second, Act 64's insistence that political parties abide by exactly the same low contribution limits that apply to other contributors threatens harm to a particularly important political right, the right to associate in a political party.

Third, the Act's treatment of volunteer services aggravates the problem. Like its federal statutory counterpart, the Act excludes from its definition of "contribution" all "services provided without compensation by individuals volunteering their time on behalf of a candidate." But the Act does not exclude the expenses those volunteers incur, such as travel expenses, in the course of campaign activities. The Act's broad definitions would seem to count those expenses against the volunteer's contribution limit, at least where the spending was facilitated or approved by campaign officials. The absence of some such exception may matter in the present context, where contribution limits are very low.

Fourth, unlike the contribution limits we upheld in *Shrink*, Act 64's contribution limits are not adjusted for inflation. Its limits decline in real value each year.

Fifth, we have found nowhere in the record any special justification that might warrant a contribution limit so low or so restrictive as to bring about the serious associational and expressive problems that we have described. Rather, the basic justifications the State has advanced in support of such limits are those present in *Buckley*. The record contains no indication that, for example, corruption (or its appearance) in Vermont is significantly more serious a matter than elsewhere.

Justice ALITO, concurring in part and concurring in the judgment.

Whether or not a case can be made for reexamining *Buckley* in whole or in part, what matters is that respondents do not do so here, and so I think it unnecessary to reach the issue.

Justice KENNEDY, concurring in the judgment.

The Court decides the constitutionality of the limitations Vermont places on campaign expenditures and contributions. I agree that both limitations violate the First Amendment. As the plurality notes, our cases hold that expenditure limitations "place substantial and direct restrictions on the ability of candidates, citizens, and associations to engage in protected political expression, restrictions that the First Amendment cannot tolerate."

The universe of campaign finance regulation is one this Court has in part created and in part permitted by its course of decisions. That new order may cause more problems than it solves. On a routine, operational level the present system requires us to explain why $200 is too restrictive a limit while $1,500 is not. Our own experience gives us little basis to make these judgments, and certainly no traditional or well-established body of law exists to offer guidance. On a broader, systemic level political parties have been denied basic First Amendment rights. Entering to fill the void have been new entities such as political action committees, which are as much the creatures of law as of traditional forces of speech and association. Those entities can manipulate the system and attract their own elite power brokers, who operate in ways obscure to the ordinary citizen. Viewed within the legal universe we have ratified and helped create, the result the plurality reaches is correct; given my own skepticism regarding that system and its operation, however, it seems to me appropriate to concur only in the judgment.

Justice THOMAS, with whom Justice SCALIA joins, concurring in the judgment.

Although I agree with the plurality that Act 64, is unconstitutional, I disagree with its rationale for striking down that statute. I continue to believe that *Buckley* provides insufficient protection to political speech, the core of the First Amendment. The illegitimacy of *Buckley* is further underscored by the continuing inability of the Court (and the plurality here) to apply *Buckley* in a coherent and principled fashion. As a result, stare decisis should pose no bar to overruling *Buckley* and replacing it with a standard faithful to the First Amendment. Accordingly, I concur only in the judgment.

I adhere to my view that this Court erred in *Buckley* when it distinguished between contribution and expenditure limits, finding the former to be a less severe infringement on First Amendment rights. Likewise, *Buckley's* suggestion that contribution caps only marginally restrict speech, because "[a] contribution serves as a general expression of support for the candidate and his views, but does not communicate the underlying basis for the support," even if descriptively accurate, does not support restrictions on contributions.

The plurality opinion, far from making the case for Buckley as a rule of law, itself demonstrates that Buckley's limited scrutiny of contribution limits is "insusceptible of principled application," and accordingly is not entitled to stare decisis effect. Today's newly minted, multifactor test, particularly when read in combination with the Court's decision in *Shrink*, places this Court in the position of addressing the propriety of regulations of political speech based upon little more than its impression of the appropriate limits.

Given that these contribution limits severely impinge on the ability of candidates to run campaigns and on the ability of citizens to contribute to campaigns, and do so without any demonstrable need to avoid corruption, they cannot possibly satisfy even *Buckley's* ambiguous level of scrutiny.

Justice STEVENS, dissenting.

I am convinced that *Buckley's* holding on expenditure limits is wrong, and that the time has come to overrule it. I have not reached this conclusion lightly. As Justice Breyer correctly observes, stare decisis is a principle of "fundamental importance." But it is not an inexorable command, and several factors, taken together, provide special justification for revisiting the constitutionality of statutory limits on candidate expenditures.

To begin with, *Buckley's* holding on expenditure limits itself upset a long-established practice. For the preceding 65 years, congressional races had been subject to statutory limits on both expenditures and contributions. There are further reasons for reexamining *Buckley's* holding on candidate expenditure limits that do not apply to its holding on candidate contribution limits.

The interest in freeing candidates from the fundraising straitjacket is even more compelling. Without expenditure limits, fundraising devours the time and attention of political leaders, leaving them too busy to handle their public responsibilities effectively.

Additionally, there is no convincing evidence that these important interests favoring expenditure limits are fronts for incumbency protection. And only by "permit[ting] States nationwide to experiment with these critically needed reforms,"—as 18 States urge us to do—will we enable further research on how expenditure limits relate to our incumbent reelection rates. In the meantime, a legislative judgment that "enough is enough" should command the greatest possible deference from judges interpreting a constitutional provision that, at best, has an indirect relationship to activity that affects the quantity—rather than the quality or the content—of repetitive speech in the marketplace of ideas.

Justice SOUTER, with whom Justice GINSBURG joins, and with whom Justice STEVENS joins dissenting.

In 1997, the Legislature of Vermont passed Act 64 after a series of public hearings persuaded legislators that rehabilitating the State's political process required campaign finance reform. A majority of the Court today decides that the expenditure and contribution limits enacted are irreconcilable with the Constitution's guarantee of free speech. I would adhere to the Court of Appeals's decision to remand for further enquiry bearing on the limitations on candidates' expenditures, and I think the contribution limits satisfy controlling precedent. I respectfully dissent.

We said in *Buckley* that "expenditure limitations impose far greater restraints on the freedom of speech and association than do . . . contribution limitations," but the *Buckley* Court did not categorically foreclose the possibility that some spending limit might comport with the First Amendment. Instead, *Buckley* held that the constitutionality of an expenditure limitation "turns on whether the governmental interests advanced in its support satisfy the [applicable] exacting scrutiny." In applying that standard in *Buckley* itself, the Court gave no indication that it had given serious consideration to an aim that Vermont's statute now pursues: to alleviate the drain on candidates' and officials' time caused by the endless fundraising necessary to aggregate many small contributions to meet the opportunities for ever more expensive campaigning.

Vermont's argument therefore does not ask us to overrule *Buckley*; it asks us to apply *Buckley's* framework to determine whether its evidence here on a need to slow the fundraising treadmill suffices to support the enacted limitations. Vermont's claim is serious. Three decades of experience since *Buckley* have taught us much, and the findings made by the Vermont Legislature on the pernicious effect of the nonstop pursuit of money are significant. Thus, the constitutionality of the expenditure limits was not conclusively decided by the Second Circuit, and I believe the evidentiary work that remained to be done would have raised the prospect for a sound answer to that question, whatever the answer might have been. Instead, we are left with an unresolved question of narrow tailoring and with consequent doubt about the justifiability of the spending limits as necessary and appropriate correctives. This is not the record on which to foreclose the ability of a State to remedy the impact of the money chase on the democratic process. I would not, therefore, disturb the Court of Appeals's stated intention to remand.

II.

Although I would defer judgment on the merits of the expenditure limitations, I believe the Court of Appeals correctly rejected the challenge to the contribution limits. Low though they are, one cannot say that "the contribution limitation[s are] so radical in effect as to render political association ineffective, drive the sound of a candidate's voice below the level of notice, and render contributions pointless."

The limits set by Vermont are not remarkable departures either from those previously upheld by this Court or from those lately adopted by other States.

Still, our cases do not say deference should be absolute. We can all imagine dollar limits that would be laughable, and per capita comparisons that would be meaningless because aggregated donations simply could not sustain effective campaigns. The plurality thinks that point has been reached in Vermont, and in particular that the low contribution limits threaten the ability of challengers to run effective races against incumbents. Thus, the plurality's limit of deference is substantially a function of suspicion that political incumbents in the legislature set low contribution limits because their public recognition and easy access to free publicity will effectively augment their own spending power beyond anything a challenger can muster. The suspicion is, in other words, that incumbents cannot be trusted to set fair limits, because facially neutral limits do not in fact give challengers an even break. But this received suspicion is itself a proper subject of suspicion. The petitioners offered, and the plurality invokes, no evidence that the risk of a pro-incumbent advantage has been realized; in fact, the record evidence runs the other way, as the plurality concedes.

Because I would not pass upon the constitutionality of Vermont's expenditure limits prior to further enquiry into their fit with the problem of fundraising demands on candidates, and because I do not see the contribution limits as depressed to the level of political inaudibility, I respectfully dissent.

D. *What Places Are Available for Speech?*

3. Speech in Authoritarian Environments: Military, Prisons, and Schools

b. *Prisons (casebook, p. 1380)*

In *Beard v. Banks*, below, the Court upheld a Pennsylvania prison regulation that prevented some inmates from having any access to newspapers or magazines. The 6-3 decision, without a majority opinion, reflected great judicial deference to prison authorities.

BEARD v. BANKS

126 S.Ct. 2572 (2006)

Justice BREYER announced the judgment of the Court, and delivered an opinion, in which THE CHIEF JUSTICE, Justice KENNEDY, and Justice SOUTER join.

We here consider whether a Pennsylvania prison policy that "denies newspapers, magazines, and photographs" to a group of specially dangerous and recalcitrant inmates "violate[s] the First Amendment." While we do not deny the constitutional importance of the interests in question, we find, on the basis of the record now before us, that prison officials have set forth adequate legal support for the policy. And the plaintiff, a prisoner who attacks the policy, has failed to set forth "specific facts" that, in light of the deference that courts must show to the prison officials, could warrant a determination in his favor.

I

The prison regulation at issue applies to certain prisoners housed in Pennsylvania's Long Term Segregation Unit. The LTSU is the most restrictive of the three special units that Pennsylvania maintains for difficult prisoners. [T]hey (unlike all other prisoners in the Commonwealth) are restricted in the manner at issue here: They have no access to newspapers, magazines, or personal photographs. They are nonetheless permitted legal and personal correspondence, religious and legal materials, two library books, and writing paper.

II

Turner v. Safley (1987), and *Overton v. Bazzetta* (2003), contain the basic substantive legal standards governing this case. This Court recognized in *Turner* that imprisonment does not automatically deprive a prisoner of certain important constitutional protections, including those of the First Amendment. But at the same time the Constitution sometimes permits greater restriction of such rights in a prison than it would allow elsewhere. *Turner* [held] that restrictive prison regulations are permissible if they are " 'reasonably related' to legitimate penological interests," and are not an "exaggerated response" to such objectives.

Turner also sets forth four factors "relevant in determining the reasonableness of the regulation at issue." First, is there a " 'valid, rational connection' between the prison regulation and the legitimate governmental interest put forward to justify it"? Second, are there "alternative means of exercising the right that remain open to prison inmates"? Third, what "impact" will "accommodation of the asserted constitutional right . . . have on guards and other inmates, and on the allocation of prison resources generally"? And, fourth, are "ready alternatives" for furthering the governmental interest available?

III

The Secretary in his motion set forth several justifications for the prison's policy, including the need to motivate better behavior on the part of particularly difficult prisoners, the need to minimize the amount of property they control in their cells, and the need to assure prison safety, by, for example, diminishing the amount of material a prisoner might use to start a cell fire. We need go no further than the first justification, that of providing increased incentives for better prison behavior. Applying the well-established substantive and procedural standards set forth in Part II, we find, on the basis of the record before us, that the Secretary's justification is adequate. And that finding here warrants summary judgment in the Secretary's favor.

The Secretary rested his motion for summary judgment primarily upon the statement of undisputed facts along with Deputy Prison Superintendent Dickson's affidavit. The statement of undisputed facts says that the LTSU's 40 inmates, about 0.01 percent of the total prison population, constitute the " 'worst of the worst,' " those who "have proven by the history of their behavior in prison, the necessity of holding them in the rigorous regime of confinement" of the LTSU. It then sets forth three "penological rationales" for the Policy, summarized from the Dickson deposition:

(1) to "motivat[e]" better "behavior" on the part of these "particularly difficult prisoners," by providing them with an incentive to move to level 1, or out of the LTSU altogether, and to "discourage backsliding" on the part of level 1 inmates;

(2) to minimize the amount of property controlled by the prisoners, on the theory that the "less property these high maintenance, high supervision, obdurate troublemakers have, the easier it is for . . . correctional officer [s] to detect concealed contraband [and] to provide security"; and

(3) to diminish the amount of material (in particular newspapers and magazines) that prisoners might use as weapons of attack in the form of "spears" or "blow guns," or that they could employ "as tools to catapult feces at the guards without the necessity of soiling one's own hands," or use "as tinder for cell fires."

As we have said we believe that the first rationale itself satisfies Turner's requirements. First, the statement and deposition set forth a "valid, rational connection" between the Policy and "legitimate penological objectives." The articulated connections between newspapers and magazines, the deprivation of virtually the last privilege left to an inmate, and a significant incentive to improve behavior, are logical ones. Thus, the first factor supports the Policy's "reasonableness."

As to the second factor, the statement and deposition make clear that, as long as the inmate remains at level 2, no "alternative means of exercising the right" remain open to him. The absence of any alternative thus provides "some evidence that the regulations [a]re unreasonable," but is not "conclusive" of the reasonableness of the Policy.

As to the third factor, the statement and deposition indicate that, were prison authorities to seek to "accommodat[e] . . . the asserted constitutional right," the resulting "impact" would be negative. That circumstance is also inherent in the nature of the Policy: If the Policy (in the authorities' view) helps to produce better behavior, then its absence (in the authorities' view) will help to produce worse behavior, e.g., "backsliding" (and thus the expenditure of more "resources" at level 2). Similarly, as to the fourth factor, neither the statement nor the deposition describes, points to, or calls to mind any "alternative method of accommodating the claimant's constitutional complaint . . . that fully accommodates the prisoner's rights at de minimis cost to valid penological interests."

Here prison authorities responded adequately through their statement and deposition to the allegations in the complaint. And the plaintiff failed to point to "specific facts" in the record that could "lead a rational trier of fact to find" in his favor.

Justice THOMAS, with whom Justice SCALIA joins, concurring in the judgment.

Judicial scrutiny of prison regulations is an endeavor fraught with peril. Just last Term, this Court invalidated California's policy of racially segregating prisoners in its reception centers, notwithstanding that State's warning that its policy was necessary to prevent prison violence. See *Johnson v. California* (2005). California subsequently experienced several instances of severe race-based prison violence, including a riot that resulted in 2 fatalities and more than 100 injuries, and significant fighting along racial lines between newly arrived inmates, the very inmates that were subject to the policy invalidated by the Court in *Johnson*. This powerful reminder of the grave dangers inherent in prison administration confirms my view that the framework I set forth in *Overton v. Bazzetta* (2003) is the least perilous approach for resolving challenges to prison regulations, as well as the approach that is most faithful to the Constitution. Accordingly, I concur only in the judgment of the Court.

Both the plurality and the dissent evaluate the regulations challenged in this case pursuant to the approach set forth in *Turner v. Safley*, which permits prison regulations that "imping[e] on inmates' constitutional rights" if the regulations are "reasonably related to legitimate penological interests." But as I explained in *Overton*, *Turner* and its progeny "rest on the unstated (and erroneous) presumption that the Constitution contains an implicit definition of incarceration." Because the Constitution contains no such definition, "States are free to define and redefine all types of punishment, including imprisonment, to encompass various types of deprivations— provided only that those deprivations are consistent with the Eighth Amendment." Respondent has not challenged Pennsylvania's prison policy as a violation of the Eighth Amendment.

Although Pennsylvania "is free to alter its definition of incarceration to include the retention" of unfettered access to magazines, newspapers, and photographs, it appears that the Commonwealth instead sentenced respondent against the backdrop of its traditional conception of imprisonment, which affords no such privileges. Accordingly, respondent's challenge to Pennsylvania's prison regulations must fail.

Justice STEVENS, with whom Justice GINSBURG joins, dissenting.

By ratifying the Fourteenth Amendment, our society has made an unmistakable commitment to apply the rule of law in an evenhanded manner to all persons, even those who flagrantly violate their social and legal obligations. Thus, it is well settled that even the "'worst of the worst'" prisoners retain constitutional protection, specifically including their First Amendment rights. When a prison regulation impinges upon First Amendment freedoms, it is invalid unless "it is reasonably related to legitimate penological interests." *Turner v. Safley* (1987). Under this standard, a prison regulation cannot withstand constitutional scrutiny if "the logical connection between the regulation and the asserted goal is so remote as to render the policy arbitrary or irrational," or if the regulation represents an "exaggerated response" to legitimate penological objectives.

In this case, Pennsylvania prison officials have promulgated a rule that prohibits inmates in Long Term Segregation Unit, level 2 (LTSU-2), which is the most restrictive condition of confinement statewide, from possessing any secular, nonlegal newspaper, newsletter, or magazine during the indefinite duration of their solitary confinement. A prisoner in LTSU-2 may not even receive an individual article clipped from such a news publication unless the article relates to him or his family. In addition, under the challenged rule, any personal photograph, including those of spouses, children, deceased parents, or inspirational mentors, will be treated as contraband and confiscated.

It is indisputable that this prohibition on the possession of newspapers and photographs infringes upon respondent's First Amendment rights. Plainly, the rule at issue in this case strikes at the core of the First Amendment rights to receive, to read, and to think.

Petitioner does not dispute that the prohibition at issue infringes upon rights protected by the First Amendment. Instead, petitioner posits two penological interests, which, in his view, are sufficient to justify the challenged rule notwithstanding these constitutional infringements: prison security and inmate rehabilitation. Although these interests are certainly valid, petitioner has failed to establish, as a matter of law, that the challenged rule is reasonably related to these interests.

Turning first to the security rationale, which the plurality does not discuss, the Court of Appeals persuasively explained why, in light of the amount of materials LTSU-2 inmates may possess in their cells, petitioner has failed to demonstrate that the prohibition on newspapers, magazines, and photographs is likely to have any marginal effect on security.

The second rationale posited by petitioner in support of the prohibitions on newspapers, newsletters, magazines, and photographs is rehabilitation. According to petitioner, the ban "provides the [l]evel 2 inmates with the prospect of earning a privilege through compliance with orders and remission of various negative behaviors and serves to encourage the progress and discourage backsliding by the level 1 inmates." In the plurality's view, in light of the present record, this rationale is sufficient to warrant a reversal of the judgment below.

Rehabilitation is undoubtedly a legitimate penological interest. However, the particular theory of rehabilitation at issue in this case presents a special set of concerns for courts considering whether a prison regulation is consistent with the First Amendment. Specifically, petitioner advances a deprivation theory of rehabilitation: Any deprivation of something a prisoner desires gives him an added incentive to improve his behavior. This justification has no limiting principle; if sufficient, it would provide a "rational basis" for any regulation that deprives a prisoner of a constitutional right so long as there is at least a theoretical possibility that the prisoner can regain the right at some future time by modifying his behavior. Indeed, the more important the constitutional right at stake (at least from the prisoners' perspective), the stronger the justification for depriving prisoners of that right.

Indeed, the strong form of the deprivation theory of rehabilitation would mean that the prison rule we invalidated in *Turner* would have survived constitutional scrutiny if the State had simply posited an interest in rehabilitating prisoners through deprivation. In *Turner*, we held that a Missouri regulation that forbade inmates from marrying except with the permission of the prison superintendent was facially unconstitutional. We rejected the State's proffered security and rehabilitation concerns as not reasonably related to the marriage ban. Taken to its logical conclusion, however, the deprivation theory of rehabilitation would mean that the marriage ban in *Turner* could be justified because the prohibition furnished prisoners with an incentive to behave well and thus earn early release.

In sum, rehabilitation is a valid penological interest, and deprivation is undoubtedly one valid tool in promoting rehabilitation. Nonetheless, to ensure that Turner continues to impose meaningful limits on the promulgation of rules that infringe upon inmates' constitutional rights, courts must be especially cautious in evaluating the constitutionality of prison regulations that are supposedly justified primarily on that basis. When, as here, a reasonable factfinder could conclude that challenged deprivations have a tenuous logical connection to rehabilitation, or are exaggerated responses to a prison's legitimate interest in rehabilitation, prison officials are not entitled to judgment as a matter of law.

In any event, if we consider the severity of the other conditions of confinement in LTSU-2, it becomes obvious that inmates have a powerful motivation to escape those conditions irrespective of the ban on newspapers, magazines, and personal photographs. Inmates in LTSU-2 face 23 hours a day in solitary confinement, are allowed only one visitor per month, may not make phone calls except in cases of emergency, lack any access to radio or television, may not use the prison commissary, are not permitted General Educational Development (GED) or special education study, and may not receive compensation under the inmate compensation system if they work as a unit janitor. The logical conclusion from this is that, even if LTSU-2 prisoners were not deprived of access to newspapers and personal photographs, they would still have a strong incentive to gain promotion to LTSU-1.

In sum, the logical connection between the ban on newspapers and (especially) the ban on personal photographs, on one hand, and the rehabilitation interests posited by petitioner, on the other, is at best highly questionable. Moreover, petitioner did not introduce evidence that his proposed theory of behavior modification has any basis in human psychology, or that the challenged rule has in fact had any rehabilitative effect on LTSU-2 inmates.

What is perhaps most troubling about the prison regulation at issue in this case is that the rule comes perilously close to a state-sponsored effort at mind control. In this case, the complete prohibition on secular, nonlegal newspapers, newsletters, and magazines prevents prisoners from "receiv[ing] suitable access to social, political, esthetic, moral, and other ideas," which are central to the development and preservation of individual identity, and are clearly protected by the First Amendment. Similarly, the ban on personal photographs, for at least some inmates, interferes with the capacity to remember loved ones, which is undoubtedly a core part of a person's "sphere of intellect and spirit." Moreover, it is difficult to imagine a context in which these First Amendment infringements could be more severe; LTSU-2 inmates are in solitary confinement for 23 hours a day with no access to radio or television, are not permitted to make phone calls except in cases of emergency, and may only have one visitor per month. They are essentially isolated from any meaningful contact with the outside world. The severity of the constitutional deprivations at issue in this case should give us serious pause before concluding, as a matter of law, that the challenged regulation is consistent with the sovereign's duty to treat prisoners in accordance with "the ethical tradition that accords respect to the dignity and worth of every individual."

d. The Speech Rights of Government Employees (new)

The Supreme Court has held that the government may not punish the speech of public employees if it involves matters of public concern unless the state can prove that the needs of the government outweigh the speech rights of the employee. In other words, speech by public employees is clearly less protected than other speech; First Amendment protection does not exist unless the expression is about public concern, and even then, the employee can be disciplined or fired if the government can show, on balance, that the efficient operation of the office justified the action. *See, e.g., Pickering v. Board of Education*, 391 U.S. 563 (1968).

In *Garcetti v. Ceballos*, below, the Court imposed a significant new limit on constitutional protection for the speech of government employees. The Court held that such speech is not protected if it is by a government employee while on the job and as part of his or her duties.

GARCETTI v. CEBALLOS
126 S. Ct. 1951 (2006)

Justice KENNEDY delivered the opinion of the Court.

It is well settled that "a State cannot condition public employment on a basis that infringes the employee's constitutionally protected interest in freedom of expression." *Connick v. Myers* (1983). The question presented by the instant case is whether the First Amendment protects a government employee from discipline based on speech made pursuant to the employee's official duties.

I

Respondent Richard Ceballos has been employed since 1989 as a deputy district attorney for the Los Angeles County District Attorney's Office. During the period relevant to this case, Ceballos was a calendar deputy in the office's Pomona branch, and in this capacity he exercised certain supervisory responsibilities over other lawyers. In February 2000, a defense attorney contacted Ceballos about a pending criminal case. The defense attorney said there were inaccuracies in an affidavit used to obtain a critical search warrant. The attorney informed Ceballos that he had filed a motion to traverse, or challenge, the warrant, but he also wanted Ceballos to review the case. According to Ceballos, it was not unusual for defense attorneys to ask calendar deputies to investigate aspects of pending cases. After examining the affidavit and visiting the location it described, Ceballos determined the affidavit contained serious misrepresentations. The affidavit called a long driveway what Ceballos thought should have been referred to as a separate roadway. Ceballos also questioned the affidavit's statement that tire tracks led from a stripped-down truck to the premises covered by the warrant. His doubts arose from his conclusion that the roadway's composition in some places made it difficult or impossible to leave visible tire tracks.

Ceballos spoke on the telephone to the warrant affiant, a deputy sheriff from the Los Angeles County Sheriff's Department, but he did not receive a satisfactory explanation for the perceived inaccuracies. He relayed his findings to his supervisors, petitioners Carol Najera and Frank Sundstedt, and followed up by preparing a disposition memorandum. The memo explained Ceballos' concerns and recommended dismissal of the case.

Despite Ceballos' concerns, Sundstedt decided to proceed with the prosecution, pending disposition of the defense motion to traverse. The trial court held a hearing on the motion. Ceballos was called by the defense and recounted his observations about the affidavit, but the trial court rejected the challenge to the warrant.

Ceballos claims that in the aftermath of these events he was subjected to a series of retaliatory employment actions. The actions included reassignment from his calendar deputy position to a trial deputy position, transfer to another courthouse, and denial of a promotion. 25 S.Ct. 1395, 161 L.Ed.2d 188 (2005), and we now reverse.

II

As the Court's decisions have noted, for many years "the unchallenged dogma was that a public employee had no right to object to conditions placed upon the terms of employment—including those which restricted the exercise of constitutional rights." That dogma has been qualified in important respects. The Court has made clear that public employees do not surrender all their First Amendment rights by reason of their employment. Rather, the First Amendment protects a public employee's right, in certain circumstances, to speak as a citizen addressing matters of public concern.

Pickering and the cases decided in its wake identify two inquiries to guide interpretation of the constitutional protections accorded to public employee speech. The first requires determining whether the employee spoke as a citizen on a matter of public concern. If the answer is no, the employee has no First Amendment cause of action based on his or her employer's reaction to the speech. If the answer is yes, then the possibility of a First Amendment claim arises. The question becomes whether the relevant government entity had an adequate justification for treating the employee differently from any other member of the general public. This consideration reflects the importance of the relationship between the speaker's expressions and employment. A government entity has broader discretion to restrict speech when it acts in its role as employer, but the restrictions it imposes must be directed at speech that has some potential to affect the entity's operations.

When a citizen enters government service, the citizen by necessity must accept certain limitations on his or her freedom. Government employers, like private employers, need a significant degree of control over their employees' words and actions; without it, there would be little chance for the efficient provision of public services. Public employees, moreover, often occupy trusted positions in society. When they speak out, they can express views that contravene governmental policies or impair the proper performance of governmental functions.

At the same time, the Court has recognized that a citizen who works for the government is nonetheless a citizen. The First Amendment limits the ability of a public employer to leverage the employment relationship to restrict, incidentally or intentionally, the liberties employees enjoy in their capacities as private citizens. So long as employees are speaking as citizens about matters of public concern, they must face only those speech restrictions that are necessary for their employers to operate efficiently and effectively.

III

With these principles in mind we turn to the instant case. Respondent Ceballos believed the affidavit used to obtain a search warrant contained serious misrepresentations. He conveyed his opinion and recommendation in a memo to his supervisor. That Ceballos expressed his views inside his office, rather than publicly, is not dispositive. Employees in some cases may receive First Amendment protection for expressions made at work. Many citizens do much of their talking inside their respective workplaces, and it would not serve the goal of treating public employees like "any member of the general public," to hold that all speech within the office is automatically exposed to restriction.

The memo concerned the subject matter of Ceballos' employment, but this, too, is nondispositive. The First Amendment protects some expressions related to the speaker's job.

The controlling factor in Ceballos' case is that his expressions were made pursuant to his duties as a calendar deputy. That consideration – the fact that Ceballos spoke as a prosecutor fulfilling a responsibility to advise his supervisor about how best to proceed with a pending case – distinguishes Ceballos' case from those in which the First Amendment provides protection against discipline. We hold that when public employees make statements pursuant to their official duties, the employees are not speaking as citizens for First Amendment purposes, and the Constitution does not insulate their communications from employer discipline. Ceballos wrote his disposition memo because that is part of what he, as a calendar deputy, was employed to do. It is immaterial whether he experienced some personal gratification from writing the memo; his First Amendment rights do not depend on his job satisfaction. The significant point is that the memo was written pursuant to Ceballos' official duties. Restricting speech that owes its existence to a public employee's professional responsibilities does not infringe any liberties the employee might have enjoyed as a private citizen. It simply reflects the exercise of employer control over what the employer itself has commissioned or created.

Ceballos did not act as a citizen when he went about conducting his daily professional activities, such as supervising attorneys, investigating charges, and preparing filings. In the same way he did not speak as a citizen by writing a memo that addressed the proper disposition of a pending criminal case. When he went to work and performed the tasks he was paid to perform, Ceballos acted as a government employee. The fact that his duties sometimes required him to speak or write does not mean his supervisors were prohibited from evaluating his performance.

This result is consistent with our precedents' attention to the potential societal value of employee speech. Our holding likewise is supported by the emphasis of our precedents on affording government employers sufficient discretion to manage their operations. Employers have heightened interests in controlling speech made by an employee in his or her professional capacity. Official communications have official consequences, creating a need for substantive consistency and clarity. Supervisors must ensure that their employees' official communications are accurate, demonstrate sound judgment, and promote the employer's mission. Ceballos' memo is illustrative. It demanded the attention of his supervisors and led to a heated meeting with employees from the sheriff's department. If Ceballos' superiors thought his memo was inflammatory or misguided, they had the authority to take proper corrective action.

Ceballos' proposed contrary rule, adopted by the Court of Appeals, would commit state and federal courts to a new, permanent, and intrusive role, mandating judicial oversight of communications between and among government employees and their superiors in the course of official business. This displacement of managerial discretion by judicial supervision finds no support in our precedents. When an employee speaks as a citizen addressing a matter of public concern, the First Amendment requires a delicate balancing of the competing interests surrounding the speech and its consequences. When, however, the employee is simply performing his or her job duties, there is no warrant for a similar degree of scrutiny. To hold otherwise would be to demand permanent judicial intervention in the conduct of governmental operations to a degree inconsistent with sound principles of federalism and the separation of powers.

Exposing governmental inefficiency and misconduct is a matter of considerable significance. As the Court noted in Connick, public employers should, "as a matter of good judgment," be "receptive to constructive criticism offered by their employees." The dictates of sound judgment are reinforced by the powerful network of legislative enactments—such as whistle-blower protection laws and labor codes—available to those who seek to expose wrongdoing. Cases involving government attorneys implicate additional safeguards in the form of, for example, rules of conduct and constitutional obligations apart from the First Amendment. These imperatives, as well as obligations arising from any other applicable constitutional provisions and mandates of the criminal and civil laws, protect employees and provide checks on supervisors who would order unlawful or otherwise inappropriate actions.

We reject, however, the notion that the First Amendment shields from discipline the expressions employees make pursuant to their professional duties. Our precedents do not support the existence of a constitutional cause of action behind every statement a public employee makes in the course of doing his or her job.

Justice STEVENS, dissenting.

The proper answer to the question "whether the First Amendment protects a government employee from discipline based on speech made pursuant to the employee's official duties," is "Sometimes," not "Never." Of course a supervisor may take corrective action when such speech is "inflammatory or misguided." But what if it is just unwelcome speech because it reveals facts that the supervisor would rather not have anyone else discover?

As Justice Souter explains, public employees are still citizens while they are in the office. The notion that there is a categorical difference between speaking as a citizen and speaking in the course of one's employment is quite wrong. Over a quarter of a century has passed since then-Justice Rehnquist, writing for a unanimous Court, rejected "the conclusion that a public employee forfeits his protection against governmental abridgment of freedom of speech if he decides to express his views privately rather than publicly." *Givhan v. Western Line Consol. School Dist.* (1979). We had no difficulty recognizing that the First Amendment applied when Bessie Givhan, an English teacher, raised concerns about the school's racist employment practices to the principal. Our silence as to whether or not her speech was made pursuant to her job duties demonstrates that the point was immaterial. That is equally true today, for it is senseless to let constitutional protection for exactly the same words hinge on whether they fall within a job description. Moreover, it seems perverse to fashion a new rule that provides employees with an incentive to voice their concerns publicly before talking frankly to their superiors.

Justice SOUTER, with whom Justice STEVENS and Justice GINSBURG join, dissenting.

The Court holds that "when public employees make statements pursuant to their official duties, the employees are not speaking as citizens for First Amendment purposes, and the Constitution does not insulate their communications from employer discipline." I respectfully dissent. I agree with the majority that a government employer has substantial interests in effectuating its chosen policy and objectives, and in demanding competence, honesty, and judgment from employees who speak for it in doing their work. But I would hold that private and public interests in addressing official wrongdoing and threats to health and safety can outweigh the government's stake in the efficient implementation of policy, and when they do public employees who speak on these matters in the course of their duties should be eligible to claim First Amendment protection.

Open speech by a private citizen on a matter of public importance lies at the heart of expression subject to protection by the First Amendment. At the other extreme, a statement by a government employee complaining about nothing beyond treatment under personnel rules raises no greater claim to constitutional protection against retaliatory response than the remarks of a private employee. In between these points lies a public employee's speech unwelcome to the government but on a significant public issue. Such an employee speaking as a citizen, that is, with a citizen's interest, is protected from reprisal unless the statements are too damaging to the government's capacity to conduct public business to be justified by any individual or public benefit thought to flow from the statements. *Pickering v. Board of Ed. of Township High School Dist.* 205, Will Cty. (1968). Entitlement to protection is thus not absolute.

This significant, albeit qualified, protection of public employees who irritate the government is understood to flow from the First Amendment, in part, because a government paycheck does nothing to eliminate the value to an individual of speaking on public matters, and there is no good reason for categorically discounting a speaker's interest in commenting on a matter of public concern just because the government employs him. Still, the First Amendment safeguard rests on something more, being the value to the public of receiving the opinions and information that a public employee may disclose. "Government employees are often in the best position to know what ails the agencies for which they work." The reason that protection of employee speech is qualified is that it can distract co-workers and supervisors from their tasks at hand and thwart the implementation of legitimate policy, the risks of which grow greater the closer the employee's speech gets to commenting on his own workplace and responsibilities. It is one thing for an office clerk to say there is waste in government and quite another to charge that his own department pays full-time salaries to part-time workers. Even so, we have regarded eligibility for protection by *Pickering* balancing as the proper approach when an employee speaks critically about the administration of his own government employer.

Nothing, then, accountable on the individual and public side of the *Pickering* balance changes when an employee speaks "pursuant" to public duties. On the side of the government employer, however, something is different, and to this extent, I agree with the majority of the Court. The majority is rightly concerned that the employee who speaks out on matters subject to comment in doing his own work has the greater leverage to create office uproars and fracture the government's authority to set policy to be carried out coherently through the ranks. "Official communications have official consequences, creating a need for substantive consistency and clarity. Supervisors must ensure that their employees' official communications are accurate, demonstrate sound judgment, and promote the employer's mission." Up to a point, then, the majority makes good points: government needs civility in the workplace, consistency in policy, and honesty and competence in public service.

But why do the majority's concerns, which we all share, require categorical exclusion of First Amendment protection against any official retaliation for things said on the job? Is it not possible to respect the unchallenged individual and public interests in the speech through a *Pickering* balance without drawing the strange line I mentioned before? This is, to be sure, a matter of judgment, but the judgment has to account for the undoubted value of speech to those, and by those, whose specific public job responsibilities bring them face to face with wrongdoing and incompetence in government, who refuse to avert their eyes and shut their mouths. And it has to account for the need actually to disrupt government if its officials are corrupt or dangerously incompetent. It is thus no adequate justification for the suppression of potentially valuable information simply to recognize that the government has a huge interest in managing its employees and preventing the occasionally irresponsible one from turning his job into a bully pulpit. Even there, the lesson of *Pickering* (and the object of most constitutional adjudication) is still to the point: when constitutionally significant interests clash, resist the demand for winner-take-all; try to make adjustments that serve all of the values at stake.

Justice BREYER, dissenting.

This case asks whether the First Amendment protects public employees when they engage in speech that both (1) involves matters of public concern and (2) takes place in the ordinary course of performing the duties of a government job. The majority answers the question by holding that "when public employees make statements pursuant to their official duties, the employees are not speaking as citizens for First Amendment purposes, and the Constitution does not insulate their communications from employer discipline." Ante, at 1960. In a word, the majority says, "never." That word, in my view, is too absolute.

Like the majority, I understand the need to "affor[d] government employers sufficient discretion to manage their operations." And I agree that the Constitution does not seek to "displac[e] . . . managerial discretion by judicial supervision." Nonetheless, there may well be circumstances with special demand for constitutional protection of the speech at issue, where governmental justifications may be limited, and where administrable standards seem readily available—to the point where the majority's fears of department management by lawsuit are misplaced. In such an instance, I believe that courts should apply the *Pickering* standard, even though the government employee speaks upon matters of public concern in the course of his ordinary duties.

This is such a case. The respondent, a government lawyer, complained of retaliation, in part, on the basis of speech contained in his disposition memorandum that he says fell within the scope of his obligations under *Brady v.*

Maryland (1963). The facts present two special circumstances that together justify First Amendment review.

First, the speech at issue is professional speech—the speech of a lawyer. Such speech is subject to independent regulation by canons of the profession. Those canons provide an obligation to speak in certain instances. And where that is so, the government's own interest in forbidding that speech is diminished.

Second, the Constitution itself here imposes speech obligations upon the government's professional employee. A prosecutor has a constitutional obligation to learn of, to preserve, and to communicate with the defense about exculpatory and impeachment evidence in the government's possession. Hence, I would find that the Constitution mandates special protection of employee speech in such circumstances. Thus I would apply the *Pickering* balancing test here.

I conclude that the First Amendment sometimes does authorize judicial actions based upon a government employee's speech that both (1) involves a matter of public concern and also (2) takes place in the course of ordinary job-related duties. But it does so only in the presence of augmented need for constitutional protection and diminished risk of undue judicial interference with governmental management of the public's affairs. In my view, these conditions are met in this case and *Pickering* balancing is consequently appropriate.

Chapter 10

First Amendment: Religion

B. The Free Exercise Clause (casebook, p. 1463)

Is a law to protect free exercise of religion a violation of the Establishment Clause? As described in Employment Division v. Smith (casebook, p. 1464), the Court narrowly interpreted the protections of the Free Exercise Clause of the First Amendment. The Religious Freedom Restoration Act was adopted in 1993 to restore religious freedom by statute to what it previously had been under the Constitution (casebook, p. 1477). But in City of Boerne v. Flores (casebook, p. 216), this law was declared unconstitutional as applied to state and local governments. Congress then adopted the Religious Land Use and Institutionalized Persons Act. It requires strict scrutiny for state and local government actions that significantly burden religion concerning land use or institutionalized persons. In *Cutter v. Wilkinson*, the Court considered whether this law violates the Establishment Clause.

CUTTER v. WILKINSON
125 S. Ct. 2113 (2005)

Justice GINSBURG delivered the opinion of the Court.

Section 3 of the Religious Land Use and Institutionalized Persons Act of 2000 (RLUIPA), provides in part: "No government shall impose a substantial burden on the religious exercise of a person residing in or confined to an institution," unless the burden furthers "a compelling governmental interest," and does so by "the least restrictive means." Plaintiffs below, petitioners here, are current and former inmates of institutions operated by the Ohio Department of Rehabilitation and Correction and assert that they are adherents of "nonmainstream" religions: the Satanist, Wicca, and Asatru religions, and the Church of Jesus Christ Christian. They complain that Ohio prison officials (respondents here), in violation of RLUIPA, have failed to accommodate their religious exercise "in a variety of different ways, including retaliating and discriminating against them for exercising their nontraditional faiths, denying them access to religious literature, denying them the same opportunities for group worship that are granted to adherents of mainstream religions, forbidding them to adhere to the dress and appearance mandates of their religions, withholding religious ceremonial items that are substantially identical to those that the adherents of mainstream religions are permitted, and failing to provide a chaplain trained in their faith."

In response to petitioners' complaints, respondent prison officials have mounted a facial challenge to the institutionalized-persons provision of RLUIPA; respondents contend that the Act improperly advances religion in violation of the First Amendment's Establishment Clause. The District Court denied respondents' motion to dismiss petitioners' complaints, but the Court of Appeals reversed that determination. The appeals court held, as the prison officials urged, that the portion of RLUIPA applicable to institutionalized persons violates the Establishment Clause. We reverse the Court of Appeals' judgment.

"This Court has long recognized that the government may . . . accommodate religious practices . . . without violating the Establishment Clause." Just last Term, in Locke v. Davey (2004), the Court reaffirmed that "there is room for play in the joints between" the Free Exercise and Establishment Clauses, allowing the government to accommodate religion beyond free exercise requirements, without offense to the Establishment Clause. "At some point, accommodation may devolve into an unlawful fostering of religion." But § 3 of RLUIPA, we hold, does not, on its face, exceed the limits of permissible government accommodation of religious practices.[1]

The Religion Clauses of the First Amendment provide: "Congress shall make no law respecting an establishment of religion, or prohibiting the free exercise thereof." The first of the two Clauses, commonly called the Establishment Clause, commands a separation of church and state. The second, the Free Exercise Clause, requires government respect for, and noninterference with, the religious beliefs and practices of our Nation's people. While the two Clauses express complementary values, they often exert conflicting pressures.

Our decisions recognize that "there is room for play in the joints" between the Clauses, some space for legislative action neither compelled by the Free Exercise Clause nor prohibited by the Establishment Clause. In accord with the majority of Courts of Appeals that have ruled on the question, we hold that § 3 of RLUIPA fits within the corridor between the Religion Clauses: On its face, the Act qualifies as a permissible legislative accommodation of religion that is not barred by the Establishment Clause.

Foremost, we find RLUIPA's institutionalized-persons provision compatible with the Establishment Clause because it alleviates exceptional government-created

---

1. Respondents argued below that RLUIPA exceeds Congress' legislative powers under the Spending and Commerce Clauses and violates the Tenth Amendment. The Sixth Circuit, having determined that RLUIPA violates the Establishment Clause, did not rule on respondents' further arguments. Respondents renew those arguments in this Court. Because these defensive pleas were not addressed by the Court of Appeals, and mindful that we are a court of review, not of first view, we do not consider them here. [Footnote by Justice Ginsburg.]

burdens on private religious exercise. Furthermore, the Act on its face does not founder on shoals our prior decisions have identified: Properly applying RLUIPA, courts must take adequate account of the burdens a requested accommodation may impose on nonbeneficiaries, and they must be satisfied that the Act's prescriptions are and will be administered neutrally among different faiths.

"[T]he 'exercise of religion' often involves not only belief and profession but the performance of . . . physical acts [such as] assembling with others for a worship service [or] participating in sacramental use of bread and wine . . . . " Section 3 covers state-run institutions—mental hospitals, prisons, and the like— in which the government exerts a degree of control unparalleled in civilian society and severely disabling to private religious exercise. RLUIPA thus protects institutionalized persons who are unable freely to attend to their religious needs and are therefore dependent on the government's permission and accommodation for exercise of their religion.

We note in this regard the Federal Government's accommodation of religious practice by members of the military. In Goldman v. Weinberger (1986), we held that the Free Exercise Clause did not require the Air Force to exempt an Orthodox Jewish officer from uniform dress regulations so that he could wear a yarmulke indoors. Congress responded to Goldman by prescribing that "a member of the armed forces may wear an item of religious apparel while wearing the uniform," unless "the wearing of the item would interfere with the performance [of] military duties [or] the item of apparel is not neat and conservative."

We do not read RLUIPA to elevate accommodation of religious observances over an institution's need to maintain order and safety. Our decisions indicate that an accommodation must be measured so that it does not override other significant interests. We have no cause to believe that RLUIPA would not be applied in an appropriately balanced way, with particular sensitivity to security concerns. While the Act adopts a "compelling governmental interest" standard, "[c]ontext matters" in the application of that standard. Lawmakers supporting RLUIPA were mindful of the urgency of discipline, order, safety, and security in penal institutions. They anticipated that courts would apply the Act's standard with "due deference to the experience and expertise of prison and jail administrators in establishing necessary regulations and procedures to maintain good order, security and discipline, consistent with consideration of costs and limited resources."

Finally, RLUIPA does not differentiate among bona fide faiths. RLUIPA presents no such defect. It confers no privileged status on any particular religious sect, and singles out no bona fide faith for disadvantageous treatment.

The Sixth Circuit misread our precedents to require invalidation of RLUIPA as "impermissibly advancing religion by giving greater protection to religious rights than to other constitutionally protected rights." Were the Court of Appeals' view the correct reading of our decisions, all manner of religious accommodations would fall. Congressional permission for members of the military to wear religious apparel while in uniform would fail, as would accommodations Ohio itself makes. Ohio could not, as it now does, accommodate "traditionally recognized" religions. The State provides inmates with chaplains "but not with publicists or political consultants," and allows "prisoners to assemble for worship, but not for political rallies."

In upholding RLUIPA's institutionalized-persons provision, we emphasize that respondents "have raised a facial challenge to [the Act's] constitutionality, and have not contended that under the facts of any of [petitioners'] specific cases . . . [that] applying RLUIPA would produce unconstitutional results." Should inmate requests for religious accommodations become excessive, impose unjustified burdens on other institutionalized persons, or jeopardize the effective functioning of an institution, the facility would be free to resist the imposition. In that event, adjudication in as-applied challenges would be in order.

Justice THOMAS, concurring.

I join the opinion of the Court. I agree with the Court that the Religious Land Use and Institutionalized Persons Act of 2000 (RLUIPA) is constitutional under our modern Establishment Clause case law. I write to explain why a proper historical understanding of the Clause as a federalism provision leads to the same conclusion.[2]

The Establishment Clause provides that "Congress shall make no law respecting an establishment of religion." Amdt. 1. As I have explained, an important function of the Clause was to "ma[ke] clear that Congress could not interfere with state establishments." The Clause, then, "is best understood as a federalism provision" that "protects state establishments from federal interference." In other words, Ohio asserts that the Clause protects the States from federal interference with otherwise constitutionally permissible choices regarding religious policy. In Ohio's view, RLUIPA intrudes on such state policy choices and hence violates the Clause.

Ohio's vision of the range of protected state authority overreads the Clause. Ohio and its amici contend that, even though "States can no longer establish preferred churches" because the Clause has been incorporated against the States through the Fourteenth Amendment, "Congress is as unable as ever to contravene constitutionally permissible State choices regarding religious policy." That is not what the Clause says. The Clause prohibits Congress from enacting legislation "respecting an establishment of religion"; it does not prohibit Congress from enacting legislation "respecting religion" or "taking cognizance of religion."

As noted above, RLUIPA may well exceed the spending power. Nonetheless, while Congress' condition stands, the States subject themselves to that condition

---

2. [T]though RLUIPA is entirely consonant with the Establishment Clause, it may well exceed Congress' authority under either the Spending Clause or the Commerce Clause. See Sabri v. United States (2004) (Thomas, J., concurring in judgment) (for a spending clause condition on a State's receipt of funds to be "Necessary and Proper" to the expenditure of the funds, there must be "some obvious, simple, and direct relation" between the condition and the expenditure of the funds). [Footnote by Justice Thomas.]

by voluntarily accepting federal funds. The States' voluntary acceptance of Congress' condition undercuts Ohio's argument that Congress is encroaching on its turf.

In *Gonzales v. O Centro Espirita Beneficente Uniao Do*, 126 S.Ct. 1211 (2006), the Supreme Court applied the Religious Freedom Restoration Act to the federal government. Although the Court did not expressly address the issue of whether the statute is constitutional as applied to the federal government, the Court did use the Act to rule in favor of a religion and against the federal government. The case involved a small religion, with relatively few adherents in the United States, whose members receive communion by drinking hoasca, a tea brewed from plants unique to the Amazon rainforest that contains a hallucinogen regulated under Schedule I of the Controlled Substances Act. Members of the religion brought a suit seeking a declaratory judgment that their use of the tea was protected by the Religious Freedom Restoration Act.

Chief Justice Roberts wrote for a unanimous Court and ruled in favor of the religion. In response to the government's claim of a need to stop the availability of hallucinogenic drugs, the Court stated: "RFRA requires the Government to demonstrate that the compelling interest test is satisfied through application of the challenged law 'to the person'—the particular claimant whose sincere exercise of religion is being substantially burdened. RFRA expressly adopted the compelling interest test 'as set forth in *Sherbert v. Verner* (1963) and *Wisconsin v. Yoder* (1972).' In each of those cases, this Court looked beyond broadly formulated interests justifying the general applicability of government mandates and scrutinized the asserted harm of granting specific exemptions to particular religious claimants."

Applying this test, the Court concluded: "Under the more focused inquiry required by RFRA and the compelling interest test, the Government's mere invocation of the general characteristics of Schedule I substances, as set forth in the Controlled Substances Act, cannot carry the day. It is true, of course, that Schedule I substances are exceptionally dangerous. Nevertheless, there is no indication that Congress considered the harms posed by the particular use at issue here — the circumscribed, sacramental use of hoasca by [this religion]."

The case indicates that RFRA is applicable to the federal government and that the Court approves a rigorous application of strict scrutiny under the statute.

C. The Establishment Clause

1. Competing Theories of the Establishment Clause (casebook, p. 1486)

The competing theories of the Establishment Clause were very much in evidence in two Supreme Court decisions concerning Ten Commandments displays: McCreary County,. v. ACLU of Kentucky and Van Orden v. Perry. In reading these cases, it is important to identify the different approaches that the Justices take with regard to the Establishment Clause. The Court declared the display in *McCreary County* unconstitutional, but upheld the display in *Van Orden*. In reading the decisions, consider whether there is a meaningful distinction between these cases. Also, it is important to consider what lower courts should do, in light of these decisions, if they are confronted with cases involving Ten Commandments monuments or other religious symbols.

MCCREARY COUNTY v. AMERICAN CIVIL LIBERTIES UNION OF KENTUCKY
125 S. Ct. 2722 (2005)

Justice SOUTER delivered the opinion of the Court

Executives of two counties posted a version of the Ten Commandments on the walls of their courthouses. After suits were filed charging violations of the Establishment Clause, the legislative body of each county adopted a resolution calling for a more extensive exhibit meant to show that the Commandments are Kentucky's "precedent legal code." The result in each instance was a modified display of the Commandments surrounded by texts containing religious references as their sole common element. After changing counsel, the counties revised the exhibits again by eliminating some documents, expanding the text set out in another, and adding some new ones.

The issues are whether a determination of the counties' purpose is a sound basis for ruling on the Establishment Clause complaints, and whether evaluation of the counties' claim of secular purpose for the ultimate displays may take their evolution into account. We hold that the counties' manifest objective may be dispositive of the constitutional enquiry, and that the development of the presentation should be considered when determining its purpose.

I

In the summer of 1999, petitioners McCreary County and Pulaski County, Kentucky (hereinafter Counties), put up in their respective courthouses large, gold-framed copies of an abridged text of the King James version of the Ten Commandments, including a citation to the Book of Exodus. In McCreary County, the placement of the Commandments responded to an order of the county legislative body requiring "the display [to] be posted in 'a very high traffic area' of the courthouse." In Pulaski County, amidst reported controversy over the propriety of the display, the Commandments were hung in a ceremony presided over by the county Judge-Executive, who called them "good rules to live by" and who recounted the story of an astronaut who became convinced "there must be a divine God" after viewing the Earth from the moon.

In November 1999, respondents American Civil Liberties Union of Kentucky et al. sued the Counties in Federal District Court and sought a preliminary injunction against maintaining the displays, which the ACLU charged were violations of the prohibition of religious establishment included in the First Amendment of the Constitution. Within a month, and before the District Court had responded to the request for injunction, the legislative body of each County authorized a second, expanded display, by nearly identical resolutions reciting that the Ten Commandments are "the precedent legal code upon which the civil and criminal codes of . . . Kentucky are founded," and stating several grounds for taking that position: that "the Ten Commandments are codified in Kentucky's civil and criminal laws"; that the Kentucky House of Representatives had in 1993 "voted unanimously . . . to adjourn . . . 'in remembrance and honor of Jesus Christ, the Prince of Ethics'"; that the "County Judge and . . . magistrates agree with the arguments set out by Judge [Roy] Moore" in defense of his "display [of] the Ten Commandments in his courtroom"; and that the "Founding Father[s] [had an] explicit understanding of the duty of elected officials to publicly acknowledge God as the source of America's strength and direction."

As directed by the resolutions, the Counties expanded the displays of the Ten Commandments in their locations, presumably along with copies of the resolution, which instructed that it, too, be posted. In addition to the first display's large framed copy of the edited King James version of the Commandments, the second included eight other documents in smaller frames, each either having a religious theme or excerpted to highlight a religious element. The documents were the "endowed by their Creator" passage from the Declaration of Independence; the Preamble to the Constitution of Kentucky; the national motto, "In God We Trust"; a page from the Congressional Record of February 2, 1983, proclaiming the Year of the Bible and including a statement of the Ten Commandments; a proclamation by President Abraham Lincoln designating April 30, 1863, a National Day of Prayer and Humiliation; an excerpt from President Lincoln's "Reply to Loyal Colored People of Baltimore upon Presentation of a Bible," reading that "[t]he Bible is the best gift God has ever given to man"; a proclamation by President Reagan marking 1983 the Year of the Bible; and the Mayflower Compact.

After argument, the District Court entered a preliminary injunction on May 5, 2000, ordering that the "display . . . be removed from [each] County Courthouse IMMEDIATELY" and that no county official "erect or cause to be erected similar displays."

The Counties filed a notice of appeal from the preliminary injunction but voluntarily dismissed it after hiring new lawyers. They then installed another display in each courthouse, the third within a year. No new resolution authorized this one, nor did the Counties repeal the resolutions that preceded the second. The posting consists of nine framed documents of equal size, one of them setting out the Ten Commandments explicitly identified as the "King James Version" at Exodus 20:3-17 and quoted at greater length than before:

Thou shalt have no other gods before me.

Thou shalt not make unto thee any graven image, or any likeness of any thing that is in heaven above, or that is in the earth beneath, or that is in the water underneath the earth: Thou shalt not bow down thyself to them, nor serve them: for I the LORD thy God am a jealous God, visiting the iniquity of the fathers upon the children unto the third and fourth generation of them that hate me.

Thou shalt not take the name of the LORD thy God in vain: for the LORD will not hold him guiltless that taketh his name in vain.

Remember the sabbath day, to keep it holy.

Honour thy father and thy mother: that thy days may be long upon the land which the LORD thy God giveth thee.

Thou shalt not kill.

Thou shalt not commit adultery.

Thou shalt not steal.

Thou shalt not bear false witness against thy neighbour.

Thou shalt not covet thy neighbour's house, thou shalt not covet th[y] neighbor's wife, nor his manservant, nor his maidservant, nor his ox, nor his ass, nor anything that is th[y] neighbour's.

Assembled with the Commandments are framed copies of the Magna Carta, the Declaration of Independence, the Bill of Rights, the lyrics of the Star Spangled Banner, the Mayflower Compact, the National Motto, the Preamble to the Kentucky Constitution, and a picture of Lady Justice. The collection is entitled "The Foundations of American Law and Government Display" and each document comes with a statement about its historical and legal significance. The comment on the Ten Commandments reads:

> The Ten Commandments have profoundly influenced the formation of Western legal thought and the formation of our country. That influence is clearly seen in the Declaration of Independence, which declared that "We hold these truths to be self-evident, that all men are created equal, that they are endowed by their Creator with certain unalienable Rights, that among these are Life, Liberty, and the pursuit of Happiness." The Ten Commandments provide the moral background of the Declaration of Independence and the foundation of our legal tradition.

II

Twenty-five years ago in a case prompted by posting the Ten Commandments in Kentucky's public schools, this Court recognized that the Commandments "are undeniably a sacred text in the Jewish and Christian faiths" and held that their display in public classrooms violated the First Amendment's bar against establishment of religion. Stone v. Graham (1980). *Stone* found a predominantly religious purpose in the government's posting of the Commandments, given their prominence as "'an instrument of religion.'" The Counties ask for a different approach here by arguing that official purpose is unknowable and the search for it inherently vain. In the alternative, the Counties would avoid the District Court's conclusion by having us limit the scope of the purpose enquiry so severely that any trivial rationalization would suffice, under a standard oblivious to the history of religious government action like the progression of exhibits in this case.

A

Ever since Lemon v. Kurtzman (1971) summarized the three familiar considerations for evaluating Establishment Clause claims, looking to whether government action has "a secular legislative purpose" has been a common, albeit seldom dispositive, element of our cases. Though we have found government action motivated by an illegitimate purpose only four times since *Lemon*, and "the secular purpose requirement alone may rarely be determinative . . . , it nevertheless serves an important function."

The touchstone for our analysis is the principle that the "First Amendment mandates governmental neutrality between religion and religion, and between religion and nonreligion." When the government acts with the ostensible and predominant purpose of advancing religion, it violates that central Establishment Clause value of official religious neutrality, there being no neutrality when the government's ostensible object is to take sides. Manifesting a purpose to favor one faith over another, or adherence to religion generally, clashes with the "understanding, reached . . . after decades of religious war, that liberty and social stability demand a religious tolerance that respects the religious views of all citizens. . . . " By showing a purpose to favor religion, the government "sends the . . . message to . . . nonadherents 'that they are outsiders, not full members of the political community, and an accompanying message to adherents that they are insiders, favored members. . . . '"

Indeed, the purpose apparent from government action can have an impact more significant than the result expressly decreed: when the government maintains Sunday closing laws, it advances religion only minimally because many working people would take the day as one of rest regardless, but if the government justified its decision with a stated desire for all Americans to honor Christ, the divisive thrust of the official action would be inescapable. This is the teaching of McGowan v. Maryland (1961), which upheld Sunday closing statutes on practical, secular grounds after finding that the government had forsaken the religious purposes behind centuries-old predecessor laws.

B

Despite the intuitive importance of official purpose to the realization of Establishment Clause values, the Counties ask us to abandon *Lemon*'s purpose test, or at least to truncate any enquiry into purpose here. Their first argument is that the very consideration of purpose is deceptive: according to them, true "purpose" is unknowable, and its search merely an excuse for courts to act selectively and unpredictably in picking out evidence of subjective intent. The assertions are as seismic as they are unconvincing.

Examination of purpose is a staple of statutory interpretation that makes up the daily fare of every appellate court in the country, and governmental purpose is a key element of a good deal of constitutional doctrine, e.g., Washington v. Davis (1976) (discriminatory purpose required for Equal Protection violation); Hunt v. Washington State Apple Advertising Comm'n (1977) (discriminatory purpose relevant to dormant Commerce Clause claim); Church of Lukumi Babalu Aye, Inc. v. Hialeah (1993) (discriminatory purpose raises level of scrutiny required by free exercise claim). With enquiries into purpose this common, if they were nothing but hunts for mares' nests deflecting attention from bare judicial will, the whole notion of purpose in law would have dropped into disrepute long ago.

But scrutinizing purpose does make practical sense, as in Establishment Clause analysis, where an understanding of official objective emerges from readily discoverable fact, without any judicial psychoanalysis of a drafter's heart of hearts. The eyes that look to purpose belong to an "'objective observer,'" one who takes account of the traditional external signs that show up in the "'text, legislative history, and implementation of the statute,'" or comparable official act. There is, then, nothing hinting at an unpredictable or disingenuous exercise when a court enquires into purpose after a claim is raised under the Establishment Clause.

Nor is there any indication that the enquiry is rigged in practice to finding a religious purpose dominant every time a case is filed. In the past, the test has not been fatal very often, presumably because government does not generally act unconstitutionally, with the predominant purpose of advancing religion. That said, one consequence of the corollary that Establishment Clause analysis does not look to the veiled psyche of government officers could be that in some of the cases in which establishment complaints failed, savvy officials had disguised their religious intent so cleverly that the objective observer just missed it. But that is no reason for great constitutional concern. If someone in the government hides religious motive so well that the "'objective observer, acquainted with the text, legislative history, and implementation of the statute,'" cannot see it, then without something more the government does not make a divisive announcement that in itself amounts to taking religious sides. A secret motive stirs up no strife and does nothing to make outsiders of non-adherents, and it suffices to wait and see whether such government action turns out to have (as it may even be likely to have) the illegitimate effect of advancing religion.

C

After declining the invitation to abandon concern with purpose wholesale, we also have to avoid the Counties' alternative tack of trivializing the enquiry into it. The Counties would read the cases as if the purpose enquiry were so naive that any transparent claim to secularity would satisfy it, and they would cut context out of the enquiry, to the point of ignoring history, no matter what bearing it actually had on the significance of current circumstances. There is no precedent for the Counties' arguments, or reason supporting them.

Lemon said that government action must have "a secular . . . purpose," and after a host of cases it is fair to add that although a legislature's stated reasons will generally get deference, the secular purpose required has to be genuine, not a sham, and not merely secondary to a religious objective.

The Counties' second proffered limitation can be dispatched quickly. They argue that purpose in a case like this one should be inferred, if at all, only from the latest news about the last in a series of governmental actions, however close they may all be in time and subject. But the world is not made brand new every morning, and the Counties are simply asking us to ignore perfectly probative evidence; they want an absentminded objective observer, not one presumed to be familiar with the history of the government's actions and competent to learn what history has to show. The Counties' position just bucks common sense: reasonable observers have reasonable memories, and our precedents sensibly forbid an observer "to turn a blind eye to the context in which [the] policy arose."

III

This case comes to us on appeal from a preliminary injunction. We accordingly review the District Court's legal rulings de novo, and its ultimate conclusion for abuse of discretion.

We take *Stone* as the initial legal benchmark, our only case dealing with the constitutionality of displaying the Commandments. *Stone* recognized that the Commandments are an "instrument of religion" and that, at least on the facts before it, the display of their text could presumptively be understood as meant to advance religion: although state law specifically required their posting in public school classrooms, their isolated exhibition did not leave room even for an argument that secular education explained their being there. But *Stone* did not purport to decide the constitutionality of every possible way the Commandments might be set out by the government, and under the Establishment Clause detail is key. Hence, we look to the record of evidence showing the progression leading up to the third display of the Commandments.

The display rejected in *Stone* had two obvious similarities to the first one in the sequence here: both set out a text of the Commandments as distinct from any traditionally symbolic representation, and each stood alone, not part of an arguably secular display. *Stone* stressed the significance of integrating the Commandments into a secular scheme to forestall the broadcast of an otherwise clearly religious message, and for good reason, the Commandments being a central point of reference in the religious and moral history of Jews and Christians. They proclaim the existence of a monotheistic god (no other gods). They regulate details of religious obligation (no graven images, no sabbath breaking, no vain oath swearing). And they unmistakably rest even the universally accepted prohibitions (as against murder, theft, and the like) on the sanction of the divinity proclaimed at the beginning of the text. Displaying that text is thus different from a symbolic depiction, like tablets with 10 roman numerals, which could be seen as alluding to a general notion of law, not a sectarian conception of faith. Where the text is set out, the insistence of the religious message is hard to avoid in the absence of a context plausibly suggesting a message going beyond an excuse to promote the religious point of view. The display in *Stone* had no context that might have indicated an object beyond the religious character of the text, and the Counties' solo exhibit here did nothing more to counter the sectarian implication than the postings at issue in *Stone*. Actually, the posting by the Counties lacked even the *Stone* display's implausible disclaimer that the Commandments were set out to show their effect on the civil law. What is more, at the ceremony for posting the framed Commandments in Pulaski County, the county executive was accompanied by his pastor, who testified to the certainty of the existence of God. The reasonable observer could only think that the Counties meant to emphasize and celebrate the Commandments' religious message.

This is not to deny that the Commandments have had influence on civil or secular law; a major text of a majority religion is bound to be felt. The point is simply that the original text viewed in its entirety is an unmistakably religious statement dealing with religious obligations and with morality subject to religious sanction. When the government initiates an effort to place this statement alone in public view, a religious object is unmistakable.

Once the Counties were sued, they modified the exhibits and invited additional insight into their purpose in a display that hung for about six months. This new one was the product of forthright and nearly identical Pulaski and McCreary County resolutions listing a series of American historical documents with theistic and Christian references, which were to be posted in order to furnish a setting for displaying the Ten Commandments and any "other Kentucky and American historical documen[t]" without raising concern about "any Christian or religious references" in them. As mentioned, the resolutions expressed support for an Alabama judge who posted the Commandments in his courtroom, and cited the fact the Kentucky Legislature once adjourned a session in honor of "Jesus Christ, Prince of Ethics."

In this second display, unlike the first, the Commandments were not hung in isolation, merely leaving the Counties' purpose to emerge from the pervasively religious text of the Commandments themselves. Instead, the second version was required to include the statement of the government's purpose expressly set out in the county resolutions, and underscored it by juxtaposing the Commandments to other documents with highlighted references to God as their sole common element. The display's unstinting focus was on religious passages, showing that the Counties were posting the Commandments precisely because of their sectarian content. That demonstration of the government's objective was enhanced by serial religious references and the accompanying resolution's claim about the embodiment of ethics in Christ. Together, the display and resolution presented an indisputable, and undisputed, showing of an impermissible purpose.

Today, the Counties make no attempt to defend their undeniable objective, but instead hopefully describe version two as "dead and buried." Their refusal to defend the second display is understandable, but the reasonable observer could not forget it.

After the Counties changed lawyers, they mounted a third display, without a new resolution or repeal of the old one. The result was the "Foundations of American Law and Government" exhibit, which placed the Commandments in the company of other documents the Counties thought especially significant in the historical foundation of American government.

These new statements of purpose were presented only as a litigating position, there being no further authorizing action by the Counties' governing boards. And although repeal of the earlier county authorizations would not have erased them from the record of evidence bearing on current purpose, the extraordinary resolutions for the second display passed just months earlier were not repealed or otherwise repudiated. Indeed, the sectarian spirit of the common resolution found enhanced expression in the third display, which quoted more of the purely religious language of the Commandments than the first two displays had done. No reasonable observer could swallow the claim that the Counties had cast off the objective so unmistakable in the earlier displays.

In holding the preliminary injunction adequately supported by evidence that the Counties' purpose had not changed at the third stage, we do not decide that the Counties' past actions forever taint any effort on their part to deal with the subject matter. We hold only that purpose needs to be taken seriously under the Establishment Clause and needs to be understood in light of context; an implausible claim that governmental purpose has changed should not carry the day in a court of law any more than in a head with common sense. It is enough to say here that district courts are fully capable of adjusting preliminary relief to take account of genuine changes in constitutionally significant conditions.

Nor do we have occasion here to hold that a sacred text can never be integrated constitutionally into a governmental display on the subject of law, or American history. We do not forget, and in this litigation have frequently been reminded, that our own courtroom frieze was deliberately designed in the exercise of governmental authority so as to include the figure of Moses holding tablets exhibiting a portion of the Hebrew text of the later, secularly phrased Commandments; in the company of 17 other lawgivers, most of them secular figures, there is no risk that Moses would strike an observer as evidence that the National Government was violating neutrality in religion.

IV

The importance of neutrality as an interpretive guide is no less true now than it was when the Court broached the principle in Everson v. Board of Ed. of Ewing (1947), and a word needs to be said about the different view taken in today's dissent. We all agree, of course, on the need for some interpretative help. The First Amendment contains no textual definition of "establishment," and the term is certainly not self-defining. No one contends that the prohibition of establishment stops at a designation of a national (or with Fourteenth Amendment incorporation, a state) church, but nothing in the text says just how much more it covers. There is no simple answer, for more than one reason.

The prohibition on establishment covers a variety of issues from prayer in widely varying government settings, to financial aid for religious individuals and institutions, to comment on religious questions. In these varied settings, issues of about interpreting inexact Establishment Clause language, like difficult interpretative issues generally, arise from the tension of competing values, each constitutionally respectable, but none open to realization to the logical limit.

The dissent, however, puts forward a limitation on the application of the neutrality principle, with citations to historical evidence said to show that the Framers understood the ban on establishment of religion as sufficiently narrow to allow the government to espouse submission to the divine will. The dissent identifies God as the God of monotheism, all of whose three principal strains (Jewish, Christian, and Muslim) acknowledge the religious importance of the Ten Commandments. On the dissent's view, it apparently follows that even rigorous espousal of a common element of this common monotheism is consistent with the establishment ban.

But the dissent's argument for the original understanding is flawed from the outset by its failure to consider the full range of evidence showing what the Framers believed. The dissent is certainly correct in putting forward evidence that some of the Framers thought some endorsement of religion was compatible with the establishment ban.

But the fact is that we do have more to go on, for there is also evidence supporting the proposition that the Framers intended the Establishment Clause to require governmental neutrality in matters of religion, including neutrality in statements acknowledging religion. The very language of the Establishment Clause represented a significant departure from early drafts that merely prohibited a single national religion, and, the final language instead "extended [the] prohibition to state support for 'religion' in general."

The historical record, moreover, is complicated beyond the dissent's account by the writings and practices of figures no less influential than Thomas Jefferson and James Madison. Jefferson, for example, refused to issue Thanksgiving Proclamations because he believed that they violated the Constitution. And Madison, whom the dissent claims as supporting its thesis, criticized Virginia's general assessment tax not just because it required people to donate "three pence" to religion, but because "it is itself a signal of persecution. It degrades from the equal rank of Citizens all those whose opinions in Religion do not bend to those of the Legislative authority."

The fair inference is that there was no common understanding about the limits of the establishment prohibition, and the dissent's conclusion that its narrower view was the original understanding stretches the evidence beyond tensile capacity. What the evidence does show is a group of statesmen, like others before and after them, who proposed a guarantee with contours not wholly worked out, leaving the Establishment Clause with edges still to be determined. And none the worse for that. Indeterminate edges are the kind to have in a constitution meant to endure, and to meet "exigencies which, if foreseen at all, must have been seen dimly, and which can be best provided for as they occur."

While the dissent fails to show a consistent original understanding from which to argue that the neutrality principle should be rejected, it does manage to deliver a surprise. As mentioned, the dissent says that the deity the Framers had in mind was the God of monotheism, with the consequence that government may espouse a tenet of traditional monotheism. This is truly a remarkable view. Today's dissent, however, apparently means that government should be free to approve the core beliefs of a favored religion over the tenets of others, a view that should trouble anyone who prizes religious liberty. Certainly history cannot justify it; on the contrary, history shows that the religion of concern to the Framers was not that of the monotheistic faiths generally, but Christianity in particular, a fact that no member of this Court takes as a premise for construing the Religion Clauses.

Historical evidence thus supports no solid argument for changing course (whatever force the argument might have when directed at the existing precedent), whereas public discourse at the present time certainly raises no doubt about the value of the interpretative approach invoked for 60 years now. We are centuries away from the St. Bartholomew's Day massacre and the treatment of heretics in early Massachusetts, but the divisiveness of religion in current public life is inescapable. This is no time to deny the prudence of understanding the Establishment Clause to require the Government to stay neutral on religious belief, which is reserved for the conscience of the individual.

Justice O'CONNOR, concurring.

I join in the Court's opinion. The First Amendment expresses our Nation's fundamental commitment to religious liberty by means of two provisions—one protecting the free exercise of religion, the other barring establishment of religion.

They were written by the descendents of people who had come to this land precisely so that they could practice their religion freely. Together with the other First Amendment guarantees—of free speech, a free press, and the rights to assemble and petition— the Religion Clauses were designed to safeguard the freedom of conscience and belief that those immigrants had sought. They embody an idea that was once considered radical: Free people are entitled to free and diverse thoughts, which government ought neither to constrain nor to direct.

Reasonable minds can disagree about how to apply the Religion Clauses in a given case. But the goal of the Clauses is clear: to carry out the Founders' plan of preserving religious liberty to the fullest extent possible in a pluralistic society.

By enforcing the Clauses, we have kept religion a matter for the individual conscience, not for the prosecutor or bureaucrat. At a time when we see around the world the violent consequences of the assumption of religious authority by government, Americans may count themselves fortunate: Our regard for constitutional boundaries has protected us from similar travails, while allowing private religious exercise to flourish. The well-known statement that "[w]e are a religious people" has proved true. Americans attend their places of worship more often than do citizens of other developed nations, and describe religion as playing an especially important role in their lives. Those who would renegotiate the boundaries between church and state must therefore answer a difficult question: Why would we trade a system that has served us so well for one that has served others so poorly?

When we enforce these restrictions, we do so for the same reason that guided the Framers—respect for religion's special role in society. Our Founders conceived of a Republic receptive to voluntary religious expression, and provided for the possibility of judicial intervention when government action threatens or impedes such expression. Voluntary religious belief and expression may be as threatened when government takes the mantle of religion upon itself as when government directly interferes with private religious practices. When the government associates one set of religious beliefs with the state and identifies nonadherents as outsiders, it encroaches upon the individual's decision about whether and how to worship. In the marketplace of ideas, the government has vast resources and special status. Government religious expression therefore risks crowding out private observance and distorting the natural interplay between competing beliefs. Allowing government to be a potential mouthpiece for competing religious ideas risks the sort of division that might easily spill over into suppression of rival beliefs. Tying secular and religious authority together poses risks to both.

Given the history of this particular display of the Ten Commandments, the Court correctly finds an Establishment Clause violation. The purpose behind the counties' display is relevant because it conveys an unmistakable message of endorsement to the reasonable observer. It is true that many Americans find the Commandments in accord with their personal beliefs. But we do not count heads before enforcing the First Amendment. Nor can we accept the theory that

Americans who do not accept the Commandments' validity are outside the First Amendment's protections. There is no list of approved and disapproved beliefs appended to the First Amendment—and the Amendment's broad terms do not admit of such a cramped reading.

It is true that the Framers lived at a time when our national religious diversity was neither as robust nor as well recognized as it is now. They may not have foreseen the variety of religions for which this Nation would eventually provide a home. They surely could not have predicted new religions, some of them born in this country. But they did know that line-drawing between religions is an enterprise that, once begun, has no logical stopping point. They worried that "the same authority which can establish Christianity, in exclusion of all other Religions, may establish with the same ease any particular sect of Christians, in exclusion of all other Sects." The Religion Clauses, as a result, protect adherents of all religions, as well as those who believe in no religion at all.

We owe our First Amendment to a generation with a profound commitment to religion and a profound commitment to religious liberty—visionaries who held their faith "with enough confidence to believe that what should be rendered to God does not need to be decided and collected by Caesar." In my opinion, the display at issue was an establishment of religion in violation of our Constitution. For the reasons given above, I join in the Court's opinion.

Justice SCALIA, with whom THE CHIEF JUSTICE and Justice THOMAS join, and with whom Justice KENNEDY joins as to Parts II and III, dissenting.

I would uphold McCreary County and Pulaski County, Kentucky's (hereinafter Counties) displays of the Ten Commandments. I shall discuss first, why the Court's oft repeated assertion that the government cannot favor religious practice is false; second, why today's opinion extends the scope of that falsehood even beyond prior cases; and third, why even on the basis of the Court's false assumptions the judgment here is wrong.

I

A

On September 11, 2001 I was attending in Rome, Italy an international conference of judges and lawyers, principally from Europe and the United States. That night and the next morning virtually all of the participants watched, in their hotel rooms, the address to the Nation by the President of the United States concerning the murderous attacks upon the Twin Towers and the Pentagon, in which thousands of Americans had been killed. The address ended, as Presidential addresses often do, with the prayer "God bless America." The next afternoon I was approached by one of the judges from a European country, who, after extending his profound condolences for my country's loss, sadly observed "How I wish that the Head of State of my country, at a similar time of national tragedy and distress, could conclude his address 'God bless _____.' It is of course absolutely forbidden."

That is one model of the relationship between church and state—a model spread across Europe by the armies of Napoleon, and reflected in the Constitution of France, which begins "France is [a] ... secular ... Republic." France Const., Art. 1. Religion is to be strictly excluded from the public forum. This is not, and never was, the model adopted by America. George Washington added to the form of Presidential oath prescribed by Art. II, § 1, cl. 8, of the Constitution, the concluding words "so help me God." The Supreme Court under John Marshall opened its sessions with the prayer, "God save the United States and this Honorable Court." The First Congress instituted the practice of beginning its legislative sessions with a prayer. The same week that Congress submitted the Establishment Clause as part of the Bill of Rights for ratification by the States, it enacted legislation providing for paid chaplains in the House and Senate. The day after the First Amendment was proposed, the same Congress that had proposed it requested the President to proclaim "a day of public thanksgiving and prayer, to be observed, by acknowledging, with grateful hearts, the many and signal favours of Almighty God." President Washington offered the first Thanksgiving Proclamation shortly thereafter, devoting November 26, 1789 on behalf of the American people "'to the service of that great and glorious Being who is the beneficent author of all the good that is, that was, or that will be,'" thus beginning a tradition of offering gratitude to God that continues today. The same Congress also reenacted the Northwest Territory Ordinance of 1787, Article III of which provided: "Religion, morality, and knowledge, being necessary to good government and the happiness of mankind, schools and the means of education shall forever be encouraged." And of course the First Amendment itself accords religion (and no other manner of belief) special constitutional protection.

These actions of our First President and Congress and the Marshall Court were not idiosyncratic; they reflected the beliefs of the period. Those who wrote the Constitution believed that morality was essential to the well-being of society and that encouragement of religion was the best way to foster morality. The "fact that the Founding Fathers believed devotedly that there was a God and that the unalienable rights of man were rooted in Him is clearly evidenced in their writings, from the Mayflower Compact to the Constitution itself."

Nor have the views of our people on this matter significantly changed. Presidents continue to conclude the Presidential oath with the words "so help me God." Our legislatures, state and national, continue to open their sessions with prayer led by official chaplains. The sessions of this Court continue to open with the prayer "God save the United States and this Honorable Court." Invocation of the Almighty by our public figures, at all levels of government, remains commonplace. Our coinage bears the motto "IN GOD WE TRUST." And our Pledge of Allegiance contains the acknowledgment that we are a Nation "under God." As one of our Supreme Court opinions rightly observed, "We are a religious people whose institutions presuppose a Supreme Being." Zorach v. Clauson (1952).

With all of this reality (and much more) staring it in the face, how can the Court possibly assert that "'the First Amendment mandates governmental neutrality between . . . religion and nonreligion,'" and that "[m]anifesting a purpose to favor . . . adherence to religion generally," is unconstitutional? Who says so? Surely not the words of the Constitution. Surely not the history and traditions that reflect our society's constant understanding of those words. Surely not even the current sense of our society, recently reflected in an Act of Congress adopted unanimously by the Senate and with only 5 nays in the House of Representatives, criticizing a Court of Appeals opinion that had held "under God" in the Pledge of Allegiance unconstitutional. Nothing stands behind the Court's assertion that governmental affirmation of the society's belief in God is unconstitutional except the Court's own say-so, citing as support only the unsubstantiated say-so of earlier Courts going back no farther than the mid-20th century. And it is, moreover, a thoroughly discredited say-so. It is discredited, to begin with, because a majority of the Justices on the current Court (including at least one Member of today's majority) have, in separate opinions, repudiated the brainspun *Lemon* test" that embodies the supposed principle of neutrality between religion and irreligion. And it is discredited because the Court has not had the courage (or the foolhardiness) to apply the neutrality principle consistently.

What distinguishes the rule of law from the dictatorship of a shifting Supreme Court majority is the absolutely indispensable requirement that judicial opinions be grounded in consistently applied principle. That is what prevents judges from ruling now this way, now that—thumbs up or thumbs down—as their personal preferences dictate.

Besides appealing to the demonstrably false principle that the government cannot favor religion over irreligion, today's opinion suggests that the posting of the Ten Commandments violates the principle that the government cannot favor one religion over another. That is indeed a valid principle where public aid or assistance to religion is concerned, or where the free exercise of religion is at issue, but it necessarily applies in a more limited sense to public acknowledgment of the Creator. If religion in the public forum had to be entirely nondenominational, there could be no religion in the public forum at all. One cannot say the word "God," or "the Almighty," one cannot offer public supplication or thanksgiving, without contradicting the beliefs of some people that there are many gods, or that God or the gods pay no attention to human affairs. With respect to public acknowledgment of religious belief, it is entirely clear from our Nation's historical practices that the Establishment Clause permits this disregard of polytheists and believers in unconcerned deities, just as it permits the disregard of devout atheists. The Thanksgiving Proclamation issued by George Washington at the instance of the First Congress was scrupulously nondenominational—but it was monotheistic. In Marsh v. Chambers (1983), we said that the fact the particular prayers offered in the Nebraska Legislature were "in the Judeo-Christian tradition" posed no additional problem, because "there is no indication that the prayer opportunity has been exploited to proselytize or advance any one, or to disparage any other, faith or belief."

Historical practices thus demonstrate that there is a distance between the acknowledgment of a single Creator and the establishment of a religion. The former is, as Marsh v. Chambers put it, "a tolerable acknowledgment of beliefs widely held among the people of this country." The three most popular religions in the United States, Christianity, Judaism, and Islam—which combined account for 97.7% of all believers—are monotheistic. All of them, moreover (Islam included), believe that the Ten Commandments were given by God to Moses, and are divine prescriptions for a virtuous life. Publicly honoring the Ten Commandments is thus indistinguishable, insofar as discriminating against other religions is concerned, from publicly honoring God. Both practices are recognized across such a broad and diverse range of the population—from Christians to Muslims—that they cannot be reasonably understood as a government endorsement of a particular religious viewpoint.

B

A few remarks are necessary in response to the criticism of this dissent by the Court. What is more probative of the meaning of the Establishment Clause than the actions of the very Congress that proposed it, and of the first President charged with observing it?

I must respond to Justice Stevens' assertion that I would "marginaliz[e] the belief systems of more than 7 million Americans" who adhere to religions that are not monotheistic. Surely that is a gross exaggeration. The beliefs of those citizens are entirely protected by the Free Exercise Clause, and by those aspects of the Establishment Clause that do not relate to government acknowledgment of the Creator. Invocation of God despite their beliefs is permitted not because nonmonotheistic religions cease to be religions recognized by the religion clauses of the First Amendment, but because governmental invocation of God is not an establishment. Justice Stevens fails to recognize that in the context of public acknowledgments of God there are legitimate competing interests: On the one hand, the interest of that minority in not feeling "excluded"; but on the other, the interest of the overwhelming majority of religious believers in being able to give God thanks and supplication as a people, and with respect to our national endeavors. Our national tradition has resolved that conflict in favor of the majority. It is not for this Court to change a disposition that accounts, many Americans think, for the phenomenon remarked upon in a quotation attributed to various authors, including Bismarck, but which I prefer to associate with Charles de Gaulle: "God watches over little children, drunkards, and the United States of America."

II

As bad as the *Lemon* test is, it is worse for the fact that, since its inception, its seemingly simple mandates have been manipulated to fit whatever result the Court aimed to achieve. Today's opinion is no different. In two respects it modifies *Lemon* to ratchet up the Court's hostility to religion. First, the Court justifies inquiry into legislative purpose, not as an end itself, but as a means to ascertain the appearance of the government action to an "'objective observer.'" Because in the Court's view the true danger to be guarded against is that the objective observer would feel like an "outside[r]" or "not [a] full membe[r] of the political community," its inquiry focuses not on the actual purpose of government action, but the "purpose apparent from government action." Under this approach, even if a government could show that its actual purpose was not to advance religion, it would presumably violate the Constitution as long as the Court's objective observer would think otherwise.

I have remarked before that it is an odd jurisprudence that bases the unconstitutionality of a government practice that does not actually advance religion on the hopes of the government that it would do so. But that oddity pales in comparison to the one invited by today's analysis: the legitimacy of a government action with a wholly secular effect would turn on the misperception of an imaginary observer that the government officials behind the action had the intent to advance religion.

Second, the Court replaces *Lemon*'s requirement that the government have "a secular . . . purpose" with the heightened requirement that the secular purpose "predominate" over any purpose to advance religion. The Court treats this extension as a natural outgrowth of the longstanding requirement that the government's secular purpose not be a sham, but simple logic shows the two to be unrelated. If the government's proffered secular purpose is not genuine, then the government has no secular purpose at all. The new demand that secular purpose predominate contradicts *Lemon*'s more limited requirement, and finds no support in our cases.

I have urged that *Lemon*'s purpose prong be abandoned, because (as I have discussed in Part I) even an exclusive purpose to foster or assist religious practice is not necessarily invalidating. But today's extension makes things even worse. By shifting the focus of *Lemon*'s purpose prong from the search for a genuine, secular motivation to the hunt for a predominantly religious purpose, the Court converts what has in the past been a fairly limited inquiry into a rigorous review of the full record. Those responsible for the adoption of the Religion Clauses would surely regard it as a bitter irony that the religious values they designed those Clauses to protect have now become so distasteful to this Court that if they constitute anything more than a subordinate motive for government action they will invalidate it.

III

Even accepting the Court's *Lemon*-based premises, the displays at issue here were constitutional. To any person who happened to walk down the hallway of the McCreary or Pulaski County Courthouse during the roughly nine months when the Foundations Displays were exhibited, the displays must have seemed unremarkable—if indeed they were noticed at all. The walls of both courthouses were already lined with historical documents and other assorted portraits; each Foundations Display was exhibited in the same format as these other displays and nothing in the record suggests that either County took steps to give it greater prominence. On its face, the Foundations Displays manifested the purely secular purpose that the Counties asserted before the District Court: "to display documents that played a significant role in the foundation of our system of law and government." That the Displays included the Ten Commandments did not transform their apparent secular purpose into one of impermissible advocacy for Judeo-Christian beliefs.

Acknowledgment of the contribution that religion has made to our Nation's legal and governmental heritage partakes of a centuries-old tradition. Display of the Ten Commandments is well within the mainstream of this practice of acknowledgment. Federal, State, and local governments across the Nation have engaged in such display. The Supreme Court Building itself includes depictions of Moses with the Ten Commandments in the Courtroom and on the east pediment of the building, and symbols of the Ten Commandments "adorn the metal gates lining the north and south sides of the Courtroom as well as the doors leading into the Courtroom." Similar depictions of the Decalogue appear on public buildings and monuments throughout our Nation's Capital. The frequency of these displays testifies to the popular understanding that the Ten Commandments are a foundation of the rule of law, and a symbol of the role that religion played, and continues to play, in our system of government.

VAN ORDEN v. PERRY
125 S. Ct. 2854 (2005)

Chief Justice REHNQUIST announced the judgment of the Court and delivered an opinion, in which Justice SCALIA, Justice KENNEDY, and Justice THOMAS join.

The question here is whether the Establishment Clause of the First Amendment allows the display of a monument inscribed with the Ten Commandments on the Texas State Capitol grounds. We hold that it does.

The 22 acres surrounding the Texas State Capitol contain 17 monuments and 21 historical markers commemorating the "people, ideals, and events that compose Texan identity." The monolith challenged here stands 6-feet high and 3½ feet wide. It is located to the north of the Capitol building, between the Capitol and the Supreme Court building. Its primary content is the text of the Ten Commandments. An eagle grasping the American flag, an eye inside of a pyramid, and two small tablets with what appears to be an ancient script are carved above the text of the Ten Commandments. Below the text are two Stars of David and the superimposed Greek letters Chi and Rho, which represent Christ. The bottom of the monument bears the inscription "PRESENTED TO THE PEOPLE AND YOUTH OF TEXAS BY THE FRATERNAL ORDER OF EAGLES OF TEXAS 1961."

The legislative record surrounding the State's acceptance of the monument from the Eagles—a national social, civic, and patriotic organization—is limited to legislative journal entries. After the monument was accepted, the State selected a site for the monument based on the recommendation of the state organization responsible for maintaining the Capitol grounds. The Eagles paid the cost of erecting the monument, the dedication of which was presided over by two state legislators.

Petitioner Thomas Van Orden is a native Texan and a resident of Austin. At one time he was a licensed lawyer, having graduated from Southern Methodist Law School. Van Orden testified that, since 1995, he has encountered the Ten Commandments monument during his frequent visits to the Capitol grounds. Forty years after the monument's erection and six years after Van Orden began to encounter the monument frequently, he sued numerous state officials in their official capacities seeking both a declaration that the monument's placement violates the Establishment Clause and an injunction requiring its removal.

Our cases, Januslike, point in two directions in applying the Establishment Clause. One face looks toward the strong role played by religion and religious traditions throughout our Nation's history. The other face looks toward the principle that governmental intervention in religious matters can itself endanger religious freedom.

This case, like all Establishment Clause challenges, presents us with the difficulty of respecting both faces. Our institutions presuppose a Supreme Being, yet these institutions must not press religious observances upon their citizens. One face looks to the past in acknowledgment of our Nation's heritage, while the other looks to the present in demanding a separation between church and state. Reconciling these two faces requires that we neither abdicate our responsibility to maintain a division between church and state nor evince a hostility to religion by disabling the government from in some ways recognizing our religious heritage.

These two faces are evident in representative cases both upholding and invalidating laws under the Establishment Clause. Over the last 25 years, we have sometimes pointed to Lemon v. Kurtzman (1971) as providing the governing test in Establishment Clause challenges. Yet, just two years after *Lemon* was decided, we noted that the factors identified in *Lemon* serve as "no more than helpful signposts." Many of our recent cases simply have not applied the *Lemon* test. Others have applied it only after concluding that the challenged practice was invalid under a different Establishment Clause test.

Whatever may be the fate of the *Lemon* test in the larger scheme of Establishment Clause jurisprudence, we think it not useful in dealing with the sort of passive monument that Texas has erected on its Capitol grounds. Instead, our analysis is driven both by the nature of the monument and by our Nation's history.

As we explained in Lynch v. Donnelly (1984): "There is an unbroken history of official acknowledgment by all three branches of government of the role of religion in American life from at least 1789." For example, both Houses passed resolutions in 1789 asking President George Washington to issue a Thanksgiving Day Proclamation to "recommend to the people of the United States a day of public thanksgiving and prayer, to be observed by acknowledging, with grateful hearts, the many and signal favors of Almighty God." President Washington's proclamation directly attributed to the Supreme Being the foundations and successes of our young Nation.

Recognition of the role of God in our Nation's heritage has also been reflected in our decisions. We have acknowledged, for example, that "religion has been closely identified with our history and government," and that "[t]he history of man is inseparable from the history of religion." This recognition has led us to hold that the Establishment Clause permits a state legislature to open its daily sessions with a prayer by a chaplain paid by the State. Marsh v. Chambers (1982). With similar reasoning, we have upheld laws, which originated from one of the Ten Commandments, that prohibited the sale of merchandise on Sunday. McGowan v. Maryland (1961).

In this case we are faced with a display of the Ten Commandments on government property outside the Texas State Capitol. Such acknowledgments of the role played by the Ten Commandments in our Nation's heritage are common throughout America. We need only look within our own Courtroom. Since 1935, Moses has stood, holding two tablets that reveal portions of the Ten Commandments written in Hebrew, among other lawgivers in the south frieze. Representations of the Ten Commandments adorn the metal gates lining the north and south sides of the Courtroom as well as the doors leading into the Courtroom. Moses also sits on the exterior east facade of the building holding the Ten Commandments tablets.

Similar acknowledgments can be seen throughout a visitor's tour of our Nation's Capital. For example, a large statue of Moses holding the Ten Commandments, alongside a statue of the Apostle Paul, has overlooked the rotunda of the Library of Congress' Jefferson Building since 1897. And the Jefferson Building's Great Reading Room contains a sculpture of a woman beside the Ten Commandments with a quote above her from the Old Testament (Micah 6:8). A medallion with two tablets depicting the Ten Commandments decorates the floor of the National Archives. Inside the Department of Justice, a statue entitled "The Spirit of Law" has two tablets representing the Ten Commandments lying at its feet. In front of the Ronald Reagan Building is another sculpture that includes a depiction of the Ten Commandments. So too a 24-foot-tall sculpture, depicting, among other things, the Ten Commandments and a cross, stands outside the federal courthouse that houses both the Court of Appeals and the District Court for the District of Columbia. Moses is also prominently featured in the Chamber of the United States House of Representatives.

Of course, the Ten Commandments are religious—they were so viewed at their inception and so remain. The monument, therefore, has religious significance. According to Judeo-Christian belief, the Ten Commandments were given to Moses by God on Mt. Sinai. But Moses was a lawgiver as well as a religious leader. And the Ten Commandments have an undeniable historical meaning, as the foregoing examples demonstrate. Simply having religious content or promoting a message consistent with a religious doctrine does not run afoul of the Establishment Clause.

There are, of course, limits to the display of religious messages or symbols. For example, we held unconstitutional a Kentucky statute requiring the posting of the Ten Commandments in every public schoolroom. Stone v. Graham (1980) (per curiam). In the classroom context, we found that the Kentucky statute had an improper and plainly religious purpose.

The placement of the Ten Commandments monument on the Texas State Capitol grounds is a far more passive use of those texts than was the case in *Stone*, where the text confronted elementary school students every day. Indeed, Van Orden, the petitioner here, apparently walked by the monument for a number of years before bringing this lawsuit. Texas has treated her Capitol grounds monuments as representing the several strands in the State's political and legal history. The inclusion of the Ten Commandments monument in this group has a dual significance, partaking of both religion and government. We cannot say that Texas' display of this monument violates the Establishment Clause of the First Amendment.

Justice SCALIA, concurring.

I join the opinion of The Chief Justice because I think it accurately reflects our current Establishment Clause jurisprudence—or at least the Establishment Clause jurisprudence we currently apply some of the time. I would prefer to reach the same result by adopting an Establishment Clause jurisprudence that is in accord with our Nation's past and present practices, and that can be consistently applied—the central relevant feature of which is that there is nothing unconstitutional in a State's favoring religion generally, honoring God through public prayer and acknowledgment, or, in a nonproselytizing manner, venerating the Ten Commandments.

Justice THOMAS, concurring.

The Court holds that the Ten Commandments monument found on the Texas State Capitol grounds does not violate the Establishment Clause. Rather than trying to suggest meaninglessness where there is meaning, The Chief Justice rightly recognizes that the monument has "religious significance." He properly recognizes the role of religion in this Nation's history and the permissibility of government displays acknowledging that history. For those reasons, I join The Chief Justice's opinion in full.

This case would be easy if the Court were willing to abandon the inconsistent guideposts it has adopted for addressing Establishment Clause challenges, and return to the original meaning of the Clause. I have previously suggested that the Clause's text and history "resis[t] incorporation" against the States. If the Establishment Clause does not restrain the States, then it has no application here, where only state action is at issue.

Even if the Clause is incorporated, or if the Free Exercise Clause limits the power of States to establish religions, our task would be far simpler if we returned to the original meaning of the word "establishment" than it is under the various approaches this Court now uses. The Framers understood an establishment "necessarily [to] involve actual legal coercion." "In other words, establishment at the founding involved, for example, mandatory observance or mandatory payment of taxes supporting ministers." And "government practices that have nothing to do with creating or maintaining . . . coercive state establishments" simply do not "implicate the possible liberty interest of being free from coercive state establishments."

There is no question that, based on the original meaning of the Establishment Clause, the Ten Commandments display at issue here is constitutional. In no sense does Texas compel petitioner Van Orden to do anything. The only injury to him is that he takes offense at seeing the monument as he passes it on his way to the Texas Supreme Court Library. He need not stop to read it or even to look at it, let alone to express support for it or adopt the Commandments as guides for his life. The mere presence of the monument along his path involves no coercion and thus does not violate the Establishment Clause.

Returning to the original meaning would do more than simplify our task. It also would avoid the pitfalls present in the Court's current approach to such challenges. This Court's precedent elevates the trivial to the proverbial "federal case," by making benign signs and postings subject to challenge. Even worse, the incoherence of the Court's decisions in this area renders the Establishment Clause impenetrable and incapable of consistent application. All told, this Court's jurisprudence leaves courts, governments, and believers and nonbelievers alike confused—an observation that is hardly new.

First, this Court's precedent permits even the slightest public recognition of religion to constitute an establishment of religion. Second, in a seeming attempt to balance out its willingness to consider almost any acknowledgment of religion an establishment, in other cases Members of this Court have concluded that the term or symbol at issue has no religious meaning by virtue of its ubiquity or rote ceremonial invocation. But words such as "God" have religious significance. For example, just last Term this Court had before it a challenge to the recitation of the Pledge of Allegiance, which includes the phrase "one Nation under God." The declaration that our country is "'one Nation under God'" necessarily "entail[s] an affirmation that God exists." This phrase is thus anathema to those who reject God's existence and a validation of His existence to those who accept it. Telling either nonbelievers or believers that the words "under God" have no meaning contradicts what they know to be true. Moreover, repetition does not deprive religious words or symbols of their traditional meaning. Words like "God" are not vulgarities for which the shock value diminishes with each successive utterance.

Finally, the very "flexibility" of this Court's Establishment Clause precedent leaves it incapable of consistent application. The inconsistency between the decisions the Court reaches today in this case and in McCreary County v. American Civil Liberties Union of Ky. (2005) only compounds the confusion.

Much, if not all, of this would be avoided if the Court would return to the views of the Framers and adopt coercion as the touchstone for our Establishment Clause inquiry. Every acknowledgment of religion would not give rise to an Establishment Clause claim. Courts would not act as theological commissions, judging the meaning of religious matters. Most important, our precedent would be capable of consistent and coherent application. While the Court correctly rejects the challenge to the Ten Commandments monument on the Texas Capitol grounds, a more fundamental rethinking of our Establishment Clause jurisprudence remains in order.

Justice BREYER, concurring in the judgment.

In School Dist. of Abington Township v. Schempp (1963), Justice Goldberg, joined by Justice Harlan, wrote, in respect to the First Amendment's Religion Clauses, that there is "no simple and clear measure which by precise application can readily and invariably demark the permissible from the impermissible." One must refer instead to the basic purposes of those Clauses. They seek to "assure the fullest possible scope of religious liberty and tolerance for all." They seek to avoid that divisiveness based upon religion that promotes social conflict, sapping the strength of government and religion alike. They seek to maintain that "separation of church and state" that has long been critical to the "peaceful dominion that religion exercises in [this] country," where the "spirit of religion" and the "spirit of freedom" are productively "united," "reign[ing] together" but in separate spheres "on the same soil."

The Court has made clear, as Justices Goldberg and Harlan noted, that the realization of these goals means that government must "neither engage in nor compel religious practices," that it must "effect no favoritism among sects or between religion and nonreligion," and that it must "work deterrence of no religious belief." The government must avoid excessive interference with, or promotion of, religion. But the Establishment Clause does not compel the government to purge from the public sphere all that in any way partakes of the religious. Such absolutism is not only inconsistent with our national traditions, but would also tend to promote the kind of social conflict the Establishment Clause seeks to avoid.

Thus, as Justices Goldberg and Harlan pointed out, the Court has found no single mechanical formula that can accurately draw the constitutional line in every case. Where the Establishment Clause is at issue, tests designed to measure "neutrality" alone are insufficient, both because it is sometimes difficult to determine when a legal rule is "neutral," and because "untutored devotion to the concept of neutrality can lead to invocation or approval of results which partake not simply of that noninterference and noninvolvement with the religious which the Constitution commands, but of a brooding and pervasive devotion to the secular and a passive, or even active, hostility to the religious."

The case before us is a borderline case. It concerns a large granite monument bearing the text of the Ten Commandments located on the grounds of the Texas State Capitol. On the one hand, the Commandments' text undeniably has a religious message, invoking, indeed emphasizing, the Diety. On the other hand, focusing on the text of the Commandments alone cannot conclusively resolve this case. Rather, to determine the message that the text here conveys, we must examine how the text is used. And that inquiry requires us to consider the context of the display.

In certain contexts, a display of the tablets of the Ten Commandments can convey not simply a religious message but also a secular moral message (about proper standards of social conduct). And in certain contexts, a display of the tablets can also convey a historical message (about a historic relation between those standards and the law)—a fact that helps to explain the display of those tablets in dozens of courthouses throughout the Nation, including the Supreme Court of the United States.

Here the tablets have been used as part of a display that communicates not simply a religious message, but a secular message as well. The circumstances surrounding the display's placement on the capitol grounds and its physical setting suggest that the State itself intended the latter, nonreligious aspects of the tablets' message to predominate. And the monument's 40-year history on the Texas state grounds indicates that that has been its effect.

The group that donated the monument, the Fraternal Order of Eagles, a private civic (and primarily secular) organization, while interested in the religious aspect of the Ten Commandments, sought to highlight the Commandments' role in shaping civic morality as part of that organization's efforts to combat juvenile delinquency. The Eagles' consultation with a committee composed of members of several faiths in order to find a nonsectarian text underscores the group's ethics-based motives. The tablets, as displayed on the monument, prominently acknowledge that the Eagles donated the display, a factor which, though not sufficient, thereby further distances the State itself from the religious aspect of the Commandments' message.

The physical setting of the monument, moreover, suggests little or nothing of the sacred. The monument sits in a large park containing 17 monuments and 21 historical markers, all designed to illustrate the "ideals" of those who settled in Texas and of those who have lived there since that time. The setting does not readily lend itself to meditation or any other religious activity. But it does provide a context of history and moral ideals. It (together with the display's inscription about its origin) communicates to visitors that the State sought to reflect moral principles, illustrating a relation between ethics and law that the State's citizens, historically speaking, have endorsed.

If these factors provide a strong, but not conclusive, indication that the Commandments' text on this monument conveys a predominantly secular message, a further factor is determinative here. As far as I can tell, 40 years passed in which the presence of this monument, legally speaking, went unchallenged (until the single legal objection raised by petitioner). And I am not aware of any evidence suggesting that this was due to a climate of intimidation. Hence, those 40 years suggest more strongly than can any set of formulaic tests that few individuals, whatever their system of beliefs, are likely to have understood the monument as amounting, in any significantly detrimental way, to a government effort to favor a particular religious sect, primarily to promote religion over nonreligion, to "engage in" any "religious practic[e]," to "compel" any "religious practic[e]," or to "work deterrence" of any "religious belief." Those 40 years suggest that the public visiting the capitol grounds has considered the religious aspect of the tablets' message as part of what is a broader moral and historical message reflective of a cultural heritage.

This case, moreover, is distinguishable from instances where the Court has found Ten Commandments displays impermissible. The display is not on the grounds of a public school, where, given the impressionability of the young, government must exercise particular care in separating church and state. This case also differs from *McCreary County*, where the short (and stormy) history of the courthouse Commandments' displays demonstrates the substantially religious objectives of those who mounted them, and the effect of this readily apparent objective upon those who view them. That history there indicates a governmental effort substantially to promote religion, not simply an effort primarily to reflect, historically, the secular impact of a religiously inspired document. And, in today's world, in a Nation of so many different religious and comparable nonreligious fundamental beliefs, a more contemporary state effort to focus attention upon a religious text is certainly likely to prove divisive in a way that this longstanding, pre-existing monument has not.

For these reasons, I believe that the Texas display—serving a mixed but primarily nonreligious purpose, not primarily "advanc[ing]" or "inhibit[ing] religion," and not creating an "excessive government entanglement with religion"—might satisfy this Court's more formal Establishment Clause tests. But, as I have said, in reaching the conclusion that the Texas display falls on the permissible side of the constitutional line, I rely less upon a literal application of any particular test than upon consideration of the basic purposes of the First Amendment's Religion Clauses themselves. This display has stood apparently uncontested for nearly two generations. That experience helps us understand that as a practical matter of degree this display is unlikely to prove divisive. And this matter of degree is, I believe, critical in a borderline case such as this one.

At the same time, to reach a contrary conclusion here, based primarily upon on the religious nature of the tablets' text would, I fear, lead the law to exhibit a hostility toward religion that has no place in our Establishment Clause traditions. Such a holding might well encourage disputes concerning the removal of longstanding depictions of the Ten Commandments from public buildings across the Nation. And it could thereby create the very kind of religiously based divisiveness that the Establishment Clause seeks to avoid.

Justice STEVENS, with whom Justice GINSBURG joins, dissenting.

The sole function of the monument on the grounds of Texas' State Capitol is to display the full text of one version of the Ten Commandments. The monument is not a work of art and does not refer to any event in the history of the State. Viewed on its face, Texas' display has no purported connection to God's role in the formation of Texas or the founding of our Nation; nor does it provide the reasonable observer with any basis to guess that it was erected to honor any individual or organization. The message transmitted by Texas' chosen display is quite plain: This State endorses the divine code of the "Judeo-Christian" God.

For those of us who learned to recite the King James version of the text long before we understood the meaning of some of its words, God's Commandments may seem like wise counsel. The question before this Court, however, is whether it is counsel that the State of Texas may proclaim without violating the Establishment Clause of the Constitution. If any fragment of Jefferson's metaphorical "wall of separation between church and State" is to be preserved—if there remains any meaning to the "wholesome 'neutrality' of which this Court's [Establishment Clause] cases speak"—a negative answer to that question is mandatory.

I

In my judgment, at the very least, the Establishment Clause has created a strong presumption against the display of religious symbols on public property. The adornment of our public spaces with displays of religious symbols and messages undoubtedly provides comfort, even inspiration, to many individuals who subscribe to particular faiths. Unfortunately, the practice also runs the risk of "offend[ing] nonmembers of the faith being advertised as well as adherents who consider the particular advertisement disrespectful." Government's obligation to avoid divisiveness and exclusion in the religious sphere is compelled by the Establishment and Free Exercise Clauses, which together erect a wall of separation between church and state.

This metaphorical wall protects principles long recognized and often recited in this Court's cases. The first and most fundamental of these principles, one that a majority of this Court today affirms, is that the Establishment Clause demands religious neutrality—government may not exercise a preference for one religious faith over another. This essential command, however, is not merely a prohibition against the government's differentiation among religious sects. We have repeatedly reaffirmed that neither a State nor the Federal Government "can constitutionally pass laws or impose requirements which aid all religions as against non-believers, and neither can aid those religions based on a belief in the existence of God as against those religions founded on different beliefs." This principle is based on the straightforward notion that governmental promotion of orthodoxy is not saved by the aggregation of several orthodoxies under the State's banner.

Acknowledgments of this broad understanding of the neutrality principle are legion in our cases. In restating this principle, I do not discount the importance of avoiding an overly strict interpretation of the metaphor so often used to define the reach of the Establishment Clause. The plurality is correct to note that "religion and religious traditions" have played a "strong role . . . throughout our nation's history." Given this history, it is unsurprising that a religious symbol may at times become an important feature of a familiar landscape or a reminder of an important event in the history of a community. The wall that separates the church from the State does not prohibit the government from acknowledging the religious beliefs and practices of the American people, nor does it require governments to hide works of art or historic memorabilia from public view just because they also have religious significance.

This case, however, is not about historic preservation or the mere recognition of religion. The issue is obfuscated rather than clarified by simplistic commentary on the various ways in which religion has played a role in American life, and by the recitation of the many extant governmental "acknowledgments" of the role the Ten Commandments played in our Nation's heritage. Surely, the mere compilation of religious symbols, none of which includes the full text of the Commandments and all of which are exhibited in different settings, has only marginal relevance to the question presented in this case.

The monolith displayed on Texas Capitol grounds cannot be discounted as a passive acknowledgment of religion, nor can the State's refusal to remove it upon objection be explained as a simple desire to preserve a historic relic. This Nation's resolute commitment to neutrality with respect to religion is flatly inconsistent with the plurality's wholehearted validation of an official state endorsement of the message that there is one, and only one, God.

II

When the Ten Commandments monument was donated to the State of Texas in 1961, it was not for the purpose of commemorating a noteworthy event in Texas history, signifying the Commandments' influence on the development of secular law, or even denoting the religious beliefs of Texans at that time. To the contrary, the donation was only one of over a hundred largely identical monoliths, and of over a thousand paper replicas, distributed to state and local governments throughout the Nation over the course of several decades. This ambitious project was the work of the Fraternal Order of Eagles, a well-respected benevolent organization whose good works have earned the praise of several Presidents.

As the story goes, the program was initiated by the late Judge E. J. Ruegemer, a Minnesota juvenile court judge and then-Chairman of the Eagles National Commission on Youth Guidance. Inspired by a juvenile offender who had never heard of the Ten Commandments, the judge approached the Minnesota Eagles with the idea of distributing paper copies of the Commandments to be posted in courthouses nationwide. The State's Aerie undertook this project and its popularity spread. When Cecil B. DeMille, who at that time was filming the movie *The Ten Commandments,* heard of the judge's endeavor, he teamed up with the Eagles to produce the type of granite monolith now displayed in front of the Texas Capitol and at courthouse squares, city halls, and public parks throughout the Nation. Granite was reportedly chosen over DeMille's original suggestion of bronze plaques to better replicate the original Ten Commandments. The donors were motivated by a desire to "inspire the youth" and curb juvenile delinquency by providing children with a "code of conduct or standards by which to govern their actions."

It is the Eagles' belief that disseminating the message conveyed by the Ten Commandments will help to persuade young men and women to observe civilized standards of behavior, and will lead to more productive lives.

The desire to combat juvenile delinquency by providing guidance to youths is both admirable and unquestionably secular. But achieving that goal through biblical teachings injects a religious purpose into an otherwise secular endeavor. By spreading the word of God and converting heathens to Christianity, missionaries expect to enlighten their converts, enhance their satisfaction with life, and improve their behavior. Similarly, by disseminating the "law of God"— directing fidelity to God and proscribing murder, theft, and adultery—the Eagles hope that this divine guidance will help wayward youths conform their behavior and improve their lives. In my judgment, the significant secular byproducts that are intended consequences of religious instruction—indeed, of the establishment of most religions—are not the type of "secular" purposes that justify government promulgation of sacred religious messages.

Though the State of Texas may genuinely wish to combat juvenile delinquency, and may rightly want to honor the Eagles for their efforts, it cannot effectuate these admirable purposes through an explicitly religious medium. The reason this message stands apart is that the Decalogue is a venerable religious text. As we held 25 years ago, it is beyond dispute that "[t]he Ten Commandments are undeniably a sacred text in the Jewish and Christian faiths." For many followers, the Commandments represent the literal word of God as spoken to Moses and repeated to his followers after descending from Mount Sinai. Attempts to secularize what is unquestionably a sacred text defy credibility and disserve people of faith.

The profoundly sacred message embodied by the text inscribed on the Texas monument is emphasized by the especially large letters that identify its author: "I AM the LORD thy God." It commands present worship of Him and no other deity. It directs us to be guided by His teaching in the current and future conduct of all of our affairs. It instructs us to follow a code of divine law, some of which has informed and been integrated into our secular legal code ("Thou shalt not kill"), but much of which has not ("Thou shalt not make to thyself any graven images. . . . Thou shalt not covet").

Moreover, despite the Eagles' best efforts to choose a benign nondenominational text, the Ten Commandments display projects not just a religious, but an inherently sectarian message. There are many distinctive versions of the Decalogue, ascribed to by different religions and even different denominations within a particular faith; to a pious and learned observer, these differences may be of enormous religious significance. In choosing to display this version of the Commandments, Texas tells the observer that the State supports this side of the doctrinal religious debate.

Even if, however, the message of the monument, despite the inscribed text, fairly could be said to represent the belief system of all Judeo-Christians, it would still run afoul of the Establishment Clause by prescribing a compelled code of conduct from one God, namely a Judeo-Christian God, that is rejected by prominent polytheistic sects, such as Hinduism, as well as nontheistic religions, such as Buddhism. And, at the very least, the text of the Ten Commandments impermissibly commands a preference for religion over irreligion. Any of those bases, in my judgment, would be sufficient to conclude that the message should not be proclaimed by the State of Texas on a permanent monument at the seat of its government.

III

The plurality relies heavily on the fact that our Republic was founded, and has been governed since its nascence, by leaders who spoke then (and speak still) in plainly religious rhetoric. The speeches and rhetoric characteristic of the founding era, however, do not answer the question before us. I have already explained why Texas' display of the full text of the Ten Commandments, given the content of the actual display and the context in which it is situated, sets this case apart from the countless examples of benign government recognitions of religion. But there is another crucial difference. Our leaders, when delivering public addresses, often express their blessings simultaneously in the service of God and their constituents. Thus, when public officials deliver public speeches, we recognize that their words are not exclusively a transmission from the government because those oratories have embedded within them the inherently personal views of the speaker as an individual member of the polity. The permanent placement of a textual religious display on state property is different in kind; it amalgamates otherwise discordant individual views into a collective statement of government approval. Moreover, the message never ceases to transmit itself to objecting viewers whose only choices are to accept the message or to ignore the offense by averting their gaze. In this sense, although Thanksgiving Day proclamations and inaugural speeches undoubtedly seem official, in most circumstances they will not constitute the sort of governmental endorsement of religion at which the separation of church and state is aimed.

The plurality's reliance on early religious statements and proclamations made by the Founders is also problematic because those views were not espoused at the Constitutional Convention in 1787 nor enshrined in the Constitution's text. Thus, the presentation of these religious statements as a unified historical narrative is bound to paint a misleading picture. Ardent separationists aside, there is another critical nuance lost in the plurality's portrayal of history. Simply put, many of the Founders who are often cited as authoritative expositors of the Constitution's original meaning understood the Establishment Clause to stand for a narrower proposition than the plurality, for whatever reason, is willing to accept. Namely, many of the Framers understood the word "religion" in the Establishment Clause to encompass only the various sects of Christianity.

The original understanding of the type of "religion" that qualified for constitutional protection under the Establishment Clause likely did not include those followers of Judaism and Islam who are among the preferred "monotheistic" religions Justice Scalia has embraced in his *McCreary County* opinion. Given the original understanding of the men who championed our "Christian nation"—men who had no cause to view anti-Semitism or contempt for atheists as problems worthy of civic concern—one must ask whether Justice Scalia "has not had the courage (or the foolhardiness) to apply [his originalism] principle consistently."

Indeed, to constrict narrowly the reach of the Establishment Clause to the views of the Founders would lead to more than this unpalatable result; it would also leave us with an unincorporated constitutional provision—in other words, one that limits only the federal establishment of "a national religion." Under this view, not only could a State constitutionally adorn all of its public spaces with crucifixes or passages from the New Testament, it would also have full authority to prescribe the teachings of Martin Luther or Joseph Smith as the official state religion. Only the Federal Government would be prohibited from taking sides (and only then as between Christian sects).

A reading of the First Amendment dependent on either of the purported original meanings expressed above would eviscerate the heart of the Establishment Clause. It would replace Jefferson's "wall of separation" with a perverse wall of exclusion—Christians inside, non-Christians out. It would permit States to construct walls of their own choosing—Baptists inside, Mormons out; Jewish Orthodox inside, Jewish Reform out. A Clause so understood might be faithful to the expectations of some of our Founders, but it is plainly not worthy of a society whose enviable hallmark over the course of two centuries has been the continuing expansion of religious pluralism and tolerance.

It is our duty, therefore, to interpret the First Amendment's command that "Congress shall make no law respecting an establishment of religion" not by merely asking what those words meant to observers at the time of the founding, but instead by deriving from the Clause's text and history the broad principles that remain valid today. The principle that guides my analysis is neutrality. The basis for that principle is firmly rooted in our Nation's history and our Constitution's text. I recognize that the requirement that government must remain neutral between religion and irreligion would have seemed foreign to some of the Framers; so too would a requirement of neutrality between Jews and Christians. The evil of discriminating today against atheists, "polytheists[,] and believers in unconcerned deities," is in my view a direct descendent of the evil of discriminating among Christian sects. The Establishment Clause thus forbids it and, in turn, forbids Texas from displaying the Ten Commandments monument the plurality so casually affirms.

IV

The Eagles may donate as many monuments as they choose to be displayed in front of Protestant churches, benevolent organizations' meeting places, or on the front lawns of private citizens. The expurgated text of the King James version of the Ten Commandments that they have crafted is unlikely to be accepted by Catholic parishes, Jewish synagogues, or even some Protestant denominations, but the message they seek to convey is surely more compatible with church property than with property that is located on the government side of the metaphorical wall.

The judgment of the Court in this case stands for the proposition that the Constitution permits governmental displays of sacred religious texts. This makes a mockery of the constitutional ideal that government must remain neutral between religion and irreligion. If a State may endorse a particular deity's command to "have no other gods before me," it is difficult to conceive of any textual display that would run afoul of the Establishment Clause.

The disconnect between this Court's approval of Texas's monument and the constitutional prohibition against preferring religion to irreligion cannot be reduced to the exercise of plotting two adjacent locations on a slippery slope. Rather, it is the difference between the shelter of a fortress and exposure to "the winds that would blow" if the wall were allowed to crumble.

Justice SOUTER, with whom Justice STEVENS and Justice GINSBURG join, dissenting.

Although the First Amendment's Religion Clauses have not been read to mandate absolute governmental neutrality toward religion, the Establishment Clause requires neutrality as a general rule, and thus expresses Madison's condemnation of "employ[ing] Religion as an engine of Civil policy." A governmental display of an obviously religious text cannot be squared with neutrality, except in a setting that plausibly indicates that the statement is not placed in view with a predominant purpose on the part of government either to adopt the religious message or to urge its acceptance by others.

Until today, only one of our cases addressed the constitutionality of posting the Ten Commandments, Stone v. Graham (1980). A Kentucky statute required posting the Commandments on the walls of public school classrooms. [The Court stated:]

> The pre-eminent purpose for posting the Ten Commandments on schoolroom walls is plainly religious in nature. The Ten Commandments are undeniably a sacred text in the Jewish and Christian faiths, and no legislative recitation of a supposed secular purpose can blind us to that fact. The Commandments do not confine themselves to arguably secular matters, such as honoring one's parents, killing or murder, adultery,

stealing, false witness, and covetousness. Rather, the first part of the Commandments concerns the religious duties of believers: worshipping the Lord God alone, avoiding idolatry, not using the Lord's name in vain, and observing the Sabbath Day.

What these observations underscore are the simple realities that the Ten Commandments constitute a religious statement, that their message is inherently religious, and that the purpose of singling them out in a display is clearly the same.

In the present case, the religious purpose was evident on the part of the donating organization. When the Fraternal Order of Eagles, the group that gave the monument to the State of Texas, donated identical monuments to other jurisdictions, it was seeking to impart a religious message. Accordingly, it was not just the terms of the moral code, but the proclamation that the terms of the code were enjoined by God, that the Eagles put forward in the monuments they donated.

Thus, a pedestrian happening upon the monument at issue here needs no training in religious doctrine to realize that the statement of the Commandments, quoting God himself, proclaims that the will of the divine being is the source of obligation to obey the rules, including the facially secular ones. In this case, moreover, the text is presented to give particular prominence to the Commandments' first sectarian reference, "I am the Lord thy God." That proclamation is centered on the stone and written in slightly larger letters than the subsequent recitation. To ensure that the religious nature of the monument is clear to even the most casual passerby, the word "Lord" appears in all capital letters (as does the word "am"), so that the most eye-catching segment of the quotation is the declaration "I AM the LORD thy God." What follows, of course, are the rules against other gods, graven images, vain swearing, and Sabbath breaking. And the full text of the fifth Commandment puts forward filial respect as a condition of long life in the land "which the Lord they God giveth thee." These "[w]ords . . . make [the] . . . religious meaning unmistakably clear."

To drive the religious point home, and identify the message as religious to any viewer who failed to read the text, the engraved quotation is framed by religious symbols: two tablets with what appears to be ancient script on them, two Stars of David, and the superimposed Greek letters Chi and Rho as the familiar monogram of Christ. Nothing on the monument, in fact, detracts from its religious nature, and the plurality does not suggest otherwise. It would therefore be difficult to miss the point that the government of Texas is telling everyone who sees the monument to live up to a moral code because God requires it, with both code and conception of God being rightly understood as the inheritances specifically of Jews and Christians. And it is likewise unsurprising that the District Court expressly rejected Texas's argument that the State's purpose in placing the monument on the capitol grounds was related to the Commandments' role as "part of the foundation of modern secular law in Texas and elsewhere."

The monument's presentation of the Commandments with religious text emphasized and enhanced stands in contrast to any number of perfectly constitutional depictions of them, the frieze of our own Courtroom providing a good example, where the figure of Moses stands among history's great lawgivers. While Moses holds the tablets of the Commandments showing some Hebrew text, no one looking at the lines of figures in marble relief is likely to see a religious purpose behind the assemblage or take away a religious message from it. Only one other depiction represents a religious leader, and the historical personages are mixed with symbols of moral and intellectual abstractions like Equity and Authority. Since Moses enjoys no especial prominence on the frieze, viewers can readily take him to be there as a lawgiver in the company of other lawgivers; and the viewers may just as naturally see the tablets of the Commandments (showing the later ones, forbidding things like killing and theft, but without the divine preface) as background from which the concept of law emerged, ultimately having a secular influence in the history of the Nation. Government may, of course, constitutionally call attention to this influence, and may post displays or erect monuments recounting this aspect of our history no less than any other, so long as there is a context and that context is historical. Hence, a display of the Commandments accompanied by an exposition of how they have influenced modern law would most likely be constitutionally unobjectionable. And the Decalogue could, as *Stone* suggested, be integrated constitutionally into a course of study in public schools.

Texas seeks to take advantage of the recognition that visual symbol and written text can manifest a secular purpose in secular company, when it argues that its monument (like Moses in the frieze) is not alone and ought to be viewed as only 1 among 17 placed on the 22 acres surrounding the state capitol. Texas, indeed, says that the Capitol grounds are like a museum for a collection of exhibits, the kind of setting that several Members of the Court have said can render the exhibition of religious artifacts permissible, even though in other circumstances their display would be seen as meant to convey a religious message forbidden to the State.

But 17 monuments with no common appearance, history, or esthetic role scattered over 22 acres is not a museum, and anyone strolling around the lawn would surely take each memorial on its own terms without any dawning sense that some purpose held the miscellany together more coherently than fortuity and the edge of the grass. One monument expresses admiration for pioneer women. One pays respect to the fighters of World War II. And one quotes the God of Abraham whose command is the sanction for moral law. The themes are individual grit, patriotic courage, and God as the source of Jewish and Christian morality; there is no common denominator. In like circumstances, we rejected an argument similar to the State's, noting in *County of Allegheny* that "[t]he presence of Santas or other Christmas decorations elsewhere in the . . . [c]ourthouse, and of the nearby gallery forum, fail to negate the [crèche's] endorsement effect. . . . The record demonstrates . . . that the crèche, with its floral frame, was its own display distinct from any other decorations or exhibitions in the building."

Nor can the plurality deflect *Stone* by calling the Texas monument "a far more passive use of [the Decalogue] than was the case in *Stone*, where the text confronted elementary school students every day." Placing a monument on the ground is not more "passive" than hanging a sheet of paper on a wall when both contain the same text to be read by anyone who looks at it. The problem in *Stone* was simply that the State was putting the Commandments there to be seen, just as the monument's inscription is there for those who walk by it.

The monument in this case sits on the grounds of the Texas State Capitol. There is something significant in the common term "statehouse" to refer to a state capitol building: it is the civic home of every one of the State's citizens. If neutrality in religion means something, any citizen should be able to visit that civic home without having to confront religious expressions clearly meant to convey an official religious position that may be at odds with his own religion, or with rejection of religion.

Finally, though this too is a point on which judgment will vary, I do not see a persuasive argument for constitutionality in the plurality's observation that Van Orden's lawsuit comes "[f]orty years after the monument's erection . . . ." It is not that I think the passage of time is necessarily irrelevant in Establishment Clause analysis. Suing a State over religion puts nothing in a plaintiff's pocket and can take a great deal out, and even with volunteer litigators to supply time and energy, the risk of social ostracism can be powerfully deterrent. I doubt that a slow walk to the courthouse, even one that took 40 years, is much evidentiary help in applying the Establishment Clause.